MW00651711

The Global Business of Coaching

Coaching has become a global business phenomenon, yet the way that coaching has evolved and spread across the globe is not unproblematic. Some of these challenges include: different types/genres of coaching; understanding and relevance of different coaching philosophies and models in different cultural contexts; equivalency of qualifications and coach credentials, as well as questions over standards and governance, as part of a wider debate around professionalisation. Coaching, then, as with the transfer of knowledge and professionalisation in other disciplines, is not immune to ethnocentricity.

Through a combination of adopting a meta-analysis of coaching, supported with narratives of coaching practice drawn from different socio-political/cultural contexts, the aim of this book is to challenge current knowledge, understanding and norms of how coaching is, or should, be practised in different cultural contexts. This book will provide a foundation for further research in coaching as an academic field of study and as an emerging profession. It will resonate with critical scholars, coach educators, and coach practitioners who want to develop their praxis and enhance their reflexivity and be of interest to researchers, academics, and students in the fields of business and leadership, human resource development, organisational learning and development, mentoring, and coaching.

David Lines is the owner and founder of David Lines & Associates, Singapore.

Christina Evans is Deputy Director in the Business School at the University of Roehampton, London, UK.

Routledge Studies in Human Resource Development
Edited by Monica Lee
Lancaster University, UK

HRD theory is changing rapidly. Recent advances in theory and practice, how we conceive of organisations and of the world of knowledge, have led to the need to reinterpret the field. This series aims to reflect and foster the development of HRD as an emergent discipline.

Encompassing a range of different international, organisational, methodological and theoretical perspectives, the series promotes theoretical controversy and reflective practice.

Positive Ageing and Human Resource Development
Edited by Diane Keeble-Ramsay and Andrew Armitage

Work, Working and Work Relationships in a Changing World
Edited by Clare Kelliher and Julia Richardson

Human Resource Management in an Emerging South Asian Economy
The Case of Brunei
Edited by Tamer K Darwish and Pengiran Muda Abdul Fattaah

The Global Business of Coaching
A Meta-Analytical Perspective
David Lines and Christina Evans

Also published in the series in paperback:

Action Research in Organisations
Jean McNiff, accompanied by Jack Whitehead

Understanding Human Resource Development
A research-based approach
Edited by Jim Stewart, Jim McGoldrick, and Sandra Watson

For more information about this series, please visit: www.routledge.com/languages/series/RSHRD

The Global Business of Coaching

Coaching

A Meta-Analytical Perspective

David Lines and Christina Evans

NEW YORK AND LONDON

First published 2020
by Routledge
52 Vanderbilt Avenue, New York, NY 10017

and by Routledge
2 Park Square, Milton Park, Abingdon, Oxon OX14 4RN

Routledge is an imprint of the Taylor & Francis Group, an informa business

© 2020 **David Lines** and **Christina Evans**

British Library Cataloguing-in-Publication Data
A catalogue record for this book is available from the British Library

Library of Congress Cataloging-in-Publication Data
A catalog record for this book has been requested

ISBN: 978-1-138-60680-7 (hbk)
ISBN: 978-0-429-46753-0 (ebk)

Typeset in Sabon
by Apex CoVantage, LLC

Contents

Figures and Charts

Tables

Author Biographies

Dr David Lines

David is currently the owner and founder of David Lines & Associates, a company based in Singapore. He commutes between Hong Kong and Singapore on a regular basis working as an executive coach, researcher, and practitioner supervisor. Prior to setting up his own business he worked in the Civil Service College in Singapore as an internal consultant, developing the capacity and capability of internal facilitators of leadership practice. David moved to Asia in 2011 as the Regional Director, Lead Consultant, Asia Pacific, of a UK based leadership development consultancy. In his earlier career he worked as an educationalist in the UK National Health Service.

David researched the career paths of executive company directors for his doctorate. He has carried out research, interviewing over 50 CEOs in the FTSE 150, for KPMG, to produce a co-authored report with Peter Hamill, *Thriving in a Diverse Business World*. His current interests include executive development and coaching as a profession. He has co-authored, with Christina Evans, an article on identity work in coaching and co-presented conference papers on coaching in a global world.

Dr Christina Evans

Christina is currently Deputy Director in the Business School at the University of Roehampton— London and has taught in the Higher Education sector for around 13 years. Prior to joining Roehampton, Christina had a career as an independent HRM researcher and consultant, whilst completing her Doctorate. In her earlier career she worked in various operational roles in the Information Technology Division of a major retailer.

Christina's research interests include career development and talent management and gender and diversity management within organisations. She has published several books and commissioned reports aimed at academic and practitioner audiences. Her latest book, *Engaged With What? Employee Engagement Viewed Through a Different Lens*, was published in 2015 by bookboon.com. Other books include: *Re-Tayloring Management: Scientific Management a Century On*, a co-edited book published by Gower in 2013, and *Managing for Knowledge: HR's Strategic Role*, published by Butterworth-Heinemann in 2003.

Acknowledgements

There are many people who have helped us along the journey of writing this book. This includes coaching practitioners, those who teach on coaching programmes, as well as others working in aligned professions. Whilst we are unable to name all of the contributors personally, as many have asked not to be named, particularly coaches who are working in Hong Kong and Singapore, given how small a community this is, there are others who we would particularly like to acknowledge.

First, there are many of you, and you know who you are, including all of the coaches and coachees, in Singapore, Hong Kong, and Thailand, who have generously given time and attention during the extended conversations we had about this book. In particular we would like to thank Professor Paul Brown of Monarch Business School Switzerland, Yvonne (Hau) Thackray Founder of The Good Coach Hong Kong, Dr Paul Barber, Henry Chamberlain, Mark Day, and Graham Barkus. And a special thanks to Helena Green, who supported and encouraged this endeavour.

Second, the academics and practitioners in the Coaching and Mentoring stream at the Universities Forum for Human Resource Development's (UFHRD) annual conferences who have shared their insights and challenges associated with coaching drawn from their own research and/or practice. It was this group who inspired and encouraged us to write this book.

Third, colleagues in the Business School at Roehampton University who have performed the role of critical friends at different points during the writing of this book. In particular, Dr Michelle Hunter, Professor Carole Elliott, Dr Paul Aldrich, and former colleagues, Professor Sharon Mavin and Dr Haytham Siala.

Fourth, we would like to acknowledge the work of other authors who have written about the field of coaching. Where we have cited particular works, we hope that we have been able to do justice to your contribution whilst at the same time developing our own ideas on the business of coaching.

Finally, we appreciate the encouragement and support that we have received from the team at Routledge during the writing process and in getting this book into print.

Part I

A Meta-Analysis of Coaching

Roots, Theories, and Models
Examined Through a
Critical Lens

1 Introduction, Rationale, and Overview

Coaching has become a global business phenomenon. Yet as others and we observe, the way that coaching has evolved and spread across the globe is not unproblematic. Some of these challenges/tensions include: different types/genres of coaching; understanding and relevance of different coaching philosophies and models in different cultural contexts; equivalency of qualifications and coach credentials, as well as questions over standards and governance, as part of a wider debate around professionalisation. Coaching, then, as with the transfer of knowledge and professionalisation in other disciplines, is not immune to ethnocentricity (McLean 2017; Prasad 2016).

In discussing some of these challenges/tensions with academics (who either teach on coaching programmes or conduct research on coaching) coach practitioners, and others who have been in the field of HR and coaching as professional practitioners and are working in different contexts; we have identified a gap for a book that adopts a more critical perspective on coaching.

Within the broad discipline of Human Resource Development (HRD), there has been a growing interest in adopting a more critical perspective (Sambrook 2014; Stewart, Rigg and Trehan 2007). An approach that reflects some form of transition from one state to another, such as the transition from a taken-for-granted acceptance of a phenomenon to a more critical approach 'evidenced by a "critical mass" of researchers and practitioners' (Sambrook 2014: 1) and that critically engages with the socio-political debates and processes that shape (or have shaped) a particular phenomenon, or HRD developmental approach (Elliott and Reynolds 2014).

Our aim in writing this book was to produce something that resonates with critical scholars, coach educators, as well as coach practitioners who want to develop their praxis and enhance their reflexivity. In addition, we provide a foundation for further research in coaching as an academic field of study and as an emerging profession.

To stimulate a critical debate within the field of coaching, in this book we will address questions such as:

- What is coaching and how do coaching interventions differ from other developmental approaches? Is coaching simply old wine in new bottles?
- What are the different genres of coaching? When, how and why did these different genres emerge?
- How does coaching differ in a variety of cultural environments and how has it morphed from its original purpose of 'life coaching'?
- Is coaching a profession, or an industry? If considered a profession, what stage is coaching in terms of developing as a profession?
- Who is leading the movement towards coach credentialing and professionalisation? How do the different social actors engaged in this activity legitimise their authority to do so?
- What tensions, if any, are there between coaching evolving as a profession and the economic imperative of coaching practitioners needing to earn sufficient income from coaching to survive?

The topics that we surface and debate in this book resonate with the themes of the 2017 UFHRD Annual Conference. These include: challenging issues of ethnocentricity and colonisation of HRD and executive development, as well as surfacing tensions associated with standard-setting and standardisation within the field of HRD more generally (Anderson 2017). Through a combination of adopting a meta-analysis of coaching, supported with narratives of coaching practice drawn from different socio-political/cultural contexts, our aim is to challenge current knowledge, understanding and norms of how coaching is, or should, be practised in different cultural contexts.

In this chapter we set out our rationale for developing a meta-analysis of coaching and what we believe we can contribute to the field of coaching. We also set out our methodological approach to researching and writing this book and explain why we are adopting a grounded theory approach and a historiographical perspective of the history of coaching, and how these methodologies informed, supported, and substantiated our analysis. The chapter will conclude with an overview of the forthcoming chapters in the book.

Rationale for Adopting Grounded Theory as a Research Methodology and the Use of Historiography as an Analytical Approach to the Emergence of Coaching

The effect of the Western world (McLean 2017) on the development of coaching models and methods has created a highly focused ethnocentricity towards a Westernisation of coaching as it has been dispersed around the world, mainly through the efforts of I.C.F. as a means of dissemination. This has generated a plethora of articles, books, and training methods that mirror a Westernised approach to coaching and often contains assumptions about the manner in which coaches approach their clients. We noticed that both coaches their client's voices, in Asia, were missing from the coaching narratives and their opinions and perspectives do not seem to be represented in the literature. One of the purposes of this research, and critical analysis, is to provide a link between the mainly western literature and the Asian voices that we consider to be missing from the coaching discourses. (Lines 2004: 61)

The authors noticed in their preliminary reading for this book that the literature that purports to describe the historical emergence of coaching has been mainly descriptive and assumptive about how coaching arrived in the commercial and business worlds and how it became a global phenomenon. We wanted to adopt a critical inquiry of the history of coaching and put these assumptions into their particular historical context. Historiographical inquiry and the methods of analysis has provided us with an exemplar of how we could undertake this part of our research.

The Way We Approached This Book—Methodologies and Methods of Inquiry

We adopted a meta-analytical approach to the field of coaching in a global world. Our aim is to take a critical perspective on the implications for coaching of the various phenomenon that have and are influencing the growth of coaching, such) and as an instrument to enhance performance and organisational transformation and change. (Hamlin, Ellinger and Beattie 2008). Meta-analysis has a distinct definition in both quantitative and qualitative research approaches. According to Paterson et al. (2001: 1), a key aspect of meta-analysis is the generation of 'new ways of thinking about phenomenon.' In this book we aim to adopt a different approach from the established approach to meta-analysis that presents a detailed analysis of all of the research findings within a specific field. We suggest that before such a study can be undertaken the main phenomenon within the field will need to be identified so that more research analysis can be undertaken to focus on each of the phenomenon within the field. Accordingly we will use a meta-analysis proposed by Patton (1990: 406–407) to identify the patterns of coaching as a global phenomenon and discuss how these patterns, forms, and shapes may direct, or not, the future of coaching. This approach is related to the use of grounded theory as an approach to understanding the field as is rather than the field as we consider it to be (Glaser and Strauss 1967; Locke 2001; Strauss and Corbin 1990). We believe this approach will enable us to present a more critical perspective of how different forms of coaching, genres/philosophies of coaching, and the main phenomenon in the field have emerged and are positioned, and the implications of this for the evolution of coaching.

According to Glaser and Strauss (1967: 21ff), the underlying purpose of using grounded theory, as a research methodology is to generate a substantive theory, the theory is considered to be 'work in progress' or 'emergent' in nature (Dick 2000: 3) and, as such, can be used as a foundation for further research in the chosen field (Glaser and Strauss 1967). This is a different approach to the 'scientific' approach, as Robson (1993: 18) points out, 'the scientific approach is usually regarded as starting with theory.' It is important to point out that it is not the purpose of grounded theory to test or verify theories, rather it is used to assemble evidence, collected in terms of . . . preferably personal interviews and or surveys, to uncover ideas and fresh hypotheses from the research subjects and field (Glaser and Strauss 1967: 28–31; Gummesson 1991: 83).

> The grounded theory approach is a qualitative research method that uses a systematic set of procedures to develop an inductively derived grounded theory about a phenomenon.
>
> (Strauss and Corbin 1990: 24)

The main idea underpinning grounded theory is the constant comparative method by which the theory is developed. We interviewed some of our participants, and emailed questions to a wider range of participants, whom we were in touch with across Asia and the UK, we then analysed, compared the information, and surfaced the themes, which we then used to structure the narrative parts of the book. Glaser and Strauss (1967) and Strauss and Corbin (1990) were committed to the formation of hypotheses that reflected the field rather than taking existing theories and then looking for examples in the field to support the theory. As Lincoln & Guba state: 'Grounded theory . . . is theory that follows from data rather than preceding them (as in conventional inquiry)'(1985: 204).

Therefore, to bring an established theoretical framework from the discipline of social psychology to grounded theory research may bias the authors and prevent us from noticing what was happening in the interviews and setting in which we were researching. For example, to assume, at the beginning of the study, that the processes of the global business of coaching are the same as a typical business process may have closed the author's minds to the other possibilities that existed within the field. However, as Glaser and Strauss (1967), and Strauss and Corbin (1990), identify, it is useful during the research process to use the existing literature as another data source to compare and contrast the categories that were emerging from the data. This was then used to develop and enhance the line of research, with the proviso that the field data gathering process is the directional driver within the inquiry and that the literature remained as a supporter and challenger to the study. We therefore

gathered information from the various groups of participants and analysed these to provide the themes that we have used as a soft structure
for the chapters and then using the literature we have presented a critical
review and then in separate sections we have included the participants'
narratives and presented them as provisional narratives that require further research and inquiry.

The theory generated during grounded theory research offers perspectives and ideas for understanding the underlying problems or issues in a
particular field of research or general problem area. (Glaser and Strauss
1967) It is important to note that a substantial theory is not generalizable
outside of the context in which it has been generated and as a result will
require more research to generate a fully grounded theory. We have surfaced themes that can now be taken further, and may be used to develop
a grounded theory of coaching, that can aid practitioners and decisions
makers to design and develop effective coaching processes. We have suggested some questions at the end of each chapter that can be used to
continue research in the coaching field.

In addition, another reason for adopting a grounded theory approach
focused on access to the coaching literature. The literature appears to be
spread across multiple journals, e.g., psychology, social sciences, leadership development, and organisational development. Access to these
journals is often dependent on the following factors' membership of a
university library; journal access is often restricted via a subscription or
paywall.

Historiography

We have chosen to take a historiographical approach to the history of
coaching as a way of illustrating the, often, tenuous links between the different forms of intervention and the emergence of coaching. The context
in which coaching has grown up into an alternative approach to personal
and professional development has been included so that we can begin to
understand that over time human intervention in areas of development
has altered according the requirements of the social and political agendas
that were in vogue.

The use of historiography as a methodology provides us with a mul-
tifaceted lens that we can bring to analysing the past that has contributed to the various histories of coaching. An essential element of this
analytical process is to understand the history as it is written and ask
further questions about other factors that might have been influential
and therefore may contribute to the environment that was necessary for
change to occur. This section will widen the lens through which we perceive coaching, to include the socio-political and cultural aspects, and
the similarities and differences in the various accounts. We will surface
issues of power and the relationship of conflict between the originators

of different schools of thought, and we will illustrate how disagreements between the established way of operating and fresh thinking has shaped and created the milieu in which coaching manifests itself in the current timeframe. We also want to pay particular attention to what might have been missed in the somewhat positive transmission of the coaching stories and try to imagine which voices or representations have been left out of the current narratives.

Why Study the History of Coaching?—Rationale and Context of Historiographical Inquiry

History has been defined as being a 'continuous, typically chronological, record of important or pubic events or of a particular trend or institution' (The New Oxford Dictionary of English 1998: 869). However, as Tosh (2015: 131) points out; 'The word history carries two meanings in common parlance. It refers both to what actually happened in the past and to the representation of that past in the work of historians.' Arnold (2000: 5) uses the word ' "historiography" to mean the process of writing history and "history" to mean the end product of that process.'

> Historians inevitably decide which things can or should be said. So 'history' (the true stories historians tell about the past) is made up of only those things which have caught [their] attention, that [they] have decided to repeat for modern ears.
>
> Arnold (2000: 8)

Arnold (2000: 8) surfaces another aspect of historiography, that of the context of the event or story, from the past, that we are drawing upon to illustrate the wider themes and phenomenon of the subject or area of interest.

Arnold (2000) asserts that, 'We need to interpret the past, not simply present it. Finding a larger context for the story is an attempt to say not just 'what happened' but what it meant.' We thus endeavoured to uncover the wider context behind the histories of coaching and highlight the contexts in which these stories originated and the social phenomenon that is being represented at that time. Grafton (2006: 1–32) identifies that 'ideas do not develop in isolation from the people who create them and use them, and that one must study ideas not as distant propositions but in terms of the culture, lives and historical contexts that produced them.' Tosh (2015: 13) points out that, 'the past is itself not a narrative. In its entirety it is as chaotic, uncoordinated, and complex as life. History is about making sense of that mess, finding or creating patterns and meanings and stories from the maelstrom.' This last point is relevant particularly when we are dealing with an emerging professional group where the historical narratives are embryonic in nature and relatively undefined in terms of research and academic study.

Another aspect that is often overlooked when analysing historical accounts or artefacts is that of the intentions of writers of history which are rarely surfaced and discussed, however as Hong and Huang (2008: 2) postulate, there are deeper motives apart from the mere writing of a history as a value free account. Often the intentions are to create a narrative that legitimises, substantiates, and confirms the existence of a country, institution, profession or emerging group. Historians are, 'caught up in [their] own bundle of interests, morals, ethics, philosophies, ideas on how the world works, and why people do the things they do' (Arnold 2000: 12). Our aim then in this chapter is to examine the evidence that exists regarding the emergence of coaching and differentiate between the 'true stories' and the fables and myths associated with the history of coaching.

Tosh (2015: 11) surfaces the point that 'No human practice ever stands still; all demand a historical perspective which uncovers the dynamics of change over time.' Arnold (200: 5) adds to this perspective, 'history both begins and ends with questions; which is a way to say that it never really ends, but is a process.' This reinforces the idea that the history of coaching is on-going and in the light of its recent emergence is unfolding around us and continues to do so, as a result of those people who are involved directly and indirectly.

Understanding the written and oral history of coaching provides a deeper understanding of the events or contexts that influenced the emergence of coaching as a craft and a new professional group. The thinkers and writers that contributed to the eventual rise of coaching were responding to often-subtle elements within their discrete professional groups or within society. We will draw on the historical timeline from Socrates to the present day to illustrate and highlight the relationship between coaching and the activities and focus of deliberate and focused change, to uncover the historical processes (Tosh 2015: 10) that eventually gave rise to what we call coaching. A key part of this is to examine the atmosphere and possible perspectives and philosophies of the times that led to the formulation of particular ideas and models that coaches now draw on for their work. We will 'strive to understand each age on its own terms and to take on its own values and priorities instead of imposing ours.' Tosh (2015: 1, 6) previously points out 'that we cannot understand a situation without some perception of where it fits into a continuing process or whether it has happened before.'

This section has outlined the aspects of studying what we know of the past of a particular phenomenon, such as coaching, and some of the particular elements that are necessary for us to consider when we are reviewing the past, deciphering the stories, and assembling the history of, in this case, coaching. The point we have made that the past is different to the present and yet may contain similar elements in that we are looking at the stories of how people acted upon their environment and how they responded to changes within their lives and the wider systems with which they were involved. Deepening our understanding of the context, situations, and the continuing social and professional processes in which they lived are important, as we need to suspend our assumptions about how we consider they ought to have behaved and our preconceptions about how systems worked at that time. We consider it important to develop an understanding and perspective of the factors which people in the past responded to and their intentions and the outcomes. Coaching has risen in popularity over the past 20 or so years, and the forces that have influenced this upward trajectory require an understanding of the past and a broader view of the history that is being compiled.

Overview of the Remaining Chapters

Chapter 2: This chapter begins with an analysis of the existing literature that sets out the different narratives of the process of the emergence of coaching. Our analysis is based on adopting an historiographical approach to the emergence of coaching in the West, particularly in North America and Europe. The chapter presents a critical review of how the extant literature portrays and presents coaching as an activity that has been around for many thousands of years, as an attempt to design a history that presents coaching as an historical phenomena with sound credentials and a firm foundation of theoretical principles. This, we suggest, is part of the development of the provenance of coaching to demonstrate the legitimacy of coaching as an occupational group. We present an analysis of the claims about the historical pathways of coaching, examining the links between the main theoretical practices of psychoanalysis, psychology, education, and sport. In the second part of the chapter we extend these narratives by drawing out and discussing the socio-political and cultural elements that provided the platform for humanistic psychology, and therefore coaching, from our perspective, to fully surface. One of the themes that we cover, and address in more depth in Chapter 5, is the absence of diverse (or missing) voices in historical and contemporary accounts of coaching. Others, too, have (McLean 2016) have surfaced similar tensions and challenges, noting a mono-culture perspective, where one culture dominates the discourse of a phenomenon, in this case coaching, thus does not take into account the hidden differences that exist within coaching as a global occupation.

Chapter 3: This chapter builds on Chapter 2, charting the progression of coaching from the emphasis on life coaching and the sporting arena into the world of business. We present an analysis of the relationships between HRM and the economic climate that existed in the 1990s, thus providing a rationale for the introduction and implementation of coaching as a method for resolving people and performance issues in business. The key initiators and ideas behind this transition are discussed. We also discuss other influences such as social psychology, and cognitive psychology that have surfaced along with the ripple effect of positive psychology in the coaching narrative. The chapter introduces a number of metaphors—'The Wild West,' the 'Gold Rush,' and the 'Seafood Market'—that emerged during interviews with coaching practitioners in the Asia Pacific region. These metaphors provide us with a different lens through which we might see the overarching business of coaching. For each of these metaphors we draw out different aspects that could be useful to coaches to learn about and adapt their business according to the context within which they are operating. An example here, taken from the 'Gold Rush' metaphor, is that coaching has in a similar fashion to the 'Gold Rush' has become a market that seems to be attractive to practitioners, given the low barriers to entry and a reasonable return on investment from their training and development. Yet we suggest that in reality the market appears, as in the 'Gold Rush,' to be skewed in favour of the merchants who supply the 'miners,' i.e., the coaches. We conclude the chapter with some of the consequences and the results of coaching entering commerce and the reasons why coaching is still involved as a central and possibly essential intervention in professional and personal development. The chapter concludes with some reflective questions for commissioners of caching as well as coaching practitioners.

Chapter 4: This chapter discusses some of the contemporary debates between the notion of coaching as an emerging profession and a business entity. The chapter starts with an in-depth look at coach competencies, as specified by the different Coaching Associations, becoming a coach, and the training and educational routes and the accreditation of coaching programmes. As coaching has gained momentum, a number of tensions have emerged with respect to the underpinning knowledge base and competencies of coaching practitioners and the legitimacy of the institutions and associations that accredit the growing number of coaching qualifications. From the user's perspective this raises the question 'How do organisations and individuals ensure that they are engaging a credible coach?' The chapter concludes with an analysis of how ICF has shaped its legitimacy as the global voice on coaching and credentialing, drawing on resource mobilisation analysis as a theoretical lens for our analysis.

Chapters 5 and 6: In these chapters we present a number of narrative accounts of coaching gathered from coach practitioners, commissioners of coaching and coaches, from different geographic and cultural contexts. Our accounts are drawn from two specific regions—the Middle East (with a particular focus on Dubai and Saudi Arabia) and Asia-Pacific (with a particular focus on Singapore, Hong Kong, and Thailand). We discuss some of the some of the challenges associated with the concept of coaching, including how individuals differentiate caching from mentoring, given the differing socio-political contexts. The narrative accounts we draw on enable us to see coaching as pluralistic and in different phases of development in the countries that we have gathered our accounts. The narratives also enable us to build on the notion of 'missing voices' in the wider coaching discourse, a theme that emerged in Chapter 2.

Chapter 7: This chapter draws together some of the tensions and challenges that coaches operating in different contexts face as they develop and practice their craft. The themes include: issues relating to identity (identity in flux vs coaching as a liminal); challenges associated with meeting the expectations of different clients and other stakeholders; choices over if, when, and where to use assessment tools (e.g., psychometrics) in one's coaching practice; gathering and using feedback to get a sense of 'How well am I doing?'; and, finally, tensions with what evidence to draw on to help with decision-making in coaching. As with other chapters, the insights presented have been drawn from the field as a starting point, then further analysed with reference to other published work. The chapter concludes with some reflective questions for coaches to consider.

Chapter 8: In this chapter we build on current debates on a specific aspect of the changing coaching eco-system. Since starting the process of writing this book we have become more aware of the growing interest and debates around the adoption of AI and Automation technologies, particularly within HRM/HRD and other coaching 'reference professions.' In this chapter we discuss some of the tensions associated with the adoption of AI and Automation technologies more generally before focusing on potential tensions for coaching. Some specific questions that the chapter considers are: What impact are new technologies such as Artificial Intelligence (AI) having on the work that coaches do? Should these new technologies be perceived as an opportunity or threat for coaching? With the rise in the concept of the 'internet of things' how might this help, or hinder, the development of coaches business and/or identity? To what extent might coaching remain a viable and sustainable occupation/profession as we see more developments in the field of AI and Automation?

Chapter 9: In this concluding chapter we draw together and provide further reflections on the key themes from the book. Our aim in this chapter is to provoke further discussion and debate, which we hope will stimulate future research into the arena of coach education, practice, and governance that reflects the diversity of organisational and individual needs. We present a model of the coaching eco-system, that maps out the key influences on the phenomenon of coaching as a global business. We revisit the 'coaching as a business' success narrative, providing additional reflections on the potential for coaching to become a precarious occupation given technological, economic, and social changes. We speculate whether we might see a similar stratification emerging in coaching, possibly around a specialist/generalist divide. As the coaching market matures (and moves out of the Gold Rush phase as discussed in Chapter 3), combined with the growing acceptance of AI and Automation tools, could less experienced coaches find themselves in the lowest strata, or possibly displaced by technology as others suggest? Or might we see a new form of 'hybrid coach' emerging as in other professions? We leave these as potential questions for future research in the field.

References

Anderson, V. (2017). HRD standards and standardization where now for human resource development. *Human Resource Development International*, 20(4), 327–345.

Arnold, J.H. (2000). *History—A Very Short Introduction*. Oxford: Oxford University Press.

Dick, B. (2000). *Grounded Theory: A Thumbnail Sketch*. www.scu.edu.au/schools/gcm/ar/arp/grounded.html.

Elliott, C.J. and Reynolds, M. (2014). Participative pedagogies, group work and the international classroom: An account of students' and tutor's experiences. *Studies in Higher Education*, 39(2), 307–320.

Glaser, B. and Strauss, A. (1967). *The Discovery of Grounded Theory: Strategies for Qualitative Research*. New York: Adeline De Gruyter.

Grafton, A. (2006). The history of ideas: Precept and practice, 1950–2000 and beyond. *Journal of the History of Ideas*, 67(1), 1–32.

Gummesson, E. (1991). *Qualitative Methods in Management Research*. Newbury Park, CA: Sage Publications.

Hamlin, R.G., Ellinger, A.D. and Beattie, R.S. (2008). The emergent 'coaching industry': A wake-up call for HRD professionals. *Human Resource Development International*, 11(3), 287–305.

Hong, L. and Huang, J. (2008). *The Scripting of a National History—Singapore and Its Pasts*. Singapore: National University of Singapore Press.

Lincoln, Y. and Guba, E. (1985). *Naturalistic Inquiry*. London: Sage Publications.

Lines, D.P. (2004). *A Grounded Theory Study of How Individuals Work Their Way Towards the Executive Director Position: Balancing Visibility and Exposure in U.K. Companies*. Unpublished Ph.D. Thesis, University of Surrey, Guildford.

Locke, K. (2001). *Grounded Theory in Management Research*. London: Sage Publications.

McLean, G.N. (2016). *The Case of the Misguided Researcher: A Fairy Tale of Ethnocentricity (Evil Witch) Versus Indigenization (Good Witch)*. Conference presentation at the 18th International Conference on HRD Research and Practice Across Europe (UFHRD/AHRD) Lisbon, Portugal, 8 June.

Paterson, B.L., Thorne, S.E., Canam, C. and Jillings, C. (2001). *Meta-Study of Qualitative Health Research: A Practical Guide to Meta-Analysis and Meta-Synthesis*. Thousand Oaks, CA: Sage Publications.

Patton, M.Q. (1990). *Qualitative Evaluation and Research Methods* (Second Edition). London: Sage Publications, International Educational and Professional Publisher.

Pearsall, J. and Hanks, P. (1998). *The New Oxford Dictionary of English*. Oxford: Clarendon Press.

Prasad, A. (2016). Towards decolonizing modern western structures of knowledge: A postcolonial interrogation of (critical) management studies. In, *The Routledge Companion to Critical Management Studies*. Oxon: Routledge.

Robson, C. (1993). *Real World Research: A Resource for Social Scientists and Practitioner Researchers*. London: Blackwell Publishing.

Sambrook, S. (2014). Critical HRD. In, Chalofsky, N.E., Rocco, T.S. and Morris, M.L. (Eds.) *Handbook of Human Resource Development*. London: John Wiley & Sons.

Stewart, J., Rigg, C. and Trehan, K. (2007). *Critical Human Resource Development: Beyond Orthodoxy*. Essex: Pearson Education Limited.

Strauss, A. and Corbin, J. (1990). *Basics of Qualitative Research: Grounded Theory Procedures and Techniques*. London: Sage Publications.

Tosh, J. (2015). *The Pursuit of History: Aims, Methods and New Directions in the Study of History* (Kindle Edition). New York: Routledge, a Taylor & Francis Imprint.

2 A Meta-Analysis of Coaching
Re-tracing the Roots and Re-analysing the Coaching Story

Introduction

This chapter, which is divided into two sections, begins with an analysis of the existing literature that sets out the different narratives of the process of the emergence of coaching. In the second section we extend these narratives by drawing out and discussing the socio-political and cultural elements that provided the platform for humanistic psychology and therefore coaching, from our perspective, to fully surface.

This analysis of how coaching has emerged provides a foundation for us to examine some of the arguments that have been used to develop a sense of authenticity and provenance for coaching. Histories tend to change over time as we uncover fresh evidence or see another way of interpreting the past. The present histories of coaching (Brock 2014; O'Connor and Lages 2009; Wildflower 2013:) have developed a foundation for others to think more critically about the origins and the emergence of coaching and a place from which further discussions and interpretations can surface. No-one account is either true or false as each historian interprets and describes the past from their particular perspective and their own intentions.

As Tosh (2015: 1) points out, our understanding of the history of a phenomenon provides us with a 'storehouse of experience that is drawn on for a sense of identity and a sense of direction.' He continues with the theme that without a knowledge of the past and access to the 'collective memory' of the past we are 'effectively excluded from social and political debate.' The authors take this argument into the realm of professional coaching suggesting that without a knowledge of the emergence of coaching as a craft and as a practice coaches cannot fully enter into the discussions and debates that are and will be essential for coaching to develop as a profession. Tosh (2015: 1–2) widens his argument as he points out that,

> our political judgements are permeated by a sense of the past,
> whether we are deciding between the competing claims of political

parties or assessing the feasibility of particular policies, to understand our social arrangements, we need to have a notion of where they came from.

O'Connor and Lages (2009: 5) concur as they state, 'We believe that you can understand coaching well only if you understand its origins, otherwise you simply have a snapshot that tells you little of where it came from and less of where it is going.'

If we apply Tosh's (2015) points to coaching as a pseudo-professional group (Muzio, Kirkpatrick and Kipping 2011), we can see that understanding how the various bodies that claim to represent coaching have emerged is as essential as knowing where coaching originated. Tosh's 'social arrangements' can be seen to include the training and development of coaches, the processes of credentialing and accreditation and the organisations who are staking claims to govern coaching as a profession. We return to this discussion of the emergence of the various coaching bodies that provide coaching credentials and qualifications in Chapter 4.

The Emergence of Coaching as a Modern-Day Phenomenon

Coaching has become a key tool in the repertoire of HRD-related practices in recent years (Hamlin, Ellinger and Beatie 2008; Grant and Hartley 2013; Ellinger and Kim 2014; Grant 2017). Some writers position it as an accepted developmental approach aimed at supporting and reinforcing organisational change (Bond and Seneque 2013; Brennan 2008; Fielden 2005; Passmore and Fillery-Travis 2011) and thus a means to enhance organisational performance (Gray, Garvey and Lane 2016). The emergence and rise of coaching seems to be accepted as a stable facet of the system of organisational and corporate learning. This is more pronounced in the Western hemisphere, or in those organisations in countries where managerial approaches have been heavily influenced by Western thinking/models. Lam (2016: 57) writing from a Hong Kong perspective reiterates this point; 'Coaching has largely been driven by Western thinking and business practice.' We raised the idea of Western influence in Chapter 1 and will continue to examine the notions and implications of this form of ethnocentrism in Chapter 3.

Coaching has a number of roots historically (Garvey 2011) and more recently as the idea of coaching evolved from the world of sport (Gallwey 1986; George 2013) and entered the main stream of management and leadership development. (Anderson 2013; Grant 2017) The implication of this historical legacy and the potential consequences for coaching in a global world is something we feel needs more critical analysis, particularly as we read the current histories of coaching (O'Connor and Lages 2009; Wildflower 2013; Brock 2014). The writers in this arena are mainly descriptive and accepting of the 'stories and myths' concerning the emergence and origins of coaching. Instead, as indicated in Chapter 1, we have used an historiographical approach to our work, which provided us with a heuristic with which we could analyse and discuss the history of coaching.

Garvey (2011) points out that the term coaching first appeared in the English language in 1849 in Thackeray's novel *Pendennis*. The term derived from a scholastic perspective, to mean the role of a Tutor at Oxford University in England, and how they would tutor or coach the student in their teaching groups. The actual form this took is unclear and whether we would recognise the style and manner as coaching today is debatable. One aspect is clear that the purpose of coaching was to sharpen the academic mind in terms of argument and logical analysis, thus arguably requiring coaches to have an appreciation of the meta-narratives of knowledge (Lyotard 1984, cited in Pedler, Burgoyne and Brook 2005: 62) as cited herein:

- Speculative: knowledge for its own sake, concerned with theoretical rigour, unconcerned with application;
- Emancipatory: knowledge that helps us overcome oppression and attain the highest human potential; and
- Performative: knowledge that helps action in the world, to resolve problems, to produce better goods and services.

(Pedler, Burgoyne and Brook 2005: 62)

Where we might place coaching today on the previous framework would depend on the purpose, intentions, and underpinning philosophy of the coach and the expectations of the sponsor and/or coachee. We suggest that most coaches major in the performative arena when practicing within business organisations. In contrast it could be speculated that within non-governmental organisations the positioning of coaching may be different. Thus, elaborating on the notion of emancipatory knowledge referred to earlier, we could consider the NGO that is trying to stop child slavery or prevent human trafficking may be operating within the emancipatory category of coaching. Another example could be when working with women only groups in countries where the rights of women are not recognised or supported. In our readings the area that seems to be left out of the literature is that of speculative knowledge, acquired for its own sake, but with little concern for theoretical rigour. In a later chapter we explore the ideas and practice of evidence-based coaching we can then compare the notion of speculative knowledge with the anecdotal examples of practice that inform our understanding of coaching in action.

According to Evered and Selman (1989) [cited in Brock 2014: 112] the word coach was first used in the modern sense—that is of a sports coach—in the 1880s referring specifically to one who trained a team of athletes to win a boat race.

Treasure (Foreword of Wildflower 2013: xii) offers the following points about the origins of coaching.

> How long has coaching been going on? As a defined procedure known by its own name? Twenty years, maybe. As a formalised activity, separate from therapy or training or conversation? Maybe thirty or forty years. But—before all that—how long have people been engaging each other in the kind of conversation which, if we overheard it, we'd catch a coaching flavour? It's almost impossible to know . . . Were there particular wise and skilful teachers, mentors, priests, parents, friends, who held themselves back from persuading and instructing, who pushed aside their own needs, fears and desires for long enough to pursue open questions, with no end in view except to create, in someone else, a space for reflection? It's inconceivable that there were not; that this never occurred.

O'Connor and Lages (2009: 348–349) concur with Treasure's (Foreword in Wildflower: 2013) points and continue, 'many people have filled the role of coach through the ages: priests and philosophers, artists and professors and of course parents.' This raises questions concerning the process and the form of coaching. What do we mean by coaching? How is coaching understood in different cultural contexts? How would we differentiate coaching from other forms of interventions used when developing individuals? What is the role that the coach fulfils? We will return to these questions in Chapters 3 and 6.

In our reading of the current literature we uncovered several main narratives that identify key relationships concerning the initial emergence of coaching as a practice; they are: education and training, psychotherapy and counselling, and psychology, and we considered humanistic psychology to have exerted a pivotal influence on the emergence of coaching that we separated it out from psychology and the relationship with sport. These genres were selected as they seem to have elements of what we might call coaching embedded within the practice of the professional group.

As we retraced the history of coaching, a question that surfaced was: why is it important for coaching practitioners to know and understand the history of coaching? We will address this inquiry in the beginning of this chapter and will suggest and assume that understanding the historical narratives of coaching enables practitioners to make more informed decisions about which school of coaching to adopt and their relationship to the beliefs and ideas that the various coaching models and theories espouse. In addition, practitioners will also be able to make significant contributions to the debates and discourses that are continuing to shape coaching as a practice and as an emerging profession. Rogers (Series editor's preface cited in Wildflower 2013) argues the case for knowing about the historical aspects of coaching.

> As coaches we need to know where our ideas come from. When we are furnished with such knowledge we are in a much better position to understand where and when to call on one technique rather than another.

The history of where our ideas come from is beyond the scope of this chapter. However, we need to have a philosophical background, epistemology, as Gray (2004: 16–17) identifies, to 'decide what kinds of knowledge are legitimate, and adequate' and, 'what it means to know.' In order for us to make these decisions we also need to be able to make decisions about the categories and labels we use to describe what we do and the language used by, e.g., coaches to describe their work and their clients. It is important to examine the ontology of our thinking, as Gray (2004: 16) describes ontology as, 'understanding what is.'

Rogers (Series editor's preface cited in Wildflower 2013) continues with the following forewarning:

> We need to be able to distinguish one guru from another, including those whose promises have proved false. Knowing all of this will mean we are able to answer challenges from our clients who, today, are much more likely to ask us probing questions about which type of coaching we do as well as who and what has influenced our practice.

The previous discussion reveals some of the foundation that coaches can use to build a sense of identity as a coach and create confidence in their practice, which supports the process of inquiry with their clients. The reality of knowing where the ideas that support practice come from connects the coach to the long line of thinkers and practitioners of many disciplines whom have already walked the path. (Wildflower 2013) We will return to the point about distinguishing one guru from another in Chapter 3.

This chapter examines the arguments and claims of where coaching has emerged from and the ideas that support the form and processes of coaching. Knowing where coaching might have merged from is key to our ontological and epistemological understanding of our knowledge base and the perspectives we might hold about ourselves and others as human beings.

Tracing, Re-analysing and Critiquing the Historical Narratives of Coaching

This section focuses on providing a review of the voices and main narratives that permeate coaching. We consider that there are four main narratives regarding the emergence of coaching, some of whose voices are quieter than others and may have been drowned out through the power of marketing across the internet. The roots and sources that we discuss and analyse are the educational, the psychological, the psychotherapeutic contributions, and the influence of sport on the popularity and success of coaching, as an individual and organisational intervention. These narratives produce a series of relationships with diverse disciplines. We chose these particular narratives to represent the emergence of coaching as there are implied associations with the wider eco-system of coaching. Garvey (2011: 345) concurs with the idea that coaching has emerged from these 'core roots' listing three main roots. We have, however, separated out the roots of psychology and psychotherapy into two different strands, as we consider they serve different purposes and intentions. These groups have and continue to have different perspectives on coaching and indeed in current debates about the professionalisation of coaching, as we discuss in Chapter 4, psychologists and psychotherapists see themselves as separate professional groups, with pre-established professional associations.

The Narrative of the Relationship With Education and Training

According to Brock (2014: 6–7) 'The roots of coaching reach deep into the soil of human history.' She continues with; 'In short coaching is far, far older than the root disciplines from which it is descended.' Brock continues her argument about the length of time coaching has been established in the world; 'Whether you call them coaches, mentors, elders, or masters, they appear in the first histories of human activity, and their activity stretches in an unbroken line to the present day.' It could be considered that Brock has conflated several terms and equated them with coaching as a way of establishing a lineage of 'coaching' to support the idea that coaching is an old and established tradition and is therefore an accepted way of developing individuals and groups. However, the idea that a process can be older than the root disciplines from which it apparently emerged is an important point. It presupposes the existence of a social process that may have been adopted by the roots of coaching and then emerged later. Garvey (2011: 308) points out that many of these historical links are associative and the writers are, 'making "performative" links to coaching activity'. Garvey (2011) does not explain or explore what he means by 'performative links.' However, the term, 'performative is a complex concept that can be thought of as a language which functions as a form of social action and has the effect of change.' Cavanaugh 2015)

We consider that presenting the different and diverse activities of 'coaches, mentors, elders, or masters', as if these activities are essentially the same in terms of process, intention, and purpose, as that of coaching as we understand it today, is to deny the cultural and historical contexts that gave rise to these activities. It may also be an example of what Hong and Huang (2008: 2) identify as 'the intentions [of the writer] are to create a narrative that legitimises, substantiates and confirms the existence of a . . . profession or emerging group.'

Brock (2014: 6ff) also claims that Socrates was one of the world's first 'personal coaches.' The Socratic method is a tradition of developing people where the teacher poses questions that the student would answer, and then Socrates would ask even more questions. These questions were not necessarily non-directive or even open in form or nature. However, as one of our respondents described, the culture of Athens at this time supported an argument-based form of social discourse. Socrates was therefore developing the skills of rhetoric, defined as 'the art of effective or persuasive speaking' (Hanks and Pearsal 1989: 1591). The Socratic tradition is thus rooted in Athenian Greek values. Athens at that time was focused on developing arguments that could win debates. There were several meeting places where debates could be held. The people who were involved with this type of social interaction would deliberately choose which meeting places to attend and therefore which arguments might be favoured.

Brock (2014) asks an important question; 'What was Socrates, if not a coach?' and continues with the assertion that Plato recorded the dialogues of Socrates, 'which make it clear that Socrates did not wish to impart knowledge; he sought instead to encourage self-understanding' (Brock: 2011). Even though, as Lane, in her introduction to (2007: xvii), points out, the Dialogues were written by Plato some years after the death of Socrates and 'depict an imaginary conversation, led by Socrates' and imagined by Plato. If we consider this aspect further, we are faced with some anomalies. The first element is that, apart from Plato's 'The Republic' and a number of dialogues written by others after the death of Socrates, there are no writings left by Socrates working with the young men of Athens. Socrates seemed to have a main purpose: to train the minds of suitable young men in Athens who could then become skilled in debate and rhetoric, and to further the introduction of a new form of government and democracy based on the philosopher as ruler (Lane 2007: xxxii). It appears that Socrates was involved with social and political change and was focusing on the development of young men who were instrumental in the success of his intentions. He is assumed to have asked good questions.

The intention was to prepare, in those days, young men for being members of the Senate in Athens. This was a deliberate preparation for a political career. Coaching conversations in the style of Socrates were therefore purposeful and had a socio-political agenda. Another commentator (Brunner 1998: 516) has discussed the relevance of locating the beginning of coaching history with Socratic questioning. Garvey (2011: 12) argues that this is more 'associative rather than factual.' It could be construed that Brock (2014) is using Socrates as a cypher, or code word, to legitimise coaching. Therefore, by ascribing the beginning of coaching to Socrates is 'short hand' for legitimacy, which then closes down/eliminates further discussion and debate about the processes through which coaching became apparent. The development of stories about a new discipline produces myths about the people who are the pioneers and forefathers, or foremothers, of an emerging branch of knowledge and practice. (Ball 2018) However, we can gather that Socrates was involved with a form of socio-political change (Lane 2007: xxx, 2007). The purpose and intentions of Socrates produces a tentative associative (Gray, Garvey and Lane 2016: 12) connection with modern day coaching, even though his model or form was different from our modern understanding of coaching. The links with a classical Socratic tradition (Brock 2014) may be an example of constructing an argument for the legitimacy of coaching by connecting it to historical figures that have high academic and social capital.

The influence of mainstream education is commented on by Brock (2014: 11) coaching is the 'missing link in adult learning theory + behavior.' The notion of a 'missing link' (Reader 2011) assumes that coaching has filled a gap in adult education, and until 'coaching' appeared on the landscape, there was a fracture within the systems of adult education. The implication of which, is that coaching has provided an answer to questions of efficacy within systems of adult education. However, the concept of 'missing link' also implies that there was a form of learning that existed prior to coaching and a new form of learning that has replaced or will replace coaching. Therefore coaching might be a transitional object (Freeman and Herron 2004), within the wider field of adult education and development. The idea of coaching being an essential aspect of learning and development brings us to the point, of the purpose and function of coaching within an environment of adult learning and development. What we might have here is the blurring of the connections between coaching and adult education. In a later chapter Brock (2014: 116–119) identifies that coaching draws on the knowledge bases of adult education. According to Grant (2005: 7) the 'knowledge domains of adult education and workplace learning and development are critical and relevant to coaching, as, at the time of writing, the majority of coaching clients are adults. Thus coaches need to be able to draw on such established knowledge to inform their coaching practice.' Neither Brock (2014) nor Grant (2005) establishes a causal link between adult education and the emergence of coaching. However, they both acknowledge the importance and relationship of different theories and knowledge bases to the work of a coach. This surfaces the practice of adopting established knowledge bases from professions that existed prior to coaching. We will discuss this in a later section as part of the relationship between theory and practice in coaching. We will also explore in Chapter 4 the underpinning knowledge that coaches draw on in their work and how/where they acquire this knowledge.

Narrative of the Relationship of Coaching With Psychotherapy and Counselling

This section is focused on the relationship between psychotherapy, counselling and coaching. The main reason to include this section is to refer to two forms of working with others that are different in their orientation and raises questions and inquiries, which inform our understanding of the coaching process. We are not concerned with the history of psychotherapy and counselling except where it might inform us of the relationship with coaching. We refer again in later sections to the medical model that guides and orients our perspective of illness, injury, disease, and wellbeing. Brock (2014: 51–53) describes how, during the late 1800s, Freud developed, 'a psychotherapy model from the [then current] medical model which was pathologically based and looked at curing mental illness and disorders in people.' Brock (2014) describes a situation, based on an historical perspective that embeds some important issues and assumptions about the nature of being human that have been railed against and opposed. This is where we first meet a model of medicine, which may or may not fit with our current perceptions of medicine or being human. The value of noticing this focuses on how our personal or cultural philosophy about life and living affect how we approach our work with others. The then view, of the 'ills' of people, and may now shape how we design and utilise theories and models of intervention. R.D. Laing in his writing in (1972) surfaces the term 'medical model' describing it as, 'the "set of procedures in which all doctors are trained". It includes complaint, history, physical examination, ancillary tests if needed, diagnosis, treatment, and prognosis with and without treatment.' The series of actions as described by Laing (1972) offer doctors a schedule that can lead to establishing the most appropriate treatment or deciding that intervention is not warranted. The medical model was established as a process of decision-making based on identifying symptoms, establishing the causation of those and deciding what might be the most appropriate intervention.

According to Campbell et al. (2011: 98–101):

> Psychotherapy is the informed and intentional application of clinical methods and interpersonal stances derived from established psychological principles for the purpose of assisting people to modify their behaviors, cognitions, emotions, and/or other personal characteristics in directions that the participants deem desirable.

This definition remains clinically driven, and it encompasses a description of the person as a set of separated parts that can be seen holistically. The relationship between psychotherapy and counselling are inherently psychological. The relationship between these two fields of practice is exemplified by the dyadic nature of the encounter between the therapist/counsellor and the person who has decided to use this particular approach to resolve some of their personal, life crises, issues, or problems. The model of the dyad used in psychotherapy has been transferred into some forms of coaching.

Roger's concept of the person and the different relationship that he advocated in his work as a psychotherapist (Rogers 1942) was termed 'person centred' and was the underpinning idea of his work and his teachings (Rogers and Sanford 1985: 1374–1388). Rogers's non-directive approach appears to have migrated from the worlds of psychotherapy and counselling directly into coaching. The method of transmission appears to be less that both psychotherapy and counselling produced coaching and more that psychotherapists and counsellors transferred their time, skills, and interpersonal experience of working with others into the emerging form of coaching. Brock (2014: 90) makes the point repeatedly, 'that coaching drew its theories and techniques from many sources, that its earliest practitioners had widely divergent backgrounds, and that these factors not only determined their approaches, but the areas in which they began to practice.' This is not the same as claiming that coaching emerged from these various and divergent backgrounds, rather that coaching has borrowed and appropriated models, theories, and ideas from a vast store of established knowledge, experience, and skills that others were already using in a different field of personal and professional development. The eclectic nature of coaching is not necessarily referenced transparently in the literature. The writers we have mentioned in this chapter seem to prefer a direct causal linkage between coaching and other disciplines. We consider this has been undertaken to bolster the provenance of coaching and to support the idea that coaching is a profession in its own right. The key elements were about working with others to support and challenge them to alter their behaviour, change their leadership or management styles, and develop their sensitivity to others so they could lead people more effectively. We will discuss in a later section in this chapter how the third wave of psychology, known as humanistic psychology, supported the domain of coaching and altered the orientation of practitioners in many related disciplines. There are number of different approaches to psychotherapy and counselling, too many to list in this chapter; however, for those who might be interested, the following link illustrates the diversity and breadth (www.psychologytoday.com/us/types-of-therapy). If we assume that coaching is eclectic in its use of knowledge and experiences from other domains, we will need to ask what body of knowledge and specific skill bases mark coaching as distinctive from other established disciplines and practices (C.f. Chapter 4).

Narrative of the Relationship of Coaching With Psychology

Brock (2014: 140ff) describes the first coaches in our modern understanding of coaching as divided into three main categories: 'Originators, transmitters and influencers.' She maintains that the root disciplines of the originators influenced the emergence of coaching, psychology being the primary root discipline. In the previous section we have discussed how education, especially adult education, may have had a form of coaching embedded inside the practice of educating adults. In this section we will review the relationship of coaching with psychology. As Brock (2014: 143) points out, 'psychologists had already developed models for one-on-one interaction,' and as we identified, so may have educationalists. However, the two disciplines we suggest were motivated by different intentions and purposes. On the one hand educationalists were focused on the education of adults to form the foundations for their exam results and potential careers, whereas psychologists were using their ideas and models to help individuals with what was described as clinical problems that were amenable to the type and structure of the discussions they were having with their patients or clients. The idea that Brock (2014) identifies as important and is a thread throughout this chapter is the concept of one-to-one conversations with the intention of improving the performance or life of the individual. This idea is not new and will be explored in the section on the form and structure of coaching. Wildflower (2013: xvii) supports this idea with her assertion that coaching, 'has the capacity to make individual lives more fulfilled, but could also have a transformative impact on society.' The promise of the potential of coaching is discussed in Chapter 3. The claims of coaching are important to identify and note, as they appear to promote coaching as a new wave of human development and performance. Brock asserted (2014: 11) that 'coaching was the missing link in adult education'; it seems to be a new wave of intervening in the personal and professional development of a wide range of individuals, e.g., for the purpose of focusing one's life, developing business improvement, and developing senior executives in companies. Devine, Meyers, and Houssemand (2013: 1382–1389) identify and examine the increasing impact that coaching might have in the educational setting, learning, teaching, and educational leadership. This extension of coaching into non-commercial environments might indicate the idea that coaching as a process can be used in multiple settings and not just for the development of leaders in commercial settings.

Wildflower (2013: xvi) is open and honest about her approach to the history of coaching, as she points out: 'As a history, it is selective and not always completely objective. It is certainly not an exhaustive survey of all of the disciplines on which coaching is based.' Instead she has chosen an eclectic range of brilliant theoreticians, eccentric teachers, maverick therapists, and inspirational moments that have contributed to the profession of coaching. Both Brock (2014) and Wildflower (2013) are attempting to connect the collection of disciplines and professions that preceded the emergence of coaching as a way of creating an historical and theoretical lineage from which coaches are basing their practices and their thinking. However, their claim that coaching emerged directly from psychology is fraught with difficulties. Their claim appears to be based on the assumption that psychology led to the direct emergence of coaching as a pseudo-profession or as a craft with coaches being craft artisans (Drake 2011). What we argue is that humanistic psychology began to cultivate a field of thinking and experience of working with people that then formed an environment in which activities such as coaching could grow and develop.

Wildflower (2013) and Brock (2014) have identified the activity which we now describe as coaching has drawn upon several streams of theory and diverse disciplines to form a foundation on which coaching has been developed. Coaching however, is only recently developing research that is particular to the pseudo-profession of coaching and is beginning to lay the ground for evidence-based practice (de Hann 2008). Prior to this type of research coaching relied on models and theories that were based on existing disciplines, mainly from the psychological field, with little regard for adult education, sociology or philosophy. These 'originators' (Brock 2014) brought with them their own embedded assumptions about how coaching could be practised within the very models being adopted as a foundation for the emergence of coaching.

The relationship between coaching and psychology is an associative one that depends on the usefulness of the various models and theories being adopted. The one area of psychology that was more associated with 'coaching' appears to be clinical psychology. This relationship was still associative, as clinical psychologists used a wide range of clinical tests to diagnose and guide their 'treatment' of individuals who had been referred to their services.

Norcross (2000) identifies the points of reference of clinical psychology and also describes the other possible correlated group within psychology (i.e., counselling psychology) that is similar to coaching as we now know it. 'Clinical psychologists tend to work with more seriously disturbed populations and are more likely trained in projective assessment, whereas counselling psychology graduates work with healthier, less pathological populations and conduct more career and vocational assessment' (Brems and Johnson 1997; Fitzgerald and Osipow 1986; Watkins et al. 1986). The counselling psychologist focuses on career and vocational assessments. This remains different to the work of current established coaches. This, however, raises another perspective, the training of the counselling psychologist in comparison to the length and depth of training of the executive coach (C.f. Chapter 4). It may also surface the apparent closeness of the two groups and may inadvertently produce a situation whereby coaches see themselves as able to undertake specialist work in the arena of career assessments.

Our discussion in this section has focused on the relationship between coaching and psychology. The claim that coaching came out of or arose from of psychology has been an associative one, made, we think, to legitimize coaching as a profession. However, as the timeline between the inception of a Coaching Psychology Forum in 2002 (Palmer 2005: 1–2), which was internet based, and the introduction of a Special Group in Coaching Psychology (SGCP) in 2006, illustrates psychology as a profession adopted coaching as a legitimate part of the work of psychologists. Palmer (2005: 1) identified 'Dr Tony Grant, [as] the originator of coaching psychology.'

The SGCP was formed for the reasons outlined by Palmer and Cavanagh (2006: 1) their claims were summed up in the following statement. 'Coaching psychologists are at the fore-front of developments in the coaching field.' They go on to identify the contribution that psychologists can make to the coaching field.

> We bring more than just a framework for a conversation with a client, such as the famous GROW model. We bring a host of psychological theories and models that underpin, and bring depth to, the coaching relationship. These include an understanding of mental health; motivation; systems theory; personal and organisational growth; adaptation of therapeutic models to the field of coaching; research into effectiveness, resilience and positive psychology.
>
> Palmer & Cavanagh (2006)

This part of the discussion is linked to the process of 'claiming authority' that various groups in coaching are tussling with during this time of confirming coaching as a profession.

However, these claims need to be viewed in the light of the theoretical orientation of psychology. Joseph (2006: 47) identifies that, 'because counselling and clinical psychology have adopted the medical model as their underlying meta-theory, coaching psychology in defining itself in relation to counselling and clinical psychology, has inadvertently also adopted the medical model.' He argues that the meta-theoretical perspective of the person-centred approach (i.e., that people are intrinsically motivated towards wellbeing and optimal functioning) is more congruent with the ethos of coaching psychology. There is in this statement an invitation for the field of coaching psychology to re-orient itself to a more humanistic stance. We have no evidence that coaching psychology has become more oriented towards a humanistic perspective. However, as we can see during this section coaching psychology has brought with it theories and models that may support the process of coaching. We will discuss the medical model in relation to the rise of humanistic psychology, commonly described as the Third Wave of psychology, in a later section. This discussion opens up the relationship between the theories and models we use in coaching and the implications for our perspective of and our relationship with the coachee or client or participants in the coaching process.

Narrative of the Relationship of Coaching With Humanistic Psychology

O'Connor and Lages (2009: 33) assert that 'Humanistic psychology is one of the principal roots of coaching.' According to Benjafield (2010: 357–362), 'Humanistic psychology is a psychological perspective that rose to prominence in the mid-20th century in answer to the limitations of Sigmund Freud's psychoanalytic theory and B. F. Skinner's behaviorism.' O'Connor and Lages (2009) concur that humanistic psychology surfaced at a time when the orientations of the behaviouristic and cognitive schools of psychology and Freudian psychoanalysis were focused on the psychologist or therapist being in a position of expert power and authority in relation to their patients. Moss (1999: 12, cited in Brock 2014: 62) broadens our understanding of the historical situation. 'Each of these schools . . . displayed major blind spots, refusing to acknowledge or explore critical dimensions of human life. Human psychology emerged to address these essential deficits of understanding humans.' The orientation of behaviourism, the cognitive school and psychotherapy, began in an era when most of these professions were dominated by the medical model. Krippner (Foreword in Moss 1999) puts forward the perspective that

> Psychological theories have reflected external and internal realities in various ways. Freudian psychoanalysis was influenced by "energy" models predominant at the time, and Freud's model of the psyche resembled a hydraulic pump supplying (or denying) libido for various human activities. Watsonian behaviorism presented a model resembling a slot machine; an external stimulus produced an output,

and the inner workings of the machine were disregarded. It is not a simple matter to present a single model of humanistic psychology because each theory reflects the background and interests of its author.

The use of mechanistic metaphors that resembled the latest thinking in engineering was applied to human beings as if they were machines and were capable of being understood in those terms. The idea that human beings were significantly different to the machines that were being developed at the time did not occur to the rational thinkers of the day. Humanistic psychology has therefore reflected the 'external and internal realities' Krippner (Foreword in Moss 1999) of the times when the tensions between the established orthodoxies of cognitive and behaviourist psychologies tended to dominate psychological thinking and practice. Krippner (Foreword in Moss 1999) continues with his description of humanistic psychologies with, 'humanistic psychologies have focused on the "well" or "healthy" (and even the "exceptional") human [being] diverging from classical [psychologies] emphasis on pathology and dysfunction in . . . the human person.'

De Carvalho (1990: 1) identifies the following figures as being the main founders of humanistic psychology: Gordon Allport, Abraham Maslow, Carl Rogers, Rollo May, and James Bugental, however, it is intriguing to notice that Otto Rank, who was one of the most influential thinkers on Carl Rogers, is not identified by De Carvalho. The main theories that were brought into focus at this time were, 'Maslow's growth hypothesis; Roger's client centred approach; Allport's personality theory; and the existentialist and phenomenological orientations of May and Bugental' (De Carvalho 1990: 267, cited in Brock 2014: 62). There was no one theory of humanistic psychology as it encompassed a broader idea of being human. Krippner (Foreword: Moss 1999) acknowledges that the psychologies of humanistic psychology, 'have incorporated insights and information from psychoanalysis, behaviorism, cognitive science, and the other schools of psychology, but have added something of their own to the brew: that human beings must be appreciated on their own terms.' Humanistic psychology therefore became a blend of the old and the new ways of thinking about and perceiving human beings.

However, Moss in his introduction to the 'historical and scientific background of humanistic psychology' points out that, 'humanistic psychology developed as a response . . . to perceived deficiencies in the psychological theory and research of the 1950's' (1999: 3). McLeod (2015: 1) takes this further, asserting the movement towards humanistic psychology was a 'rebellion against what some psychologists saw as the limitations of the behaviourist and psychodynamic psychology.' Response or rebellion? Response sounds very conservative and safe. Whereas rebellion implies something is moving at a deeper level within the system of the social, professional worlds that were inhabited by the authorities of psychology, psychoanalysis, and psychotherapy. In a later section we will revisit this aspect and inquire into the social, cultural and professional tectonic plates that were moving across the Western world. However, it is important to note that previous historical accounts have been written from a Western perspective and that the contributors have largely been from the U.S., the UK, and Europe.

Wildflower (2013: 77ff) identifies the following aspects that were prevalent in the psychological and psychotherapeutic world in the 1950s. She writes,

> At a time when the vast majority of the literature and practice was based on Freudian or neo-Freudian principles, therapy involved delving into a patient's past, uncovering painful childhood experiences, and relying on the professional to guide the patient towards understanding and recovery; or it sidestepped the role of the mind altogether to focus on directly modifying observable behaviour.

The premise of expert power and authority is described clearly in this quote. The passive position of the patient as a recipient of the 'treatments' and 'directions' of the therapist or psychologist all led to a psycho-social phenomenon of deference and subjugation of the patient's needs to the jurisdiction of the professional who was responsible for the patient's recovery. The two main influences on the thinking and the work of the early humanists were Martin Buber and Otto Rank. Otto Rank was, according to Wildflower (2013: 77),

> one of the first Freudian-trained psychoanalysts to break with Freud's teachings. . . . Rank stressed the importance of the client and the therapist working together in the 'here and now'; the necessary tension between separation and connectedness for all human beings; and the importance of understanding human development as a lifelong construction.
>
> In 1924, Rank published Das Trauma der Geburt (translated into English as The Trauma of Birth in 1929), exploring how art, myth, religion, philosophy and therapy were illuminated by separation anxiety in the "phase before the development of the Oedipus complex" (1929: 216). But there was no such phase in Freud's theories. The Oedipus complex, Freud explained, was the nucleus of the neurosis and the foundational source of all art, myth, religion, philosophy, therapy—indeed of all human culture and civilization.

The animosity between Freud and Rank eventually led to disruption in the field of psychoanalysis. The disjuncture between the firmly held strategies of searching for the cause of symptoms that were obviously due to some form of Oedipal disorder producing sickness and ill-health, and the idea that not all things are as a result of an underlying pathology and therefore are a disease or sickness of some kind. Rank disagreed with Freud (Rank 1929) about the centrality of the Oedipus complex. This argument split the two apart. In many ways this pattern of disagreement between the established authority figure and the emergence of new ideas seems to have been a significant phenomenon in generating the plethora of approaches to the history of intervention in being human. The writers consider that this is a time when a revision of how we work with individuals and groups is required.

We have noticed the process of separation from the authority and 'truth' of Freudian and neo-Freudian thinking, by Rank, who challenged Freud's ideas in his seminal book (1929), eventually Maslow, 'who stressed the importance of focusing on the positive qualities in people, as opposed to treating them as a bag of symptoms.' Hoffman (1988: 109), Rogers (1951) who developed a person centred theory and who was influenced by Rank and worked with Maslow to develop what we now know to be the origins of humanistic psychology. The central tenant of which is 'self actualisation.'

Wildflower describes the relationship between coaching and humanistic psychology.

> The central hypothesis of humanistic psychology is that the individual has within herself resources for self-understanding, for altering her self-concept, changing her attitudes and self-directing her behaviour. These resources can be tapped through skilful facilitation and a climate that promotes respect for the individual. Coaching depends on an equal partnership between client and coach. Given the qualities of humanistic psychology, it is easy to see why its precepts are central to current coaching practice.
>
> (2013: 79)

The relationship between coaching and humanistic psychology is therefore deemed to be one whereby the tenants of humanistic psychology and coaching seem to be congruent and in alignment. We might need to ask why coaching did not emerge from other schools of thought. Why did the thoughts and philosophy of humanistic psychology and coaching combine? A partial answer to that question may be found in how Maslow (1943) and others construed the individual in the personal, social, and political sense.

> Instead of focusing on what goes wrong with people, Maslow wanted to focus on human potential, and how we fulfil that potential. Maslow stated that human motivation is based on people seeking fulfilment and change through personal growth.
>
> (Maslow 1943: 382–383)

The humanistic psychology movement supported the idea of self as agency. McLeod offers this perspective. 'Personal agency is the humanistic term for the exercise of free will. Personal agency refers to the choices we make in life, the paths we go down, and their consequences.' (2015: 1) This moved against the principle of 'determinism' that was an integral aspect of Freudian, neo-Freudian, behaviourism and the cognitive schools at that time. It is important to recognise that the culture of the time in which these ideas were being presented was more stable with established stratification of society. Therefore, belief in a more deterministic life could be sustained, as society, work, and life seemed to have a solid structural order.

> The humanistic approach emphasizes the personal worth of the individual, the centrality of human values, and the creative, active nature of human beings. The approach is optimistic and focuses on noble human capacity to overcome hardship, pain and despair.
>
> McLeod (2015: 2)

We will return to this discussion about the cultural and social aspects of the emergence of coaching in a later section.

Rowan (Reason and Rowan 1990: 84), when discussing Maslow's contribution, describes the humanistic approach as one where

> we have a chance of being able to describe the person holistically rather than reductively. In other words, we can see the whole person, rather than some selected split off aspect of the person. But this depends crucially on the relationship between the knower and the known. We have to approach the person as a person.

The humanistic approach to psychology thus emerged in a social and political context of affluence and the idea of the American Dream. Furthermore according to Rice (2015) the, 'Hierarchy of Needs has been accused of having a cultural bias—mainly reflecting Western values and ideologies. From the perspective of many cultural psychologists, this concept is considered relative to each culture and society and cannot be universally applied.' The relativity of the main tenets we use in humanistic psychology and therefore coaching is discussed in Chapter 3. In an introduction to the Kindle edition of Moss's book on humanistic psychology, the writer puts forward the following description of humanistic psychology.

> Humanistic Psychology began as a movement of creative individuals who sought to remake psychology in the image of a fully alive and aware human being. Humanistic psychology emphasizes liberation from personal and social oppression and the pursuit of higher levels

of human potential. Humanistic psychologists criticize scientific psychology for their emphasis on the measurement, prediction, and control of behavior, and protest the exclusion of such basic aspects of humanness as consciousness, values, freedom, love, and spirit from psychological investigation.

Moss (1999)

We can see from the previous quote that the purpose and intention of the early 'creative individuals,' who were psychologists and psychotherapists, was to recreate psychology within a humanistic paradigm. The 'image of a fully alive and aware human being,' the 'liberation from personal and social oppression,' and the pursuit of higher levels of human potential,' seemed to generate sufficient energy and enthusiasm to take the principles of humanistic psychology into many walks of life. However, we can see as coaching emerged into the world as a new, and. possibly, a professional group, that humanistic psychology put forward some promises and set expectations of new possibilities and avenues of developing the potential of individuals, businesses, and organisations, possibly education, society, and the commercial world. We can see that this movement impacted the way in which social research was conducted and opened up the process of inquiry to embrace new ideas. (Reason and Rowen 1990). The client centred approach (Rogers 1942, 1951; Rogers and Sanford 1985) seeped into and effected a multitude of professional activities, particularly the shift from pedagogy approach, to teaching and learning, towards andragogy, which formed the basis of a new approach to adult education. (Knowles 1950)

The client centred approach placed high importance on the following principles. 'Humanistic-Existential [approach] models [and values] democracy. Freedom to choose is maximized. [and there is the intention to] validate our clients' human potential.' (CRC Health Group 2015). In addition Greening (2006: 239) puts forward the following five basic principles of humanistic psychology:

The five basic principles of humanistic psychology are:

- Human beings, as human, supersede the sum of their parts. They cannot be reduced to components.
- Human beings have their existence in a uniquely human context, as well as in a cosmic ecology.
- Human beings are aware and are aware of being aware—i.e., they are conscious. Human consciousness always includes an awareness of oneself in the context of other people.
- Human beings have the ability to make choices and therefore have responsibility.
- Human beings are intentional, aim at goals, are aware that they cause future events, and seek meaning, value, and creativity.

These principles imply a certain approach and purpose to the professional's relationship with their clients, and certain beliefs about human beings that would shape the power dynamics between them. And the responsibility for the process is in the hands of both participants.

There are more questions raised here than we have discussed so far, such as is coaching still rooted inside a humanistic approach or has it adopted different roots to match different and diverse possibly cultural expectations? If so, what are the implications for the essence of coaching? Where does the concept of democracy end up in a hierarchical organisational or social structure? We will follow these points up in Chapter 3.

In our review of the relationship between humanistic psychology and coaching we have established the main links between them are related to the adoption of humanistic beliefs and principles to support and substantiate the theoretical knowledge base, the espoused values, and the relationship between the coach and the client. (O'Connor and Lages 2009; Wildflower 2013: 76–78; Brock 2014: 62–66) We acknowledge that this possibly only applies to coaches who have intentionally adopted a humanistic approach, and may not apply to those models and processes of coaching that are based on other methodologies such as psychoanalytic, behaviouristic, and cognitive focus. Coaching is therefore only based on a humanistic approach if the models and beliefs of the methodology mirrors and uses humanistic approaches.

Narrative of the Relationship of Coaching With the World of Sport

In this section we will discuss the relationship of coaching and sport. There is a clear narrative that coaching emerged from the world of sport. (Gallwey 1986; Whitmore 1992, 2002). The association with sport can be observed very clearly as we watch athletic events and team games. The idea of a coach being responsible for the results of the game can be noticed as we watch the results of our favourite teams and hear the commentators declaring that it is the fault of the coach. The idea that sport gave rise to the broader practice of coaching outside of sport is compelling. Brock asserts, 'those in the business world seem to have needed the analogy of the athletic coach in order to accept the type of support they had previously shunned, or had accepted only in secret' (2014: 111).

Brock (2014: 6) argues that the roots of coaching extend back to 'antiquity,' claiming that, 'Eastern philosophers and ancient athletic coaches were among the first practitioners.' Brock (2014) continues by stating that, 'the ancient Greek coaches—former athletes themselves—helped the competitors of their day achieve personal excellence.' We can begin to see how looking at the past through the lens of the present may lead us to superimpose our terms and concepts upon a past that appears to look the same as we consider coaching to be. It is not possible for us to go back in time to evaluate Brock's claims and use of terms such as 'coach' and 'personal excellence.'

The imposition of the word coaching to describe a process that occurred 3,000 or so years previously may accidently confuse process with terminology, given that the word coaching did not seem to have entered the English language prior to the nineteenth century. (Garvey 2011) We concur with Brock (2014) that the athletes of the Greek Games were supported in some way to progress in their art and athletic forms, just as, even today, Masters of Martial Arts enable their students to learn the art and develop their prowess. Whitmore (Quoted in Hilpern 2006: 32) makes the point that

> Historically, coaching in sport was not what we call coaching, but instead [was] instruction . . . This was based on the dominant system of psychology, that is, behavioural and cognitive psychology. What that assumes is that people do not know much and they have to learn by being told.

The sentiment underpinning Whitmore's words are echoed by the idea, and a historical picture of the sporting coach as someone who has played the sport or event to high enough level for them to be seen as capable of teaching the sport or event. (Brock 2014: 113) Their credibility and success depended on how good they were at telling the aspiring players what to do and how to play. This often meant the coach had to demonstrate the skills and show the players they were capable. The style of 'coaching' used historically appeared to be more focused on instruction and demonstration from an expert position, than on using questions and answers from an egalitarian perspective. We will discuss the term coaching in the next section and analyse the differences between instruction, training, development, and coaching. We consider that coaching has a specific process and intention that the other processes of learning may not use.

Brock (2014: 113) continues with her description of the sports coach: 'In baseball, old pitchers teach (mentor) young pitchers. Old catchers do the same. They are experts, and do not stray outside their realm of expertise.' This idea of the experienced player becoming a coach and mentor of the younger players does not necessarily match up with the model of modern coaching outside of the sporting world. We will return to this theme of the experienced person developing the inexperienced manager, leader, or executive, in a later chapter.

Sports coaching have a different relationship to coaching in the world apart from sport. Wildflower (2013: 38) identifies that '[the] field of [sports psychology] has a history going back to the 1890s in America.' Wildflower (2013) however, does not identify any links with her assertions about the advent of sports psychology. She claims (2013) that in '1921 researchers were analysing Babe Ruth's swing and measuring his reaction time.' The first sports psychology laboratory was founded by Dr Carl Diem in Berlin, in the early 1920s.' We can see that in the early twentieth century the sporting world was beginning to search for answers to the secrets of success on the field outside of the confines of physical prowess. Green and Benjamin (2009) assert that, 'In its formation, sport psychology was primarily the domain of physical educators, not researchers, which can explain the lack of a consistent history.'

The image of the more experienced 'player' teaching the less experienced person, drawn from the field of sports coaching, lingers in our popular imagination and we tend to associate coaching with that notion. However, coaching is a process using questions to encourage the recipient to think, reflect, and make sense of their own situation, whereas the image of the experienced 'player' may be more associated with mentoring. Bozeman and Feeney (2007: 719–739) from their critical inquiry into mentoring describe the process in the following way.

> Mentoring is a process for the informal transmission of knowledge, social capital, and the psychosocial support perceived by the recipient as relevant to work, career, or professional development; mentoring entails informal communication, usually face-to-face and during a sustained period of time, between a person who is perceived to have greater relevant knowledge, wisdom, or experience (the mentor) and a person who is perceived to have less [experience] (the protégé).
> (2007: 719–739)

Coaching also seems to have remnants of sporting terminology in its language and ideas: the notions of taking part in events or games as a team, or the idea of the organisation being a complete entity or macro-team dependent on the performance of individuals. Being part of the team, being a team player. These imply that the world of businesses, organisations outside of sport, and the way in which people work within organisations are somehow replicating the sporting world. In our experience we hear coaches encouraging others to motivate and encourage the members of their teams to generate higher levels of performance. Sport seems to have provided us with a way of seeing performance in organisations.

Gallwey (1974) developed what Whitmore (1992, cited in Brock 2014: 114) claims was 'a simple and comprehensive method of coaching that could be readily applied to almost any situation.' Gallwey noticed that 'something else' was happening when athletes were taking part in an event or playing a game. His expertise and his experiences in coaching tennis gave Gallwey opportunities to observe the 'games people play' Wildflower (2013: 39) Wildflower (2013) identifies the plethora of advice available for athletes at the time Gallwey introduced his ideas of the 'Inner Game,'; however, 'it was characteristically aimed at high-performing athletes. It was firmly rooted in a Western mind-set that emphasized the competitive drive; and it still tended to be dominated by quantitative, laboratory based analysis.' The essence of Gallwey's methodology challenged the traditional approach to understanding athletic performance and introduced a new way of approaching sports coaching. Instead of critical feedback about what the athlete needs to correct Gallwey (2009: xvii, cited in Wildflower 2013: 41) identified 'three principles, appear to have become foundational for coaching practice. 1) non-judgemental awareness; 2) Trust in one's own self; and 3) The exercise of free and conscious choice.' Wildflower (2013) also points out, 'Gallwey's book on tennis appeared when developments in humanistic psychology, with their more optimistic models of human nature, were becoming established in the public consciousness.' Wildflower (2013) asserts that 'the 'Inner Game' concept played a huge role in the early progress of life coaching and coaching in business and other professional fields, helping people to believe in themselves and trust their intuitive abilities.'

The Etymology of the Term Coach

The ubiquitous use of the word 'coach' has led to a generalised perspective where we all think we know what it means in modern parlance; however, we may not be describing the same phenomenon or process. There are a number of opinions concerning the history of the word coach. O'Connor and Lages (2009) offer the perspective that the word comes from a French word, *coche*, for coach or carriage. However, if we examine the etymology of the word coach (Hanks and Pearsal 1998: 349) we discover the subtle differences in the word as a noun and as a verb. As a noun the term coach does derive from French roots. Yet as a verb it means someone who coaches or carries out the function of coaching. And yet, O'Connor and Lages' (2009) description of the origins of the word coach provides us with a metaphor that we can use to develop our understanding of coaching. O'Connor and Lages (2009: 12) add their ideas to the use of this metaphor, Kocs was the name of the Hungarian town where these types of carriages were made therefore 'a 'kocs' [became known] a superior carriage, an elegant way to make a journey in quick time.' They continue with the idea that 'coaching is not just a way to reach your destination, but also the best and most elegant way to travel.' O'Connor and Lages (2009) may have inadvertently offered a subtext for coaching that the authors of this book consider is left out of the historical stories of coaching. The idea that coaching is a process for the privileged few and is therefore out of the reach of most people for reasons of economics and accessibility. This may not be a 'truth' at this period of the history of coaching, and it may well require further consideration as we notice that the human potential movement sought to democratise the development of human potential. We will continue to surface this phenomenon as we explore the main stories of the emergence of coaching.

We have an historical perspective of the word coach, and in the previous paragraph the 'modern' idea of a coach has, even as we write, an image, associated as we said in our previous section, of the word being heavily associated with the world of sport. However, we may need to pause for a moment and ask ourselves about not just the word but also the activity itself. Earlier in this chapter we commented that as we look back in time everything seems to fit into our image of coaching as long as it appears to be a relationship between two people and learning is happening; most authors have not unravelled the differences and similarities with training, instructing, personal development, professional development, teaching, and facilitating. We can organise the different activities into four categories;

- Experienced informing—this grouping may include teaching, instructing, and training. The experienced informer is someone who has significant experience in the arena and is capable of imparting that information to the benefit of others. Power is not shared even if discussion is used as a method of learning.
- Developing known potential—with a focus on a blend of experienced informing and deliberate exercises to take individuals along a prescribed path of knowledge and skills development. This is normally associated with a pedagogical approach where the experienced person is in a position of power and authority with regard to their subject and has gained sufficient knowledge and experience in their subject.
- Improving performance specific to the person's skills and capabilities.
- Facilitating human potential—the aim of this category is to create a learning environment where the power is shared equally between the people who are involved with this process. Aims and objectives are jointly set, and questions and inquiry are the main process of learning. The climate of the sessions supports the development of the potential of the people involved.

Where do we put the process of coaching? At face value coaching might resemble facilitation. We consider if coaching were in the realm of the expert informer then most of the coaching programmes that are being marketed would miss that objective. If coaching were to take their clients along a prescribed path of development, then a better use of that investment might be to attend a structured programme in person or online.

Reviewing and Re-analysing the Evolution and Emergence of Coaching

The world of a coach is not limited to the one-on-one relationships they have with their coachees. The coach and coachee live in their personal eco-systems that are part of wider systems. (We will explore the idea of the coaching eco-system later in Chapter 9) Socrates has been held up as one of the original coaches. (Brock 2014: 6) and he was part of the Athenian eco-system. However, one of the main elements of the Socratic story are the, perhaps, often left out and unfortunate consequences of Socrates' life and career as an educator of young Athenian talent. Fry (2018: 404) asserts that Socrates was accused of offending the 'gods' of Athens, and this was his major offense. We include this aspect of the story of Socrates to introduce the relationship between the coach and the types of risks that coaches might be taking when they are working with senior figures and major organisations. And the metaphorical 'gods' that are revered in organizations of which coaches might need to take account and pay attention. We cannot accurately represent what happened to this process we call coaching in between Athenian Greece and the present day. The history of how individuals and groups were developed might be attempted from a sporting, educational, or political perspective. However, as we discussed in the section about the etymology of the term coaching, it requires a longer piece of research to unravel the nature and the actual process of this phenomenon. Nevertheless, it opens up an historical inquiry that prompts us to ask how coaching appeared to emerge, as if from nowhere.

Social and Cultural Currents That Created an Atmosphere in Which Coaching Could Emerge and Thrive

There are a number of factors that, possibly due to lack of space in past articles or book chapters have, to date, been left out of the historical narrative. One aspect that has been left out of the established histories of coaching is the influence of the Baby Boomer Generation, when a swell of children were born into western countries following WWII (Croker 2007) These children grew up in a different atmosphere to their parents, benefiting from better educational opportunities and improved health care (https://en.wikipedia.org/wiki/Mid-twentieth_century_baby_boom). The effect and influence of television provoked diverse ways of perceiving the world that were distinctly different to the attitudes and assumptions of their parents (Twenge 2006). They were encouraged to think for themselves and develop their own points of view. Their thoughts and feelings became more important to this generation and were paid more attention Twenge (2006: 72). This rise in emphasis on the importance of personal perspectives and the advent of more time to think and consider themselves has possibly produced a generation of people who were more receptive to the ideas that support coaching and personal improvement.

It is in the political and social turmoil of the mid-1960s that saw the Western world going through a process of changing attitudes towards the methods and processes of education; the exact nature of some of these forces generating these changes has been discussed by Postman and Weingartner (1969: 11ff). In summary, there was increasing unrest with the provision of education and the increasing alienation of the students from the mainstream process of education. There was increasing recognition of the place that change was and still is playing in our experience of the world. Postman and Weingartner (1969: 13) assert that 'change—constant, accelerating, ubiquitous—is the most striking characteristic of the world we live in and that [the] educational system has not yet recognised this fact.' They advocated a method of teaching that included the learner within the design and the delivery of education. One that supported student involvement and that took education from a mainly didactic teacher centred approach towards one where education was facilitated. The progress of their ideas took many years to take hold. Paulo Freire (1972) took this type of approach to literacy education in Brazil. Shaull, writing in the foreword (Freire 1972: 12) states that Freire's basic assumption is, 'that man's ontological vocation is to be a subject who acts upon and transforms his world, and in doing so moves towards ever new possibilities of fuller and richer life individually and collectively.'

Other factors during the 1960s that influenced the patterns of society and thinking across the U.S., the UK, and Europe included student protests against government decisions and unrest regarding various wars that were being fought by Western countries in, e.g., Vietnam. These spread across the U.S, London, Paris, Berlin, and Rome. 'The protests of 1968 comprised a worldwide escalation of social conflicts, predominantly characterized by popular rebellions against military and bureaucratic elites, who responded with an escalation of political oppression' (https://en.wikipedia.org/wiki/Protests_of_1968). The opposition to authority or anti-establishment, exemplified by the spread of popular music culture through groups such as The Beatles (Shuker 1998: 234) and an anti-authoritarian movement that spread across the UK, the U.S., and eventually across most of the Western world (https://en.wikipedia.org/wiki/Counterculture_of_the_1960s), this provided a fertile ground for protests and countercultural ideas. We can begin to see the environment in which different individuals and groups began to exert their individuality and personalities in the form of diverse ideas regarding how 'things ought to be done.' It is against this backdrop that we can see how different forms of thinking began to emerge. Even though Maslow's ideas began in the 1940s, his thinking challenged the prevailing mores of the time regarding how to approach the psychology of individuals (Maslow 1943). His contribution was to move the focus of psychology from a position of developing a diagnosis and ascribing a known pathological definition to an individual's dilemma towards one where the person's needs were paramount and there was a more positive orientation towards the individual.

During this time there were shifts in the distribution of power in Western societies. There was the general acceptance, supported by humanistic psychology, that individuals were powerful in their own right. These changes were important, as coaching with its emphasis on the individual taking responsibility for their own development, entered with the coach as a facilitator of learning rather than as an expert who was supposed to instruct and teach.

We argue that without the countercultural revolutions that swept the U.S., the UK, and Europe, humanistic psychology, Esalen, and other places, where different ways of thinking and approaches to education and psychology could develop, coaching would have entered a world that was unprepared for the challenges that coaching has brought to the practice of personal and professional change. Esalen, founded by Dick Price and Michael Murphy (www.esalen.org/about), was a response and challenge to the more traditional approaches to psychology, psychotherapy, and psychiatry that prevailed at that time. The emphasis on healing the whole person was influenced by humanistic psychology and was a definitive move away from the more pathological based approaches dealing with the human condition.

Puttick (2004: 399) concurs that the Human Potential Movement was a reaction to established ways of approaching human development.

> The human potential movement (HPM) originated in the 1960s as a counter-cultural rebellion against mainstream psychology and organised religion. It is not in itself a religion, new or otherwise, but a psychological philosophy and framework, including a set of values that have made it one of the most significant and influential forces in modern Western society.
>
> Puttick (2004: 399)

The emergence of the Human Potential Movement (HPM) in the 1960s, with the growth of a humanistic psychology based on the work of Abraham Maslow (1943), paved the way for a humane approach to individuals that emphasised the normality of being human rather than focusing on a pathological approach to human beings. This was a move away from the traditional approaches to the psychology of the individual. Barber (2006: 22–23) describes humanistic psychology in the following way:

> a humanistic value-base . . . suggests [that] an individual's mind and body, as well as their intellectual, emotional and spiritual being are indivisibly related to the other. That given resources, individuals have the potential to work towards resolving their own problems. That it is important to meet life in an open, inquiring and creative way in order to maximise their growth as individuals. That reason and democratic process should underpin all we do individually and socially.
>
> Barber (2006: 22–23)

The emphasis on the resources of the individual and the belief in their capacity to resolve their own problems is central to humanistic psychology. These ideas permeated the consciousness of the HPM and formed an approach to personal development that was fundamentally different to formerly established approaches. The move from a hierarchical approach by a psychologist or psychiatrist with their patients towards a more egalitarian relationship formed the foundation for a hopeful approach to resolving human situations. This is in tune with the ideas put forward previously about the separation of the individual from the hierarchical traditional and pathological approach to human development. In Chapter 3 we will follow the philosophical traditions that have influenced the development of coaching, in particular Neuro-Linguistic- Programming and Positive Psychology. We will discuss how these ideas have brought heuristics for coaches to use in their practice.

The background described previously provided a fertile milieu for different forms of disruption and unrest. Opportunities that were not possible in the more authoritarian forms of society and government emanated from young people born in times of scarcity and now living in the apparent abundance of the 1960s and 70s.

The Provenance of Coaching

The previous sections in this chapter have briefly and critically outlined the narratives on which the provenance of coaching has been founded. Other writers (Brock 2014; Wildflower 2013; O'Connor and Lages 2009), on whose ideas we have built our critical analysis, have developed arguments about the 'origins,' 'sources,' and the roots of coaching. This has been important, as Rogers (Foreword of Wildflower 2013) has described,

> As coaches we need to know where our ideas come from. When we are furnished with such knowledge we are in a much better position to understand where and when to call on one technique rather than another.

What Rogers (Foreword of Wildflower 2013) appears to be referring to here aligns with the concepts of ontology and epistemology, key concepts that need to be considered in any human enquiry (Heron 1981). As Heron (1981) argues, when engaging in any enquiry we need to be mindful of different types of knowledge: propositional (i.e., assertions of facts and truths) and experiential (i.e., knowing about an entity, which could be a person, thing, or a process) that the enquirer has encountered in a face-to-face encounter and interaction. He suggests that 'Experiential knowledge through encounter or acquaintance with what is before me involves more than just the bare or minimal perception. It involves familiarity with the encountered entity through sustained interaction' (Heron 1981: 27–28).

Heron (1981) elaborates by referring to the notion of 'propositional construing' and 'presentational construing.' Propositional construing recognition he argues is aligned to use of language, which in itself brings certain complexities given that as individuals, whilst we may use the same language, we can associate different meanings. This seems to be particularly relevant when coaches are working in a language, such as English, across cultural and linguistic boundaries. Presentational construing, according to Heron (1981) involves interweaving language with other non-linguistic and other non-verbal cues. What Heron (1981: 28–29) appears to be referring to here is the need to adopt a more holistic approach to enquiry which is 'not only a means of experiential knowing, it is a fundamental kind of practical knowledge . . . not just as presentations of a spatio-temporal whole that transcends its immediate presentations but also as the presentations of a *presence* in space and time.'

Returning to the quote by Rogers (Cited in Wildflower 2013) surfaces a question about how coaches acquire and make sense of different types of knowledge in order to build and develop their practice. This is a theme that we come back to in Chapter 4, where we set out and discuss coaching qualifications and credentials. One of the issues that we raise in Chapter 4 is how the equivalency of the knowledge gained on a short (weeklong) coach training programme and an extended (one to two years) coaching academic qualification can be identified and evaluated. The foundation for effective coaching may need to include the linguistic and contextual aspects of the engagement. We will return to this theme in Chapter 9 when we discuss the wider eco-system of coaching.

The histories of coaching that have been created include those aspects and those thinkers and originators whom the writers consider as being a key part of the 'provenances' of coaching, and the social and political context within which particular authors have developed their ideas and thinking. We have discussed elsewhere in this chapter about the predominance of Western thought in the coaching literature, particularly the influence of the North American originators.

One of the questions that surfaces at this point, in our discussions, focuses on what has been inadvertently due possibly to lack of space or reasons of focus and coherence left out of the histories. The purposes of creating a successful provenance is the creation of a rational and logical succession for the group's story, for the development of a clear identity, and high credibility of the emerging occupation and potential 'new' profession. One of the intentions of describing the provenance or authenticity of a professional group is to provide ideas and narratives that instil public trust and confidence in the emerging occupation.

Provenance is created as part of the argument about the value, importance, and the worth of an object or service. In this case the effectiveness of the process of coaching and the validity of the promises or claims being made. And provenance therefore serves as an importance element in the coaching business cycle. (We will follow this discussion up in Chapter 3.)

The main focus of this section is to develop what Arnold (2000: 8) identifies as, 'the context of the story.' We will draw on a few illustrations from the historical narratives to highlight those elements and possible voices that we, taking a wider lens, have deduced might be missing from the established and generally accepted historical accounts.

In this chapter we have argued that in most cases the links between the 'forefathers' of coaching, models, theories, and practice are mainly associative in nature (Gray, Garvey and Lane 2016: 12). These associations, with possibly high status individuals, convey a stronger sense of provenance supporting the assumptions about the status and credibility of coaching that occur as a result of those associative or assumptive connections. The narrative, as we have elaborated in this chapter, contains the foundations of the process of creating a suitable provenance, thus implying that coaching has a valued status, high prestige, and is a valuable service.

The value of being associated with Socrates, Maslow, Perls, Gallwey, Whitmore, and others provides substance and higher degrees of confidence in the process of coaching. However, the wider context or ecosystem of, e.g., Maslow, Perls, or Whitmore, might be ignored or masked in some way so that the connections can appear to be easily transferred to the modern or postmodern environment, strengthening the idea of causal connections that may not exist over time and space. Connections that cannot be proven beyond reasonable doubt. We argue that for many of the characters that have been identified as key players in the creation of coaching as a process and as an emerging occupation, their appearance in the narrative has provided correlational authenticity to coaching as an emerging profession. The adoption of models created by these historical figures, e.g., Maslow's theory and model of human needs, has strengthened the relationship between coaching and the apparent pathway to the present day. However, as we examine the wider context, several aspects emerge that might have been assumed as part of the general knowledge landscape of our current times. These silent assumptions are rarely brought to the forefront of discussions about coaching and therefore remain embedded and unexamined in our thinking about coaching. In our readings about coaching we have noticed that writers and espousers of coaching generally accept that coaching is a 'good thing.' Western (2012: 23) concurs with this sentiment.

> The coaching gospel has been a marketer's dream and coaching success can be found everywhere—popular magazines, websites, books journals and through narrative accounts. We hear less about the challenges and limitations, as coaching has focused very successfully on spreading the 'good news'—that is changes lives and improves work performance.

The assumption about the 'good news' of coaching may therefore act as an interference pattern as the development and evolution of coaching occurs over time. (We will return to this discussion in Chapter 9.) The possible negative or dark aspects of coaching are ignored until there is a breakdown in the coaching systems, and we are woken up to the possibilities of the less than good sides of coaching.

In the next section we will begin to surface those phenomena that have not been discussed in the literature.

The Hidden Networks of Coaching

Networks exist in all walks of life, from family groups to friendships, work relationships, and ad hoc encounters. Brock (2014: 134) 'discovered that many of the key influencers [i.e., people who had a direct or personal influence on coaching] and the early coaches knew each other, even though they lived in different countries and worked in several different fields.' We cannot be sure why this observation seems to be so important for Brock. However, she has surfaced an element of the development of coaching that may continue to influence how coaching is evolving.

With the idea of 'knowing each other, even though separated by countries and fields of work,' Brock (2014: 134) creates a number of questions about the processes that might be at work here, in order for these people to become connected, other than by random chance or a process of synchronicity. Navidi's (2017) work on Superhubs and networks, in the financial world, illuminates some possibilities for a hypothesis that might add to our understanding. One part of this is to search for and locate a 'hub' where most of the key influencers might have met. Wildflower (2013: 16) identifies Esalen as a place where this could have happened. 'Esalen was becoming an epicentre of the 1960s social revolution . . . it attracted people who wanted to push the boundaries of the self and break free of society's constraints.' O'Connor and Lages (2009: 35) list many of the people who visited Esalen, these included, Maslow, Fritz, and Laura Perls, John Whitmore, Gallwey, and others. O'Connor and Lages (2009: 35) claim that 'all of the important humanistic psychologists taught at Esalen' at Big Sur, California. Whether Esalen was the only hub where the early influencers (Brock 2014: 134) met and began conversations is more difficult to answer. There is a possibility that other hubs existed in many countries and were connected through both the literature and practices of humanistic psychology, or through direct communication. One such hub existed in the 1980s, located in a portakabin, in the grounds of the University of Surrey in Guildford, in the UK known as Hut 10. This was the home of the Human Potential Research Group, initiated by John Heron from 1970–1977. The research group continued until the mid-1990s. The H.P.R.G. was the first university-based centre for humanistic and transpersonal psychology and education in Europe. This might be an example of the network that was being created across the UK and Europe and can conceivably be seen as another hub within the humanistic network. The claim that Esalen attracted the people who initiated and convened coaching into a coherent form leaves out those people who did not attend Esalen directly but were influenced and engaged with humanistic psychology and the implications for the development of human potential. These additional connections were not restricted to the U.S. but were spread out across Europe. We discussed earlier in this chapter about how the social protests across Europe were producing tensions between established hierarchies and young people who wanted different forms of government and more emancipation and the freedom to be themselves. The social and cultural atmosphere was changing, and as a result movements, such as the H.P.M. and the promise of an increase on the potential of individuals were synchronistic and aligned with the vision and promises of coaching.

Esalen could be seen to be a place where 'magic' happened, with a 'romantic' notion of 'becoming a better person.' A place that Wildflower (2013: 16) encapsulates as, 'Literally, "on the edge", perched on steep hills high above the Pacific Ocean.' It is possible that 'word' was spread through the networks of Humanistic Psychology that were spread across the world. Hence how people in different countries came to know about the diversity of ideas and the potential of the people who facilitated and taught in the Institute. The concerns of business in developing their executives and senior leaders were, as we will discuss in the next chapter, being addressed through diverse interventions including, psychotherapy, clinical psychology, and counselling. However the creation of Life Coaching by Leonard (Brock 2014: 197) and 'The Inner Game' by Gallwey (date), led to a form of working with people that was significantly different to the practices listed previously and began to tip the balance between the established orthodoxies and the emergence of fresh ways of developing others.

Accessing Esalen—Resources That Were Required

The process of bringing people together, gathering them into a place that begins to generate an attractive energy, is a myriad one with many elements. If we examine Esalen more closely we can surface the elements of a desire and willingness to pursue developmental activities, personal accessibility, investment of the time, the energy, and the knowledge base to contribute and have the access to the economic implications of using these resources. Therefore we can infer that the people who sought out Esalen, either as a place where they could contribute their ideas or as a place of personal development, had access to sufficient time and economic support that could provide them with the freedom to visit California in the 1960s.

The trip within the U.S. seems to be an easier one; however, we do not want to under estimate the distances involved with the U.S. In comparison with the UK and Europe, the transportation links might have been more straightforward. Whereas traveling from Europe involved taking up to two commercial flights and possibly a hired car, that would have been outside the reach of the majority of people with the UK and Europe. We ask the question: is it possible that the individuals, who arrived in Esalen in those early days, represented a section of society that had time and money on their hands? However, this analysis is in contrast to Wildflower's (2013: 16) statement. 'They were forging an inclusive community that was intellectually exciting, personally challenging, and held the promise of expansive spiritual growth.'

The reason why this discussion is salient for our understanding of the emergence of coaching is as Navidi (2017: Kindle Loc 503) identifies, 'the decisions of anonymous individuals lead to collective activity. Who are the key players?' Navidi's question is critical if we are to understand who the decision makers might be in the networked world of coaching. The networks might be hidden from view to the main body of coaches and due to the spread of the internet some individuals and coaching organisations might appear to be more widespread than they are in reality. We have noticed independent coaches advertising themselves as if they are a larger organisation and appear to be representing the entire coaching profession. We discuss in a further chapter that this could lead to confusion for the new entrant into coaching, as they make decisions about which path to take at the beginning of their coaching career or which organisations to trust. This is another aspect that, perhaps using network science, could be examined further. Brock (2014: 362) expands the ideas of a hidden exclusive group further by identifying the existence of what she describes as 'Conversations Among Masters. . . . an annual invitation only conference designed specifically for and limited to, master-level (experienced successful) coaches.' This surfaces the idea that within coaching is an exclusive group. How influential this group might be inside the world of coaching is outside the scope of this chapter. However, we are left with the anomaly of knowing what Brock (2014) means by her use of the words 'experienced successful coaches.' We do not have any reference to the assumptions behind the phrase or any comment about the generation of an exclusive group within the world of coaching. The question that surfaces at this point is: is there a hidden form of elitism in coaching and how might this affect the structure and governance of coaching? And conversations amongst experienced coaches might be developmental and useful to take the occupation of coaching into the future. The key point is if we hide these conversations away from the majority of other coaches are we becoming an exclusive club or a democratic occupation?

The Missing Voices of Coaching

It might seem paradoxical to discuss the absence of voices as part of the emergence of coaching, especially as we associate coaching with the many strong and clear personalities that have co-created a new occupation that is influencing the development of an increasing number of people. However, as we identified in the previous section the voices that have been heard through the commentators and writers of the coaching narrative might have had some advantages that were and may still be preventing the majority of voices to be heard. We realise that it is impossible to include every voice in coaching; however, it is useful to examine where the predominant voices are located and whose are left out. The idea of 'missing voices' implies the presence of a process or processes that may unintentionally prevent the expression of different voices.

In this section we unpick how two of the writers (Wildflower 2013; Brock 2008, 2014) of the historical narrative of coaching arrived at their choices of whose voices they paid attention to and how this might have accidentally ignored or left out other voices. Coaching seems to have a positive press (Western 2012: 23ff), with few if any dissenting critics. As Western (2012: 23) points out, 'We hear less about the challenges and limitations, as coaching as focused on spreading the "good news"— that it changes lives and improves work performance.' This rendition of the power of coaching is cast in semi-religious phrasing implying that coaching is a process where 'life' can be changed and 'work performance' can be improved. The identified promises of coaching are alluring and may appeal to those who are working under stress and pressure as a way of altering their life and work to make it different to the pattern under which they are working. The absence of the critical voices may also correspond with the rise in 'positive psychology' that commenced with Maslow's work on human needs (1943) and was supported by Seligman's work with Petersen (2004) that challenged and brought a 'positive counterpoint' to the Diagnostic and Statistical Manual of Mental Disorders (DSM) (https://en.m.wikipedia.org/wiki/Martin Seligman). This may also have been influenced by the earlier publication of Gallwey's work on The Inner Game (1986), with its emphasis on non-judgmental feedback. The voice of the critic or even a critique of coaching may have become obscured by the 'gospel' (Western 2012) of coaching.

In order to understand, or gain an insight into, whose voices are missing and which voices seem to surface more strongly and inadvertently tend to dominate the story of coaching, we need to identify where, e.g., Brock (2008) and Wildflower (2013) obtained their informants and establish the mediums through which the voices are heard. Brock, in her original thesis (2008), identifies in her methodology chapter how she went about finding the voices she used to develop her ideas and to describe the emergence of coaching (Brock 2008: 135 ff). Brock 'used a purposive sampling method (Robson 2002) designed to elicit a minimum of 1,000 responses from a geographically dispersed sample of practitioners in coaching and related fields who may be using coaching.' However, it is unclear how geographically dispersed her sample was, she does not mention the areas or countries from which she obtained the data. There seemed to be other criteria that were applied that 'limited eligibility to complete the survey' and may have focused attention on certain types of voice. These included,

> the following, individuals and groups: established coaching organization; coach 136 training school or program; academic or education institution who offers or is considering offering coaching education; significant purchaser or provider of coaching; professional in a related profession such as psychology, organization development, human resources, among others; and professional coach.

The participants of her research were then chosen from the following range of sources.

> from the list of organizations, organized coach-training programs, and coaching professional association identified for the survey. I also included individuals selected on the basis of meeting one or more of the following criteria: from MCC and PCC holders whom I knew had extensive networks; individuals who held a key position in a professional organization; or people who had published a book or articles in recognized coaching industry journals. In addition, these individuals were selected from those having a global network.

The use of existing networks and the sources from which she drew her sample provided a template that excluded those who had not made a name for themselves or become visible enough in the global relationships, from which Brock created her sample of people and whom she interviewed for her research. In a later publication (Brock 2014: 474–477) she identifies the respondents whom she interviewed, and they appear to contain many of the shapers and influencers of the emerging occupational group of coaching. The following table identifies the wide geographical dispersion that Brock (2008: 135ff) used to eventually focus her research.

Brock (2008: 156) identifies that her respondents were dispersed over the following geographical areas.

> Of the 170 interviewees, the geographical distribution of interviewees was 75% from North America, 18% from Europe, with the remaining 7% from Australia, Asia, Middle East, and South and Central America.

Table 2.1 Geographical Dispersion of Brock's Sample

Country of Origin	Number of participants
North America	127
Europe	29
Asia—Far East	4
Australia	4
South America	2
Russia	1

Source: (Taken and adapted from Brock 2014: 474–477)

Table 2.1 illustrates more detail about this distribution and illuminates the predominance of interviewees from North America. However, North America is a large area with many states and diversity of cultures. The exact distribution in North America is unknown. It would be useful if we were able to access this information and analyse which parts of North America were best represented and which cultural dimensions were being preferred, as we could then generate some conclusions about the values and beliefs that might underpin coaching from this ethnocentric perspective. There is also the intriguing categorisation of Europe, where the UK and the different countries and cultures of Europe are blended into one unit. The use of the terms Asia and the Far East seem to symbolise a form of ethnocentrism where the variety of Asia seems to have been overlooked. We have therefore lost the information that might alert us to differences in understanding coaching from these perspectives. This may not have been Brock's (2008) intention as these broader categories might have been used because of the difficulties in representing all of the details concerning the respondents' locations. Therefore, 93% of the interviews are taken from a 'Western' perspective. If we combine these with the Westernised Australian influence we can see the representation of voices from other parts of the world has diminished. This has illustrated a possibility that Western perspectives are more dominant in coaching and may inadvertently form a cultural template from which we begin to perceive coaching. We point out that Brock's (2008) work clearly delineates the emergence of coaching from the Western perspective and that, now, the histories of coaching in other parts of the world may also require to be written, so that a more global understanding of the evolution of coaching can be developed. McLean (2017) makes the point that, 'the predominance of the English language in "so-called" International and high quality journals, may inhibit the publication of articles from authors for whom English is not their first or even their second language.' McLean's point is important in the light of the section on missing voices in coaching. The world of coaching may therefore foster the ontological position of being, that is favoured in the West, based on, 'Parmenides, circa

515–445 BC, [who] placed [the] emphasis on a permanent and unchanging world. . . . [Where] reality is seen as being composed of clearly formed entities with identifiable properties' (Gray 2004: 16). We will continue this discussion in Chapter 3 and 5 when we talk about the cultural differences between Asia and the West.

Wildflower's (2013) contribution to the historical narrative is significant as she identifies, from her perspective, writers and theorists who have created a cultural milieu from which many forms of 'talking' interventions can be developed and eventually become the backbone of coaching. However, Wildflower (2013: xvi) admits that

> As a history, it is selective and not always objective. It is certainly not an exhaustive survey of all of the disciplines on which coaching is based.

The voices she includes are an 'eclectic range,' possibly inspired by her own experience and readings. We can begin to see that for both Brock and Wildflower they began to shape a narrative of coaching that could begin to explain the emergence and existence of this, possibly, new form of development. In appreciation of Brock (2014) and Wildflower (2013), those writers that might now take a historiographical approach to the history of coaching have more material from which they can decipher and interpret the possible pathways through which coaching eventually manifested itself.

On reflection we might be able to perceive the presence of Western thought and ideas that are embedded within the structures of coaching models and as a process. We will follow up this theme in Chapter 3 and develop a discussion about the possible effects of this hegemony of Western thought.

Summary

We have analysed the historical processes of the emergence of coaching in the West, using a historiographical approach, particularly in North America and Europe. In Chapter 3 we continue our analysis of the development of coaching as a business. We have taken a critical review of how the literature portrays and presents coaching as an activity that has been around for many thousands of years, as an attempt to design a history that presents coaching as a historical phenomenon with sound credentials and a firm foundation of theoretical principles. This is part of the development of the provenance of coaching to demonstrate the legitimacy of coaching as an occupational group. We have analysed the claims about the historical pathways of coaching and examined the links between the main theoretical practices of psychoanalysis, psychology, education, and sport. The links, as Garvey cited in (Garvey, Stokes and Megginson 2018:

12) identify, that the link to classical times is probably part of the 'old as the hills discourse, and is therefore associative rather than factual,' and is therefore not necessarily an accurate account of coaching. We discussed how the links with the past have been developed as a course of action designed to promote trust and confidence in the communities that coaching began to infiltrate, especially the business world. Through a presentation of coaching being, as Brock (2014: 6) puts it, 'far, far older than the root disciplines from which it descended,' the impossibility of this statement is not questioned. How can an occupational group be older than the root disciplines, from, which it is claimed it has developed? That would make coaching the root discipline of its own roots.

We discussed the socio-political aspects of the emergence of coaching and looked at the social changes that were necessary for coaching to be accepted as a process of human development. The influence and role of the Human Potential movement and the principles of which have permeated the beliefs and practice of coaching. This discussion is picked up again in the following chapter.

In addition, we have traced the emergence of coaching and linked it to the work of Gallwey (1986) and Whitmore (2002), who with others brought coaching from the world of sport into the world of business. We will discuss the progress of this transition in Chapter 3 and examine the association of coaching with Human Resource Management and Human Resource Development (HRM & HRD).

Western's (2012: 23) critical observation of 'Coaching being a good thing.' This therefore potentially leaves out the darker aspects of coaching. The presentation of coaching as being positive and of benefit to the potential clients of coaching produces an environment where all coaches might be seen as positive and helpful. It might be construed that the results of coaching are always positive.

In contrast to the theme of 'coaching being a good thing' (Western 2012), the impact of positive conflict on the development of ideas and theories surfaces regularly in this chapter. It can be seen that most of the changes in thought and practice within the psychoanalytical and the psychological field came out of a process of disagreement with the existing status quo and the setting up of new schools and fresh approaches to human development. The disagreements between established authorities and new thinkers seem to be vital in the development of theory and practice. It would appear that maintaining an environment where critical voices and dissenters can be heard and the results of such discussions fed back into the global communities of coaching is also an imperative of continuing the development of coaching as an occupation and possible profession.

One of the themes that we will return to in Chapter 5 is the absence of diverse voices in coaching, as we identified earlier in this chapter. McClean (2017) identifies and challenges the coaching communities to be aware of how one culture can begin to dominate the discourse in coaching and influence the spread of ideas and theories from an ethnocentric perspective that does not take into account the hidden differences that exist within coaching as a global occupation.

The privilege and social capital of coaching has led to networks developing and Navidi (2017) encourages us to find out who are involved in these networks so that we can become more politically influential and astute about who are the facilitators of the thinking and the emerging ideas that are shaping the marketplaces where coaches develop their business and practice.

This chapter is not a definitive historical analysis or an exhaustive account of the way in which coaching emerged. We have presented a series of ideas and thoughts that with the intention of creating more reflection about the profession of coaching and to stimulate interest and debate within coaching circles about the models and theories that are currently underpinning coaching and the direction of this movement.

We have critically analysed the historical processes of the emergence of coaching, using an historiographical approach, in the West, particularly in North America and Europe, and we continue this discussion in Chapter 3. We have extended the narratives of coaching and discussed the socio-political and cultural aspects that provided a platform for humanistic psychology and coaching to fully surface. We have examined the claims of authors who previously have taken a descriptive approach to the histories of coaching. We have deconstructed the claims of the main relationship narratives of how coaching might have surfaced and identified the pathway from sport into business.

The theme of positive conflict surfaces regularly in this chapter. It can be seen that most of the changes in thought and practice came out of a process of disagreement with the existing status quo and the setting up of new schools and fresh approaches to human development. The disagreements between established authorities and new thinkers seem to be vital in the development of theory and practice. It would appear that maintaining an environment where critical voices and dissenters can be heard and the results of such discussions fed back into the global communities of coaching is also an imperative of continuing the development of coaching as an occupation and possible profession.

References

Anderson, V. (2013). A trojan horse? The implications of managerial coaching for leadership theory. *Human Resource Development International*, 16(3), 251–266.

Arnold, J.H. (2000). *History—A Very Short Introduction*. Oxford: Oxford University Press.

Ball, P. (2018). 'Urea and the Wohler Myth'—BBC. *Science Stories.* www.bbc. co.uk/programmes/b0b6p8g2 (accessed 12 August 2018).

Barber, P. (2006). *Becoming a Practitioner Researcher: A Gestalt Approach to Holistic Inquiry.* London: Middlesex University Press.

Benjafield, J.G. (2010). *A History of Psychology* (Third Edition). Don Mils, ON: Oxford University Press, pp. 357–362.

Bond, C. and Seneque, M. (2013). Conceptualizing coaching as an approach to management and organizational development. *Journal of Management Development*, 32(1), 57–72.

Bozeman, B. and Feeney, M.K. (2007). Toward a useful theory of mentoring: A conceptual analysis and critique. *Administration & Society*, 39(6), 719–739, October. doi:10.1177/0095399707304119. Archived from the original on 5 January 2013.

Brems, C. and Johnson, M.E. (1997). Comparison of recent graduates of clinical versus counseling psychology programs. *Journal of Psychology*, 131, 91–99.

Brennan, D. (2008). Coaching in the US: Trends and challenges. *Coaching: An International Journal of Theory, Research and Practice*, 1(2), 186–191.

Brock, V. (2008). *Grounded Theory of the Roots and Emergence of Coaching.* A Dissertation Submitted in Partial Fulfilment of the Requirements for the Degree Doctor of Philosophy in Coaching and Human Development, International University of Professional Studies, Maui, 2008.

Brock, V. (2014). *Sourcebook of Coaching History* (Second Edition). ISBN:13:978-1-46998-665-4.

Brunner, R. (1998). Psychoanalysis and coaching. *Journal of Managerial Psychology*, 13(17), 515–517.

Campbell, L.F. Norcross, J.C. Vasquez, M.J.T. and Kaslow, N.J. (2011). Recognition of psychotherapy effectiveness: The APA resolution. *Psychotherapy*, 50(1), 98–101, https://psycnet.apa.org/doi/10.1037/a0031817

Cavanaugh, Jillian R. (2015). Performativity. *Anthropology*, 10 March. doi:10.1093/OBO/9780199766567-0114 (retrieved 10 October 2017 and accessed 26 August 2019).

CRC Health Group. *Humanistic Therapy.* Web. www.crchealth.com/types-of-therapy/what-is-humanistic-therapy (accessed 29 March 2015).

Croker, R. (2007). *The Boomer Century. 1946–2046: How America's Most Influential Generation Changed Everything.* New York: Springboard Press.

De Carvalho, R.J. (1990). Contributions to the history of psychology: LXIX: Gordon Allport on the problem of method in psychology. *Psychological Reports*, 67(1), 267–275.

de Haan, E. (2008). *Relational Coaching: Journeys Towards Mastering One-to-One Learning.* Chichester: Wiley Press.

Devine, M., Meyers, R. and Houssemand, C. (2013). *How Can Coaching Make a Positive Impact Within Educational Settings.* 3rd World Conference on Learning, Teaching and Educational Leadership (WCLTA-2012). www.sciencedirect.com.

Drake, D. B. (2011). What do coaches need to know? Using the Mastery Window to assess and develop expertise. Coaching. *An International Journal of Theory, Research and Practice*, 4(2), 138–155, https://doi.org/10.1080/17521882.201 1.596486

Ellinger, A.D. and Kim, S. (2014). Coaching and human resource development. *Advances in Developing Human Resources*, 16(2), 127–138.

Evered, R.D. and Selman, J.C. (1989). *Coaching and the Art of Management*. New York, NY: American Management Association.

Fielden, S. (2005). *Literature Review: Coaching Effectiveness—A Summary*. NHS Leadership Centre. http://literacy.kent.edu/coaching/information/Research/NHS_CDWPCoachingEffectiveness.pdf (accessed 18 May 2015).

Fitzgerald, L.F. and Osipow, S.H. (1986). An occupational analysis of counseling psychology: How special is the specialty? *American Psychologist*, 41, 535–544.

Freeman, S. and Herron, J.C. (2004). *Evolutionary Analysis* (Third Edition). Upper Saddle River, NJ: Pearson Education.

Freire, P. (1972). *Pedagogy of the Oppressed*. New York: Penguin Books. Reprinted in Pelican Books 1985.

Fry, S. (2018). *Mythos—The Greek Gods Retold*. New York: Penguin Random House.

Gallwey, W.T. (1974). *The Inner Game of Tennis. The Ultimate Guide to the Mental Side of Peak Performance*. New York: Pan Books.

Gallwey, W.T. (1986). *The Inner Game of Golf*. Pan Books in association with Jonathan Cape Ltd London.

Garvey, B. (2011). *A Very Short, Fairly Interesting and Reasonably Cheap Book About Coaching and Mentoring*. London: Sage Publications.

Garvey, B. Stokes, P. and Megginson, D. (2018) Coaching and Mentoring Theory and Practice. Sage Publications Ltd. London

George, M. (2013). Seeking legitimacy: The professionalization of life coaching. *Sociological Inquiry*, 83(2), 179–208.

Goldstein, quoted in Modell, A.H. (1993). *The Private Self*. Cambridge, MA: Harvard University Press, p. 44.

Grant, A.M. (2005). What is evidence-based executive, workplace and life coaching? In, Cavanagh, M.J., Grant, A.M. and Kemp, T. (Eds.) *Evidence Based Coaching: Volume 1; Theory, Research and Practice Form the Behavioural Sciences*. Bowen Hills, QLD, Australia: Australian Academic Press, pp. 1–12.

Grant, A.M. (2017). The third 'generation' of workplace coaching: Creating a culture of quality conversations. *Coaching: An International Journal of Theory, Research and Practice*, 10(1), 37–53.

Grant, A.M. and Hartley, M. (2013). Developing the leader as coach: Insights, strategies and tips for embedding coaching skills in the workplace. *Coaching: An International Journal of Theory, Research and Practice*, 6(2), 102–115.

Gray, D.E. (2004). *Doing Research in the Real World*. Thousand Oaks, CA: Sage Publications.

Gray, D.E., Garvey, B. and Lane, D.A. (2016). *A Critical Introduction to Coaching and Mentoring*. London: Sage Publications.

Green, C.D. and Benjamin, L.T. (2009). *Psychology Gets in the Game*. Lincoln, NE: University of Nebraska Press.

Greening, T. (2006). Five basic postulates of humanistic psychology. *Journal of Humanistic Psychology*, 46, 239. Sage Publications DOI: 10.1177/002216780604600301

Hamlin, R.G., Ellinger, A.D. and Beattie, R.S. (2008). The emergent 'coaching industry': A wake-up call for HRD professionals. *Human Resource Development International*, 11(3), 287–305.

Hanks, P. (Chief Ed.) and Pearsal, J. (Ed.). (1989). *The New Oxford Dictionary of English*. Oxford: Clarendon Press.

Heron, J. (1981) Philosophical basis for a new paradigm - Chapter two in, Reason, P. and Rowen, J. (Eds.). (1990). *Human Inquiry—A Sourcebook of New Paradigm Research*. Chichester and New York: John Wiley & Sons.

Hilpern, K. (2006). Driving force: Interview with Sir John Whitmore. *Coaching at Work*, 1(6), 33–35.

Hoffman, E. (1988). *The Right to Be Human: A Biography of Abraham Maslow*. Los Angeles, CA: Jeremy P. Tarcher, Inc.

Hong, L. and Huang, J. (2008). *The Scripting of a National History—Singapore and Its Pasts*. Singapore: National University of Singapore Press.

Joseph, S. (2006). Person centred coaching psychology: A meta-theoretical perspective. *International Coaching Psychology Review*, 1(1), April. The British Psychological Society.

Knowles, M.S. (1950). *Informal Adult Education: A Guide for Administrators, Leaders, and Teachers*. New York: Association Press.

Laing, R.D. (1972). *The Politics of the Family and Other Essays*. Routledge. https://en.m.wikipedia.org/wiki/Medical_model.

Lam, P. (2016). Chinese culture and coaching in Hong Kong. *International Journal of Evidence Based Coaching and Mentoring*, 14(1), February. Full text archive. http://ijebcm.brookes.ac.uk.

Lane, M. (Ed.). (2007). Introduction. In, Lee, D. (1987). *Plato: The Republic*. London: Penguin Books.

Maslow, A.H. (1943). *A Theory of Human Motivation*. NY: Brooklyn College.

McLean, G.N. (2017). *The Case of the Misguided Researcher: A Fairy Tale of Ethnocentricity (Evil Witch) Versus Indigenization (Good Witch)*. Presentation at the 18th International Conference on HRD Research and Practice across Europe (UFHRD/AHRD) Lisbon, Portugal, 8 June.

McLeod, S.A. (2015). *Humanism*. www.simplypsychology.org/humanistic.html.

Moss, D. (Ed.). (1999). *Humanistic and Transpersonal Psychology: A Historical and Biographical Sourcebook*. Westport, CT: Greenwood.

Muzio, D., Kirkpatrick, I. and Kipping, M. (2011). Professions, organisations and the state: Applying the sociology of professions to the case of management consultancy. *Current Sociology*, 59(6), 805–824.

Navidi, S. (2017). *$uperhubs—How the Financial Elite and Their Networks Rule Our World*. Nicholas Brealey Publishing. Boston: Hachette Book Group.

Norcross, J.S. (2000). Issue of eye on Psi Chi. 5(1), 20–22, Fall. Published by Psi Chi, The National Honor Society in Psychology (Chattanooga, TN). Copyright, Psi Chi, The National Honor Society in Psychology. Norcross Web Reference. www.csun.edu/~hcpsy002/Clinical%20Versus%20Counseling%20Psychology.pdf.

O'Connor, J. and Lages, A. (2009). *How Coaching Works—The Essential Guide to the History and Practice of Effective Coaching*. London: A&C Black.

Palmer, S. (2005). Chair's update—Coaching psychology finally exists: Thank you for your support. *The Coaching Psychologist*, 1, July (Special group in Coaching Psychology). The British Psychological Society.

Palmer, S. and Cavanagh, M. (2006). Editorial—Coaching psychology: Its time has finally come. *International Coaching Psychology Review*, 1(1), April. The British Psychological Society.

Passmore, J. and Fillery-Travis, A. (2011). A critical review of executive coaching research: A decade of progress and what's to come. *Coaching: An International Journal of Theory, Research and Practice*, 4, 70–88.

Pedler, M., Burgoyne, J. and Brook, C. (2005). What has action learning learned to become? *Action Learning Research and Practice*, 2(1), 49–68.

Peterson, C. and Seligman, M. (2004). *Character Strengths and Virtues—A Handbook and Classification*. Oxford, UK: American Psychological Association and Oxford University Press.

Postman, N. and Weingartner, C. (1969). *Teaching as a Subversive Activity*. London: Penguin Education.

Puttick, E. (2004). Human potential movement. In, Hugh, C. (Ed.) *Encyclopedia of New Religions*. Oxford: Lion, p. 399. ISBN:9780745950730.

Rank, O. (1929). *The Trauma of Birth* (Dover Edition). Internet Link. https://en.wikipedia.org/wiki/Otto_Rank; https://en.m.wikipedia.org/wiki/MartinSeligman.

Reader, J. (2011). *Missing Links: In Search of Human Origins*. New York: Oxford University Press.

Reason, P. and Rowen, J. (Eds.). (1990). *Human Inquiry—A Sourcebook of New Paradigm Research*. Chichester and New York: John Wiley & Sons.

Rice, K.E. (2015). Hierarchy of needs. *Integrated Sociopsychology*, 9/12/12

Robson, C. (2002). *Real World Research: A Resource for Social Scientists and Practitioner-Researchers* (Second Edition). Oxford: Blackwell Publishers Ltd.

Rogers, C.R. (1942). *Counselling and Psychotherapy*. Cambridge, MA: Riverside Press.

Rogers, C.R. (1951). *Client-Centered Therapy: Its Current Practice, Implications and Theory*. London: Constable.

Rogers, C.R. and Sanford, R.C. (1985). Client-centered psychotherapy. In, Kaplan, H.I., Sadock, M.D. and Benjamin, J. (Eds.) *Comprehensive Textbook of Psychiatry*. Baltimore: Williams & Wilkins, pp. 1374–1388.

Shuker, R. (1998). *Key Concepts in Popular Music*. London: Routledge.

Tosh, J. (2015). *The Pursuit of History: Aims, Methods and New Directions in the Study of History* (Kindle Edition). London: Routledge, a Taylor & Francis Imprint.

Twenge, J.M. (2006). *Why Today's Young Americans Are More Confident, Assertive, Entitled and More Miserable Than Ever Before*. New York: Free Press, A Division of Simon & Schuster Inc.

Watkins, C.E., Lopez, F.G., Campbell, V.L. and Himmell, C.D. (1986). Counselling psychology and clinical psychology: Some preliminary comparative data. *American Psychologist*, 41, 581–582.

Western, S. (2012). *Coaching and Mentoring—A Critical Text*. Los Angeles, CA: Sage Publications.

Whitmore, J. (1992). *Coaching for Performance: A Practical Guide to Growing Your Own Skills*. San Diego, CA: Pfeiffer.

Whitmore, J. (2002). *Coaching for Performance* (Third Edition). London: Nicholas Brealey Publishing.

Wildflower, L. (2013). *The Hidden History of Coaching*. Maidenhead: Open University Press, McGraw-Hill Education.

3   The Global Business of Coaching

Introduction

This chapter charts the progression of coaching from the emphasis on life coaching and the sporting arena into the world of business. By presenting our analysis of the inter-relationships between HRM and the economic climate that existed in the 1990s, we provide a rationale for the introduction and implementation of coaching as a method for resolving people and performance issues in businesses. We identify some of the key initiators of this process and for the purposes of clarity examine the central ideas behind this transition. We review some of the consequences and the results of coaching entering commerce and the reasons why coaching is still involved as a central and possibly essential intervention in professional and personal development.

Grounded theory (Glaser and Strauss 1967) supports our intention to surface the voices that we considered to be missing in the coaching narratives. This approach begins with the participants' lived experiences and then relates this to relevant themes in wider literature. We chose this approach since the time period we are writing about is recent and has scant literature describing the significant processes that underpinned the migration of coaching into the world of business.

We gathered our information from a sample of individuals who were mainly UK based and have held senior positions in HR before and during the 1990s, and others who still are in senior positions. We also included clinical psychologists, experienced psychotherapy practitioners', and coaching brokers, who have seen changes in the coaching marketplace, we have labelled this group of participants as PPs. In addition, we asked for the opinions of experienced coaches in Asia, whom we also asked to identify metaphors that could describe the various phases of business development in the coaching industry.

This chapter draws on our conversations from the field in the UK and Asia to describe the way in which coaching has entered the personal and the professional development industry and critically identifies the implications and possible future trends. We will follow up the future trends in

Chapter 9. We have used the literature available on the internet and various publications to include a variety of perspectives so that the chapter can represent the field in as broad a way as possible, given the constraints of one chapter.

In this chapter we will use the following questions as a soft structure to guide our arguments and discussions:

1. What broader contextual factors have influenced the business of coaching? Who have been the key influencers/protagonists?
2. What are the organisational expectations from coaching, as distinct from other HRM/HRD systems/practices aimed at improving performance?
3. What are the tensions between coaching as performativity vs coaching as self-realisation and actualisation?
4. How do organisations know if coaching is bringing the desired performance outcomes and at what cost to individuals?

Positioning the Business of Coaching

Since the late 1980s and early 1990s, coaching has become an ever increasing and fast growing business. A cursory search of the term 'value of coaching' in Google returned 50,300,000 hits. In addition, surveys by organisations such as ICF (2016) also emphasise the organisational benefits of coaching, through enhanced individual and organisational performance. When we searched terms such as 'What is the market worth of coaching, executive coaching?,' the search returned with 40,400,000, results. However, the majority of the information was specific to the U.S. market. LaRosa (2018) identifies that 'Personal coaching is one segment of the broader personal development industry.' Boersma(2016), in quoting figures from I.C.F, 'which has a membership of close to 50,000 professionals, estimates the global coaching sector generates about $2 billion, per year, in revenue.' LaRosa (2018) locates the coaching market; this includes life coaching, and executive coaching, within the personal development industry, which has an estimated worth of $9.9 billion U.S. He states that,

> The $9.9 billion U.S. self-improvement or personal development industry is largely comprised of affluent Baby Boomers and female customers, especially for programs related to relationships, weight loss, exercise, spirituality, and Far Eastern topics. A substantial share of these customers are located on the two coasts of the United States.' This is not surprising as roughly 53% of the USA live on one or other of the coastal regions. (www.differencebetween.net/miscellaneous/geography-miscellaneous/difference-between-east-coast-and-west-coast/) It outside the scope of this chapter to discuss

any relationship between coaching and the two coasts of the USA, other than the West coast appears to be more aligned with 'free thinking and individualism.'

(LaRosa 2018)

This a vignette about the scope of the market in which coaching is situated. It is intriguing to note that the 'personal development' market is larger. These figures are U.S. centric and might not represent the global picture; it is interesting to note that Boersma (2016) is quoting I.C.F. numbers that appear to represent the global market and correspond with the U.S. centric statistics. However, Sherman and Freas (2004) state that the investment in coaching in the U.S. is equal to $1 billion. Therefore, the rest of the world might equal $1 billion. However, Bersin (2019) points out that 'The market for leadership development solutions is enormous: more than $14 billion is spent by corporations and there are more than 70,000 books and videos on the topic.' This complicates the market, mainly because coaching is often integrated with leadership development and therefore the true market figure for coaching might be more or less than the $2 billion. Segers et al. (2011: 204), citing Fillery-Travis and Lane (2006) ascertains that 'Coaching has become a $2 billion per-year global market.' The figure of $2 billion seems to have been around for a long time and has been widely quoted since at least 2006. The repetition of this figure might cause us to question if the market is actually growing or is stable at $2 billion or is an accurate estimation of the value of coaching as a global market. We can see that coaching is a much smaller market than either personal development or leadership development. The value of locating coaching in this way is to begin to see it as part of a wider landscape of activities with a longer history of customer acceptance. However, these figures do not demonstrate or indicate what the demand for coaching services might be or whether coaches can earn a living from this kind of work.

According to Sherpa Coaching (2019), 'Expectations of demand [for coaching] have finally leveled off after years of increase. From 2015 and '16, into the [current] years, . . . we see a leveling trend.' The demand for coaching appears to be waning at the same time, as more people are entering coaching. If market demand is falling (Segers et al. 2011), then why are people still training to be coaches? This observation is something that we return to later in this chapter as we examine the fuller picture of the coaching marketplace.

Whilst it is difficult to establish the actual income derived from coaching, surveys by Coaching Associations such as ICF in the U.S. and the Asia Pacific Alliances of Coaching (APAC) and Coach Training providers, e.g., Sherpa Coaching (2019), indicate that coaches charge different rates depending on the type and seniority of the coachee. APAC's 4th Asia Coaching Survey, published in 2016–2017, reports the hourly coaching rate for coaches in U.S. dollars, and the rate ranges from less than $150 up to $750 (www.apacoaches.com). In addition, APAC's 2016–2017 survey indicates that there appears to be a difference in the rates that coaches seem to charge for coaching in different countries that fall under the Asia Pacific region. Sherpa Coaching's 2018 Coaching Survey indicates that the hourly rate charged by Executive Coaches is $386 (an increase from the $350–$360 hourly rate that coaches indicated they charged in the previous three years) (www.sherpacoaching.com). The amounts quoted are indicative rather than actual. However, coaches who chose to use coaching as their main source of income can compute how many hours they will need for chargeable work and estimate how much time will be required for building the relationships that can bring in the required volume of work. Previous research by the authors (Evans and Lines 2014: 770) identified a number of activities that the independent coach would need to address as they develop the business of their coaching practice. These activities can be summarised in the following points: 'escaping the entrapment of organisational life,' 'setting up and shaping own independent box,' 'uncovering personal values,' 'becoming closer to idealised self,' 'developing a portfolio of products and services,' 'developing a viable income stream,' 'presenting a credible self to clients,' and 'gaining acceptance of clients.' These points are discussed in more detail in Evans and Lines (2014). However, the range of activities encompasses the reason why the individual might have decided to enter coaching, and how they then generate a viable income stream from the different business development activities that are needed by someone who has decided to enter coaching as a career. The need to be seen as credible in the mind of the potential and actual client base is something we identified in a previous study. Evans and Lines 2014)

The analysis in this section so far focuses on the numbers that are in general circulation on the internet. However, it does not inform us of the nature of the coaching industry, as it focuses on the potential size of the whole market. I.C.F. conducted a global survey of coaching securing 15,380 responses from 137 countries (I.C.F. 2016). Of these responses, practitioners make up 53,300, and those who use coaching skills as HR professionals or in leadership positions generated 10,900 responses. The majority of the report findings appear to be aimed at the practice of coaching even though there is some information about the amount coaches might be able to earn according to country. The report leaves out the structure and shape of the coaching industry. The focus on the practice of coaching narrows our perspective to the micro and meso aspects (see Chapter 9) of coaching as a practice, the needs of the recipients, and the requirements of the purchasers of coaching as an intervention. If we widen our viewpoint we discover that coaching has moved on from just being about independent practice to a marketplace that includes coaching brokers, who take responsibility for organising pools of suitably qualified coaches and providing matched coaches for their clients. We cannot discern how many brokers there are in the market, as one of our Professional Practitioners stated, 'when [people] talk about coaching [they] see it through a narrow view. No one knows the true picture, [of the shape and structure of the market].' In a later section we use three metaphors that have been identified by our PPs as indicative of the business and market of coaching. The financials of the market share of coaching that is taken up by brokers, training providers, third party providers of models, approaches, and advice for coaches and purchasers is hidden within the overarching figures of $2 billion. In addition to this rather fuzzy picture, some of the brokers and training providers will inevitably be providing a blend of services to include leadership, organisational development, and consultancy. There is another dimension regarding market forces. Institutions (such as universities who develop and deliver MBA programmes) are competing in a global marketplace for education and consider that they have to provide added-value learning opportunities to students, even if that is not expected, or valued, by the students attending such programmes (Herd, Gettman and Stevens 2018; Parker, Hall and Kram 2008). Is it possible that the adoption of the term 'coaching' into the title and marketing of programmes improved registration rates, because the programme purports to offer a pathway into coaching as a 'profession'? There is scope for more inquiries into the effect of the idea of coaching and its effect on current thinking about executive education.

The Business and Organisational Context of the 1990s

The drive for HR to become more strategic had been in the ether for some time. Malik (2009) charts the historical emergence of Strategic Human Resource Management, linking it to the increasing complexity of organisations and the need for HR to become involved with the business in a closer relationship. Ulrich and Brockbank (2008) have put forward a model of partnership between HR and the business as a way of conceptualising a different relationship between HR and the organisations in which they operate. They state that,

> 'all staff functions are trying to find ways to deliver more value to either top line growth or to bottom line profitability. The need for greater business performance has put all support functions under a microscope. If they are not delivering definitive and sustainable value, they have been given the mandate to change, be eliminated, or be outsourced.

In the early 1990s, there was a recession across the U.S., the UK, and Europe. This placed pressure on organisations to respond to a changing economic situation. (Walsh 1993; Gardner 1994) The response of many organisations and businesses to the economic downturn was to begin to make staff that were now considered surplus to requirements redundant. This produced an influx of educated and experienced professionals into the marketplace who were looking for work. In addition there were changes inside organisations that were beginning to affect particularly the support functions such as HR.

In the UK, the Institute of Training and Development (IDT) and the Institute of Personnel Development came together in the mid-1990s to form the CIPD (Leopold 2002). The American equivalent of CIPD, the American Society for Personnel Management in 1989, officially became the Society of Human Resource Management. The development of the overarching SHRM, and the CIPD separately responsible for the certification, training, and development of Human Resource professionals, in the U.S. and the UK, coincided with the changing demand on organisations. Jarvis (2004) represents the situation for organisations in the 1990s and identifies the following elements of the changing organisation.

- **A rapidly evolving business environment.** Targeted development interventions have become popular in helping individuals adjust to workplace changes.
- **The structural features of modern organisations.** Organisational downsizing and flatter structures mean that newly promoted individuals often have to quickly fit into the higher performance requirements of their new roles. Coaching can support individuals achieving these changes.
- **The need for targeted, individualised, just-in-time development.** The development needs of individuals can be diverse and in smaller organisations there are often too few individuals with specific development needs to warrant the design of a formal training programme. Coaching offers a flexible option, which can be delivered 'just-in-time' to strengthen under-developed skills.
- **Financial costs of the poor performance of senior managers.** There is a growing acceptance of the costs associated with poorly performing senior managers/executives. Coaching provides an opportunity to undertake pre-emptive and proactive interventions to improve their performance.
- **Improved decision-making by senior employees.** For senior level executives it can be 'lonely at the top,' as they have few people they can confide in, develop ideas and discuss decisions and concerns. A coach can be used as a 'safe and objective haven' to discuss issues and provide support.
- **Individual responsibility for development.** There is an increasing trend for individuals to take greater responsibility for their personal and professional development. Coaching can help individuals

identify development needs, plan development activities, and support
personal problem solving.

- **Support for other learning and development activities.** Coaching
provides a valuable way of providing ongoing support for personal
development plans, especially in assisting the transfer of learning in
the workplace.
- **A popular development mechanism.** People enjoy participating in
coaching as they get direct one-to-one assistance and attention that
fits in with their own timeframes and schedules. There is the potential to see quick results.

Jarvis (2004) describes the factors that were changing the business environment and the significant alterations in the psychological contract
(Argyris 1960; Coyle-Shapiro and Parzefall 2008: 17–34; Rousseau
1989) between the employee and the organisation. The cost of 'poor performance of senior managers' is exacerbated when there are fewer senior
managers, and performance issues cannot remain hidden beneath several
layers of management. Jarvis's (2004) last point surfaces some of the reasons why coaching might have become popular.

The Migration of Coaching Into Business in the UK, Singapore, and Hong Kong

We argue in this section that as coaching migrated into organisations,
professionals aligned with coaching, for example, psychotherapists,
counsellors, and psychologists, brought with them the psychological and
sociological orientations of Social Psychology, NLP, and Positive Psychology. The grafting of these orientations onto the process of coaching
began to reduce the influence of humanistic psychology on the wider
sphere of psychology. Elkins (2009: 267) identifies the process in the U.S.:

> humanistic psychology lost its power and influence, in large measure
> because it is inherently incompatible with the basic assumptions and
> values of contemporary main-stream psychology and with the con-
> servative ideologies that have increasingly gained power in American
> culture since the 1960s.

How this process affected the coaching domain is unclear; however, we
could hypothesise and suggest that as 'high performance' became the
dominant discourse in organisations, humanistic approaches that emphasised relationships, might have been seen as too 'touchy feely' (Elkins
2009: 272). The dominant discourse of 'high performance' may have
required a different language and set of assumptions. The language of
goals, targets, and outcomes became important. The ground was laid for
sporting terminology.

There are a number of people who were instrumental in aiding the migration of coaching from the sporting arena. Gallwey's (1974) concept of the 'inner game and the outer game' became pivotal in the development of a different attitude towards sports coaching, and Whitmore (1992) and others took the ideas of the 'inner game' and began disseminating a version of the process using the GROW model, a model over which more than one person has claimed ownership (Fine and Merrill 2010). The idea of the 'inner game and the outer game,' the inner game of the mind and the outer game of the organisation, and the work for which the individual is responsible, is integral to Gallwey's (1974) thesis of improvement and development.

The inner game and the outer game represent two components of the coaching process, the inner psychological 'self talk' and the outer aspect of 'personal performance.' We will return to this discussion later in the chapter, when we examine the tensions, and the synchrony, between these two aspects.

There are numerous individuals who have been identified (Brock 2014: 142) as either originators or the transmitters of coaching. Two examples of these individuals, Whitmore and Alexander (Brock 2014: 158, 274), who had been sportsmen who had performed at senior levels in their respective activities of motor racing and tennis, negotiated with Gallwey to introduce 'The Inner Game' ideas into the UK. And with this move, coaching based on the ideas of Gallwey were introduced to, first, sports coaches and then into the business world in the UK. The timeline associated with this movement from sport into business is important as it maps out how long ideas may take from inception into different markets. Gallwey's work was first published in the U.S. in 1972–1974. Whitmore and Alexander (Brock 2014: 158, 274), 'began to train people to be sports coaches using the Inner Game techniques around 1980,' Brock (2014: 274). The actual reasons that gave Whitmore and Alexander the impetus to transfer these sporting skills into the business world are not evident. However, we can hypothesise that they considered there was a new frontier or market for coaching and decided to capitalise of this business opportunity. There may have been more altruistic reasons as well; however, there is no historical record of those.

The account so far taken from the extant literature leaves out the impact of the context into which coaching was being introduced. The professional participants in our research (PP) described the emergence of coaching in the UK business world in slightly different terms, to the descriptions focused on the U.S. The situation that existed in the UK in the late 1980s and early 1990s had been influenced by a number of factors.

The following vignette describes some of the possible elements that may have paved the way for coaching to enter the business and commercial markets. Our participants identified the presence of clinical psychology, therapists, and counsellors, who were already operating within organisational and business settings. The following is a vignette from one of our professional participants (PPs) of what the situation might have been like in the UK.

> In the UK, the immediate post-war period was of re-stabilising industries that had been devoted entirely to war effort and, as a nation, getting out of bankruptcy. The spectre of the Depression that had followed the First World War was well within living memory. So job security was of paramount importance and the great companies—Unilever, Shell, ICI, Rolls Royce—appeared to offer jobs for life. Families treasured generational involvement with such companies.
>
> In 1973/4 ICI made its first ever redundancies. That sent a serious shock wave through the system. It coincided with the turbulence of the three-day working work when the miners went on strike and electricity supply was restricted to manufacturing industry for three days of the week for the first three months of 1974. Around this time (1972) an American company had been making its own foray into the European market it was the first time that what was then called Executive Career Counselling had come to the UK. At that time it was thought rather indecent in the UK to manage a career. Someone who moved companies by choice was thought to be very unstable and seriously short on loyalty. Careers happened by being in one place, working hard, doing well and being promoted. Perish the thought of self-promotion.
>
> But it was a timely arrival, and started a niche consulting industry that became executive career counselling until; in the great and productive turmoil of the Thatcher years through the 1980s British industry started making wholesale redundancies. Big contracts involving many individuals started appearing, for which there was no ready supply of skilled individual career counsellors. Therefore individual career counselling morphed into the outplacement business, and found itself also attached to the executive recruitment business, and now has many facets. So in [this participant's] professional lifetime what started as executive career counselling has returned as part of what might well happen in executive coaching. But now we have the opportunity to know so much more about the person.

As the previous vignette illustrates, when the economy alters and businesses need to adapt and change then the focus of the work with people also requires a shift. The language and needs of people development also embodies different words; thus, we see a migration to using the word coaching as part of the new vernacular. According to our PPs, the words coach and coaching were being adopted by major business schools and organisational consultancies, replacing previous terms that were aligned with psychotherapy and counselling. Another element that has been underplayed has been the migration of qualified psychotherapists, counsellors, psychologists, and educationalists into coaching, thus providing a greater sense of credibility, as their previous qualifications have added surety about the veracity of the practitioners' claims.

However, the story in Singapore seems to be slightly different. According to our sources, coaching entered Singapore as a method and means to work with the disadvantaged, to provide them with the thinking tools and ways of becoming more responsible for their own lives. And this was successful. However, as coaching began to take off, so it was seen as a means of creating a business and earning an income particularly working with business executives. Businesses and commercial organisations with a Western background, Multinational Companies (MNCs), were interested in using coaches to develop their leadership skills, acculturate new arrivals into the differences of working in an Asian culture, and how to do business in Asia. Our PPs recognised this as a turning point in the development of coaching in Singapore, which was linked to the presence of a newly created ICF chapter. The inauguration of an ICF chapter brought a sense of permanence for coaching in Singapore and with the opening of a chapter in Hong Kong coaching was in Asia to stay.

Lam (2016) identifies coaching as a, 'Western concept introduced into Hong Kong Chinese society almost two decades ago.' Bearing in mind that Lam is writing this in 2016, it can be seen that coaching has been around a long time in Hong Kong. She goes on to describe how coaching has adapted and possibly integrated the more traditional Chinese philosophies. Lam (2016: 57) identifies that 'coaching in Hong Kong has largely been driven by Western thinking and business practice,' and 'the Hong Kong International Coaching Community (HKICC) was registered in 2002 by a group of coaches who were mainly English speaking people educated in the West.' However, Lam's findings (2016: 57, 69) illustrate how the acceptance of coaching in Asia might have been influenced by the 155 years of British rule and 'still remain very Chinese.' Lam (2016: 57, 69) agrees that more research is necessary to deepen the findings. There are indications that for many people in Hong Kong coaching is an acceptable approach to professional and personal development, especially if 'it is efficient' Lam (2016: 70). It is outside the scope of this chapter to discuss if coaching is an efficient method of developing people, and this raises the question of how to research the idea and concept of the 'efficiency' of coaching. This is not the same idea as Fillery-Travis and Lane (2006), who posit, 'does coaching work?' Coaching might well work; however, if it is an efficient method of working with individuals and teams, this has not been discussed.

The Inter-relationship Between HR/HRD/OD and Coaching

Coaching appears to have become the method of choice for HR profes-sionals when they are intervening with human interactions in their organ-isation. There are a number of factors why this has become the case, which we now discuss. Our PPs suggested that the shift away from the

> old and traditional forms of developing managers with a sheep-dip approach [was] appearing less attractive as a way of tailoring devel-opment for individual managers and leaders, [particularly] those who [were expected] to thrive in the new economy and [the emerg-ing] digital environment.

The push was to develop 'truly customised approaches [to coaching], designed specifically for each individual client.' The emphasis on improv-ing performance and the impact of recession is highlighted by de Waal (2012): '[it] has spurred many companies to self-analysis and further organisational improvement. As a result, there is an increasing inter-est into the factors that determine sustainable organisational success.' Brown, Kingsley and Paterson (2015: 163) identify the changing role of HR in businesses and chart the changes that led to HR becoming more responsible for 'driving business performance—for example by work-ing on changing behaviours. . . . Staff development and training became important.' The synergy between coaching and HR professionals becomes more evident as we notice a relationship between the various activities and interests of both parties. de Waal (2012) puts forward the following observation: 'Organizations need to maintain their competitiveness and viability, by continuously adapting to changing circumstances through initiating and implementing fundamental large-scale changes in the way they operate and do business, otherwise they run the risk of going out of business.' The imperative of developing higher performance in organisa-tions has not reduced, and as organisations develop and change in line with changing trends and digitisation, so the emphasis on improving per-formance will remain paramount.

According to Jarvis (2004) another factor influencing the rise of coach-ing was the alteration towards a corporate, commercial culture of transfer-ring responsibility for the learning agenda to the individual manager and senior leader for their own development. Hakim (2003: preface to Kindle Edition) describes this transition as, 'I [the employee] am a business part-ner with integrity and a responsibility for working with the organisation and the customer, and attending to my own personal and professional development.' The part of this that is often left out of 'taking responsi-bility' is the idea of forming a 'business partnership with the organisa-tion and the customer'; this is an essential part of the 'responsibility for personal and professional development.' This does depend on whether the organisation has a culture that is set up for employee and customer partnerships. The combination of 'high performance' and the transition from a hierarchical and possibly paternalistic approach to professional development may have produced a culture whereby managers and senior leaders required a personalised approach to their learning. Our UK PPs reiterated that the aspect that coaching dovetails into is the element of 'customised development, that is designed specifically for an individual.' The other part of this is the word 'designed,' and this raises the inquiry of how often coaching interventions are actually designed for individuals and how this process is carried out, even if it appears to evolve from an open conversation. What decisions the coach is making, based on what information, and what they are doing in the moment-by-moment flow of the coaching process to ascertain the specificity of the coaching being carried out, is something that we return to in Chapter 5 as we present and analyse the responses from our coaching participants to this aspect of their practice.

It appears that coaching provides a service in which the strategic aims of organisations post the recession in the early 1990s are being addressed. Personal responsibility for learning is transferred to the individual employee, coaching supports other aspects of development, e.g., leadership development programmes. And as Jarvis (2004) points out it is a 'popular' intervention: 'People enjoy participating in coaching as they get direct one-to-one assistance and attention that fits in with their own timeframes and schedules. There is the potential to see quick results.' The essence of 'direct one-to-one . . . attention' implies a sense of privacy, confidentiality, and possibly a safe place for the client to off-load with someone whom they do not know and therefore feel able to talk about it in a more open manner.

The PPs involved in our research identified the following elements that began to change in the organisational landscape during and after the recession. There seem to be 'Increased competition and need for improved business performance against strategic objectives.' Another PP suggested that this increased the 'pace and breadth of businesses, with the increasing use of technology and ever present communications','

> and as a consequence of this accelerating pace of change the pressures facing businesses [increased] the need for efficiency and effectiveness in all operations, and leaders needed to demonstrate innovation and creativity, to take advantage of new ways of delivering products and services.

This need for improving performance, and the demands on leaders to adopt significantly different styles 'away from a command and control approach towards more collaborative leadership required a change in approach to people development.' These alterations in the business world began to shift the focus of organisational decision makers away from the established methods of resolving 'people issues' through counselling and psychotherapy towards the new approach of coaching.

Using Metaphor to Describe the Different States of Market Development in Coaching

One of our participants, who is from Hong Kong originally and is now living in Shanghai, talked about images and metaphors of coaching. We are using these in a metaphorical manner to discuss the global business of coaching. We have deliberately chosen to use these images as metaphors so that the connections between them and coaching are more immediate and present in the system. Morgan (1993: 277ff), in defence of metaphor as a method of developing understanding, asserted that,

> people . . . tend to become trapped by their perspectives and assumptions. As a result, they construct, understand, and interpret the . . . world in partial ways, creating interesting insights but obliterating others as ways of seeing become ways of not seeing.

Morgan (1993: 277ff) continues his discussion with a perspective of metaphors that might help us to understand the global business of coaching: 'metaphor is not just a literary or linguistic device for embellishing or decorating discourse. It's a prima means through which we forge our relationships with the world.' The metaphors we are using can be seen as lenses through which we can observe the states of the business of coaching rather than the different phases of traditional business development. The 'Wild West,' The Gold Rush,' and the 'Seafood Market' are all perspectives drawn from an historical and current understanding of the realities of these phenomenon. We suggest that these images hold true for coaching across the world. We argue that these are not the same as the maturation of coaching (Grant 2017) as an occupation or semi-profession; Grant (2017) argues that coaching has passed through two generations of development and is now in a 'third generation.' We assert that the practice of coaching is maturing; however, the global business of coaching remains turbulent, vacillating between the three main metaphor states without any need to stabilise and become an established presence in the business world.

Our first metaphor is 'The Wild West,' the idea of being in a territory that is not familiar and has not developed the 'rule of law' and formed itself into a stable society. (Brogan 2001: 219–248) We can see that in the development of 'Life Coaching' by Leonard (Kochman 2003) he sought to democratise coaching and make it a part of everyone's lives without the need for regulations and rules that might inadvertently exclude some and include a few others. The 'wildness' of the West or the new frontier, can be visualised in terms of individuals who need to look after themselves, a need to be self-reliant. This might be seen in terms of setting up a coaching business (Evans and Lines 2014), where the person who had been employed is now a solo entrepreneur and will need to be self-reliant and self-promoting.

In previous sections we have described a process whereby coaching migrated from sport across the new frontier of business and commerce. The frontier of business was different to the arena of sport (see Chapter 9) bringing a process of transferring sporting terms into business language. Our PPs describe how they considered that management and men dominated leadership in the 1990s. Scarborough (2018) identifies the available data on that period and comes to the same conclusion, even though women were in the workplace they were still in the minority. It can be hypothesised that these business leaders may have been more familiar with the language of sport, the idea of 'goals,' 'achievement,' 'targets,' and 'strategy and tactics' were terms that were understood. Coaching by adopting models that utilised these familiar terms could be seen as relevant to the emergence of the 'performance based organisation.'

The concept of the 'Wild West' remains a romantic notion with a cinematic vista. The idea of new frontiers can be seen in many corporate changes and possibly when businesses are introducing new ways of developing performance. There is an illusion that the 'Wild West', has been civilised. The introduction of credentialing and competencies brings a sense of the civilised and established occupation, craft, or semiprofession. However, as we have discussed previously, coaching is still an open field into which anyone can enter and 'hang out their shingle.' The frontiers remain in different forms. The introduction of coaching into an organisation, where coaching has not been utilised as a way of professional and possibly personal development, is a new frontier for the coach who is advocating this new practice of development. And it is a new frontier for the organisation that will need to alter its culture and approach to people and performance. However, as organisations change and alter their culture, purpose, and vision, coaching will continue to cross new frontiers. The rise and effects of the Fourth Industrial Revolution (Schwab 2016) will become clearer as the technologies develop and are more fully integrated into businesses. We discuss in Chapters 8 and 9 some of the potential consequences of this process. There is the possibility that there will be many subtle and conceivably hidden frontiers for coaching and coaches to cross and adapt to.

In addition, there is the concept of 'going West to gain more' (Brogan 2001: 219), the idea of entering Asia as a business opportunity. The process of entering new territories, with the prospect of what these new lands can offer new opportunities that could be developed financially, and the provision of new markets. This required creative energy and explorers who were keen to take the risks associated with breaking new ground. The Humanistic Potential Movement (CF. Chapter 2) provided such people and promised the release of hidden human potentials. The new frontier for the new and emerging occupation of coaching were the businesses and commercial organisations that were entering a recession and needed new ways of developing the performance of their executives and therefore the profitability of their businesses. This sense of the Wild West remains present, as more people enter coaching and new frontiers open up for coaches to move into.

The frontier is 'wild' because there are no established paths for individuals and organisations to follow. The original men and women who introduced coaching into organisations needed to adapt their existing frames of reference to the new country of business. Peltier (2001: 235ff) points out that the migration of counsellors and psychotherapists, who wanted to enter the world of business coaching might have a number of boundaries to cross and readjustments from their therapeutic world into the environment of business. Peltier (2001: 235) identifies a primary shift and subtle warning to the aspiring executive coach who is transferring from their therapy practice. 'Just because a new market has "buzz" doesn't mean there is a fit.' The idea of 'fit' did not surface from our participants. However, Peltier's (2001) perspective is important, as the entrants into coaching seem to be increasing, each year. The issues of identity reformation, the loss of independence, and the reduction of freedom of expression in terms of clothing and hours worked (Peltier 2001: 235–236). Peltier associates coaching with the consulting world, and his perspectives are coloured by his personal attitude towards that world. The key issues for a therapist making transitions and for many others who want to help others are outlined by Peltier (2001: 236ff) as business being about the pursuit of 'profit,': business processes are faster than the therapeutic cycle. The therapists will need to present themselves differently, and 'dress like a business person,' alter their language for example, from terms like, 'sessions,' into 'meetings,' and 'making sense' to 'ideas for action.' This is a flavour of what the transition across the frontier into coaching might entail. A detailed account of the micro-transitions and changes is outside the scope of this section. However, being aware that crossing new frontiers might involve changes in beliefs, attitudes, and relationships with other people is worth bearing in mind.

The second metaphor in terms of the business of coaching is, 'The Gold Rush.' Historically, Gold Rushes occurred around the world (Reeves, Frost and Fahey 2010: 111–128). In the case of coaching, the market began in mainly the U.S. and then moved across the world using a variety of vectors; one example has been the influence of the ICF and the establishment of 'Chapters' across the globe to support and credential coaches in different countries. In Chapter 4 we analyse the rise of ICF through the lens of resource mobilisation theory. A 'Gold Rush' is a new discovery of 'gold, that draws people in to a new market in which money can be made.' We argue that coaching became the new 'gold' in terms of developing people and the next market in terms of professional develop-ment, at a time when organisations were searching for answers to the perplexing question of how to improve their people's performance and improve the 'bottom line' of the business. We have discussed in a previ-ous section the influences on that process. We are utilising the metaphor of the 'Gold Rush' to illustrate the market development and possible returns on investment for individual coaches as the market matures. Bro-gan (2001: 10) quoting Andrews (1964: 49) points out the three stages of colonisation. 'Gold, trade, tillage represent the three stages in the history of colonisation, and the greatest of these because fundamentally essential to permanence, is tillage.' The 'Gold Rush' as a metaphor illustrates how this might be the first step towards a new form of colonialism utilising coaching as a wave of change. We also have several stages of business development embraced in this metaphor. This first is the 'rush' for the 'gold' of coaching.

The next stage of business development is the 'establishment of a mine' and staking a claim; this is not to be confused with opening a business. Another stage in the process is developing the coach to be able to extract the ore—the skills and development of the coach that are necessary in order to be able to 'mine' the 'gold' of the individual client, team, or organisation. This stage is also relevant when coaches are working with their clients; the mining process can be seen in the art of asking ques-tions that encourage reflection and uncovering the person's potential to resolve their own issues. The stage of 'staking a claim' is fraught with hidden difficulties. What happens if clients consider that the 'claim' of a coach or the 'claims' being made about the value and effectiveness of coaching are spurious and based on hype or marketing gloss. One of the issues for clients is who they can trust and how to resource the coaches that are required by the organisation. The organisational sponsor might well move onto another source for the necessary coaches who can meet the organisational needs at that time. Mines can be valuable if seams of gold can be found and recovered. How often valuable seams are discov-ered in coaching is unknown, and how often the coaching claim is found to be empty is also now known as statistics do not seem to be available to corroborate or substantiate the claims made by coaches. Informal, anecdotal information, as to the efficacy of each coach's claims, can be read on websites and in marketing articles, however, these claims are not necessarily easy to validate or confirm.

The metaphor of the 'Gold Rush' highlights a number of other business phases that are important to surface. The histories of the 'Gold Rushes' (Reeves, Frost and Fahey 2010) across the world identify the value of the return on the investment of the individual miner (www.history.com/news/8-things-you-may-not-know-about-the-california-gold-rush). The function of managing a mine was a costly enterprise, and the people who made the highest return were the merchants who sold provisions such as food and clothing, the equipment required to develop a mine, and access to water sluices, used to wash the ore and recover the gold. The maxim 'During a gold rush, sell shovels' can be interpreted as during the coaching 'gold rush,' sell training, development, and the 'equipment or tools' of coaching, in all guises and through all available channels (www.flexport.com/blog/trade-merchants-rich-california-gold-rush).

This analysis is important as coaching develops, and as we discussed earlier in this chapter when we identified the possible returns for an average coach. The investment required to train and develop to be a credentialed coach, the time and opportunity costs that will be necessary to grow a successful coaching business, have not been calculated over the coaching population, even though individual coaches and consortiums of coaches, may have personally figured these costs. Will the merchants in coaching be the real winners as coaching becomes more established? This last question raises another area of inquiry. What happened at the end of the gold rushes? During and beyond the 'Gold Rush' in California?:

> The '49ers who abandoned their golden dreams steadily accumulated modest riches painting houses, stitching clothes and baking pies. In today's money, a farmer selling onions made $160,000 in 1849; some deliverymen made six-figure salaries.

The success for the miners after the 'gold rush' was in doing the work that was required, and demanded, to support the wider eco-system of the whole community. What will be required in the wider coaching eco-system after the rush for 'executive' gold is over?

The Seafood Market—*Caveat Emptor—Buyer Beware*

This metaphor is useful for acknowledging the dynamics of a 'market place'. Pedrosa-Guitierrez and Hernandez (2017) conducted research into the activities of a seafood/fish market in central Mexico. They concluded that there were some interacting factors that allowed the fish market to prosper.

> [The market's] responses to fish market dynamics [which resulted in the market] organizing a complex network of buyers and suppliers whose relationships can be explained in the form of strong and weak ties. At the same time, reputation has been the central resource to build this social capital and also gives place to market transactions.

Our PPs identified that not knowing who to buy from in a crowded market may create the demand to buy on reputation and familiarity; the customer therefore will mainly buy on references from trusted professionals in the buyers network. However, in the case of commercial procurement the process adds a degree of scrutiny and possible protection from criticism, rather than through a relational process that places the emphasis on knowing whom you are buying from. In the Mexican example (Pedrosa-Guitierrez and Hernandez, 2017), the networks of buyers and sellers are created over time, some strong relationships and some weaker ones, that come together in a dynamic system to develop the social capital creating whole market transactions. As another of our PPS describes,

> 'The seafood metaphor is an example of market development—first, people sell sea fishes. Then they extend into other sea creatures like shell, shrimp . . . etc., and then even to fresh water creatures. Just like in the coaching market, what 'coaching' means become wider and wider . . . Thus potentially confusing to the practitioners, users and buyers. The buyer, in the coaching market is placed in a difficult position. Making choices about individual contributors to the coaching system based on reputation, appearance, and the stories being told about their success.'

The risk in buying fish when you do not know the market very well and do not necessarily trust the stallholders is considerable. You may get poisoned. In coaching you might not know if the client will benefit or not, whether they will be 'poisoned' or nourished by the process. It is difficult to ascertain the health and benefits of a particular coach's approach, style, or embedded suggestions through talking to them. Resolving the issue of performance is the priority, not necessarily the outcome in terms of individual responsibility, autonomy, or dependence (Heron 1989: 149–166). The point about the health and freshness of the fish, or the freshness of the coaching process, is one that is not necessarily written about in any detail. In our research for this book, we have not found any references to the health and wellbeing of the practitioner as being paramount in the choice of a coach. An extensive internet search of Google Scholar did not reveal any articles or books that discuss the health and wellbeing of the coach and the importance of the coach having regular supervision. However, Clutterbuck, Whitaker and Lucas (2016: 7–9) discuss the purpose of supervision and include the idea of supervision being 'restorative.' They continue with the point that,

> '[there might be an assumption] that the need for "restorative work in general might be less as . . . the coaching work will be less emotionally laden . . . [however] it is . . . likely that some of our clients issues will resonate with our own experiences. On occasion, these similarities may provoke some unfinished business . . . and also the need for restorative work remains important.

If the coach is not in supervision it might be less likely that they will notice when the overlap of the client's internal processes interrupts and triggers them. This is not necessarily accurate as some coaches we interacted with during the research for our book did recognise the need for supervision or deep discussions with fellow coaches when they felt something was not right with their practice. However, they did not receive regular supervision. We consider that the health and wellbeing of the coach is important as they interact with and develop their clients. Clutterbuck, et al. (2016) identify the possibilities for coaches to be stimulated by their clients emotional and professional journey, and therefore a potential need for coaches to seriously consider their requirements of and for supervision.

What Are the Tensions Between Coaching as Performativity vs Coaching as Self-Realisation and Actualisation?

This section is a discussion about the tensions we have uncovered as a result of writing this book. We will draw on the information provided by our participants' and form the narratives we have explored, so far, in this chapter. There seems to be a central tension between the agenda of the organisation, which primarily appears to be about improving the performance, changing the behaviour and style of the client, or altering their level of engagement. All of these might be in tension with the client's personal development requirements. However, we cannot find any research that specifically addresses these issues. Therefore, as we describe a narrative of the possible tensions that might arise in coaching we are hypothesising and suggesting these areas for further research. One of our Singaporean coaches highlighted an example of the challenges facing coaches when there is an apparent conflict between the performative aspects and the more transformational intentions of coaching. The description includes the following: the coach has been asked to provide five hours of coaching over a period of three months to a C-suite executive. The objectives have been formed from a 360-degree feedback process and are mainly behavioural. The question that is embedded in this brief description is; can coaching be effective for behavioural change within the boundaries of the assignment? What happens to the transforming nature of coaching? In the metaphor of the 'Wild West,' described previously, an observation of the type of people who ventured into the frontier, was that those who were more academic, or of a professional class were less likely to be of use to the construction of the infrastructure that transformed the Wild West. Carpenters, builders, woodsmen, and laborers who were used to building things, became a valuable resource (Brogan 2001: 219–248). The issue when we apply that metaphor to coaching is the tension between being a transformative coach and being a coach that is aligned with the actual needs of their clients. If there is a short period of time available, then maybe the coach may need to focus on what is required at that period of time. If we view coaching as part of the wider eco-system of lifelong learning (Jarvis 2002) then the coach might need to see their place as part of a lifelong process that continues after they have finished the current coaching assignment.

In the discussion so far in this chapter we have highlighted that there is a tension between the practice of being a coach and the activities associated with developing and growing a business. Businesses require clients and therefore client retention is paramount. However, the primary sponsor maybe the primary client, creating a three or even four way set of relationships for the coach. There is the relationship between the coach and the corporate sponsor, or broker, who supplies the coach with their clients. There might be strain between the coach and the client who is being coached, even if effective contracting has taken place, between the needs of the individual client, the requirements of their colleagues for the person to alter their behaviour or improve their skills of organising, and the requirements of the organisation that is economically bound into the coaching relationship. Towler (2005: 309) describes the organisation as the 'invisible client,' a hidden presence influencing the dynamics between the coach, the sponsor, the client and possible the client's colleagues. The client might also be in tension because they realise that their performance or behaviour needs to change however, they feel that they are unable to do so. This could be due to interference between their personal beliefs about themselves, their sense of self-worth, or fear about learning something new. These strains might not be evident in the coaching sessions. However, the client might not want to own up to a fear of not being good enough, one of the human fears that our participants described as being more universal than might be considered. The pressure of having to change according to a 'timetable' that has been imposed by the organisation through regulating the number of sessions and or hours that the client is allowed, might negate any real progress, or prevent the client from learning.

We begin to surface the tensions here that might also include those, unexplored areas for the coach, for example, some of our participants described how they did not take gender, or culture, into account unless the client 'brought it up.' These types of tension might not noticeably surface in the coaching process; however, they may rest at an unconscious level, possibly affecting the questions that are asked and the lines of inquiry that are avoided. We might take Towler's (2005) idea of the 'invisible client' and apply it to any pressure or unease that is affecting the coaching process. If so any undeclared self-interests on behalf of the coach or even the client, can be a source of friction between them, an example of this is the client who does not really want to be in a coaching relationship and then might pretend to be changing or achieving the objectives by creating positive stories about themselves doing well when they are not engaging in the process. Another aspect that is important to surface is the unease of working with an individual whom the coach begins to dislike, or the pressure of avoiding the possibility of emotional catharsis.

One of our participants described the world of coaching as being made up of different tribes who are 'wrapped up in what they believe'; these tribes often then 'argue against the other tribes,' creating discourses that focus on the correct way to ask questions, or the right way to address conflict, or even that there might be one way of coaching, a true way that is sacrosanct and from which the coach must never deviate. The anxiety of the novice coach might play out in being tied into a certain model or framework even if the client requires a different approach. This is not a definitive discussion on the tensions we have observed in researching this book. We suggest that the training and development of a coach might need to take these into account and prepare coaches for the 'real world' of being a coach. We revisit these in Chapters 7 and 9.

Summary and Questions for Further Reflection

We have continued to explore coaching within a specific time frame that positions the discussions in the years in which coaching emerged. We have discussed the factors that assisted the rise of this new occupation and the meso relationships that supported the growth of coaching. This chapter has built on the historical account of the evolution of coaching in Chapter 2, bringing our analysis into the current point in time. We have identified the changing nature of HRM and HRD, and the influences of these changes on the rise and utilisation of coaching. Other influences such as social psychology and cognitive psychology have been surfaced along with the ripple effect of Positive psychology in the coaching narrative.

The metaphors of 'The Wild West,' the 'Gold Rush,' and the 'Seafood Market' are ways of seeing the overarching business of coaching. In each of these metaphors we have identified different aspects from which coaches can learn about their business and adapt according to the apparent implications for their practice. One example of this taken from the 'Gold Rush' metaphor is that coaching has, in a similar fashion to the 'Gold Rush,' a market that seems to be attractive to practitioners in terms of low barriers to entry and in terms of a reasonable return on investment from their training and development. Whereas in reality the market appears, as in the 'Gold Rush,' to be skewed in favours of the merchants who supply the 'miners', i.e., the coaches. All of the metaphors describe a period of history where change was constant and the 'world' was altering. Through understanding the historical narratives of change through a wider lens than the micro aspects of the practice of coaching could lead to a deeper understanding of the macro network systems that govern and guide the future direction of this emerging occupation.

Questions for Consideration by Commissioners of Coaching

There are a number of questions that remain to be asked, and some of them follow on from our previous discussions. The key ones at this juncture in our discussions focus on the following; when selecting a coach how do you establish how skilful/qualified the people who call themselves coaches are? What has their education been? How up-to-date is it? How long has the coach been practising? Do they have specific sectorial experience? How relevant and current might that be?

Questions for Practitioners for Further Reflection

Which of the metaphors discussed in this chapter resonant most with you? Which of the metaphors might your clients identify with most and why? How do you as a coach 'fit' into the world of coaching? What adjustments have you had to make in your beliefs, attitudes, and ways of working with others? How do you as a coach position yourself in a business that appears to have a hierarchical structure? How do you create your visibility and presence in what is potentially a crowded/unclearly defined marketplace? Does your coaching work provide you with purpose and satisfaction? How do you see this continuing?

References

Andrews, C.M. (1964). *The Colonial Period of American History* (Paperback Edition). New Haven: Yale University Press, Vol. I.

Argyris, C. (1960). *Understanding Organizational Behavior*. Homewood, IU: Dorsey Press.

Bersin, J. (2019). *Why Leadership Development Feels Broken: And How We're Fixing It*. Josh Bersin Academy. https://joshbersin.com/2019/07/why-leadership-development-feels-broken-and-how-were-fixing-it/ (accessed 4 October 2019).

Boersma, M. (2016). Coaching no longer the preserve of executives. *Financial Times—Special Report*. www.ft.com/content/60d6ae0a-d0b2-11e5-92a1-c5e23ef99c77 (accessed 4 October 2019).

Brock, V.G. (2014). *Sourcebook of Coaching History* (Second Edition). ISBN:1469986655.

Brogan, H. (2001). *The Penguin History of the USA*. London, UK: Penguin Books.

Brown, P., Kingsley, J. and Paterson, S. (2015). *The Fear Free Organisation— Vital Insights from Neuroscience to Transform Your Business Culture*. London: Kogan Page.

Clutterbuck, D., Whitaker, C. and Lucas, M. (2016). *Coaching Supervision—A Practical Guide for Supervisors*. London: Routledge, Taylor & Francis Group.

Coyle-Shapiro, J.A-M. and Parzefall, M. (2008). Psychological contracts. In, Cooper, Cary L. and Barling, J. (Eds.) *The Sage Handbook of Organizational Behavior*. London: Sage Publications.

de Waal, A. (2012). Characteristics of high performance organisations: Macroth-ink institute. *Journal of Management Research*, 4(4), 39–71.

Elkins, D.N. (2009). Why humanistic psychology lost its power and influence on American psychology—Implications for advancing humanistic psychology. *Journal of Humanistic Psychology*, 49(3), 267–291.

Evans, C. and Lines, D. (2014). Which hat do I say I am wearing? Identity work of independent coaching practitioners. *European Journal of Training and Development*, 38(8), 264–779.

Fillery-Travis, A.F. and Lane, D. (2006). Does coaching work or are we asking the wrong question? *International Coaching Psychology Review*, 1, 23–36. Cited in, Segers, J., Vloeberghs, D., Henderichx, E. and Inceoglu, I. (2011). Structuring and understanding the coaching industry: The coaching cube. *Academy of Management, Learning and Education*, 10(2), 204–221.

Fine, A. and Merrill, R.R. (2010). *You Already Know How to Be Great: A Simple Way to Remove Interference and Unlock Your Greatest Potential*. New York: Portfolio Penguin.

Gallwey, W.T. (1974). *The Inner Game of Tennis* (First Edition). New York: Random House.

Gardner, Jennifer M. (1994). The 1990–1991 recession: How bad was the labor market? (PDF). *Monthly Labor Review: Bureau of Labor Statistics*, 117(6), 3–11.

Glaser, B. and Strauss, A. (1967). *The Discovery of Grounded Theory: Strategies for Qualitative Research*. New York: Adeline De Gruyter.

Grant, A.M. (2017). The third 'generation' of workplace coaching: Creating a culture of quality conversations. *Coaching: An International Journal of Theory, Research and Practice*, 10(1), 37–53.

Hakim, C. (2003). *We Are All Self Employed—How to Take Control of Your Career* (Kindle Edition). San Francisco: Berrett-Koehler Publishers Inc.

Herd, A., Gettman, H. and Stevens, C. (2018). *Coaches' and Clients' Perspectives on Using Various Assessment Tools in Executive Coaching: Toward a Data-Driven Conceptual Decision Framework*. UFHRD Annual Conference. Northumbria University, Newcastle, 6–8 June.

Heron, J. (1989) Six Category Intervention Analysis. (Third Edition) Human Potential Resource Group. University of Surrey, Guildford. Surrey. U.K.

Jarvis, J. (2004). *Coaching and Buying Coaching Services*. CIPD. http://coachingblog.lt/wp-content/uploads/2012/09/2995coachbuyingservs1.pdf (accessed 12 October 2019).

Jarvis, P. (Ed.). (2002). *The Age of Learning: Education and the Knowledge Society*. London: Kogan Page.

Kochmanm, M. (2003). Coach or couch, choose your therapy. *New York Times*, 13 July.

Lam. P. (2016) Chinese culture and coaching in Hong Kong. International Journal of Evidence Based Coaching and Mentoring. Vol. 14, No. 1, February 2016. Oxford Brookes Oxford U.K.

LaRosa, J. (2018). *U.S. Personal Coaching Industry Tops $1 Billion, and Growing*. Published by Market Research.com Market Research Blog. https://blog. marketresearch.com/us-personal-coaching-industry-tops-1-billion-and-grow ing (accessed 4 October 2019).

Leopold, J. (2002). *Human Resources in Organisations*. Harlow: Pearson Education, Financial Times Press.

Malik, N. (2009). Emergence of strategic human resource management historical perspective. *Academic Leadership: The Online Journal*, 7(1), Article 16. https://scholars.fhsu.edu/cgi/viewcontent.cgi?article=1259&context=alj (accessed 30 October 2019).

Morgan, G. (1993). *Imaginization—The Art of Creative Management*. London: Sage Publications.

Parker, P., Hall, D.T. and Kram, K.E. (2008). Peer coaching: A relational process for accelerating career learning. *Academy of Management Learning & Education*, 487–503.

Peltier, B. (2001) The Psychology of Executive Coaching. Theory and Application. Brunner-Routledge. Taylor & Francis Group. New York

Pedrosa-Guitierrez, C. and Hernandez, J.M. (2017). *Social Networks, Market Transactions, and Reputation as a Central Resource: The Mercado del Mar, a Fish Market in Central Mexico*, 10 October. https://journals.plos. org/plosone/article?id=10.1371/journal.pone.0186063#sec020 (accessed 27 October 2019).

Reeves, K., Frost, L. and Fahey, C. (2010). Integrating the historiography of the nineteenth century gold rushes: Australian economic history review. *An Asia-Pacific Journal of Economic, Business & Social History*, 50(2), 111–128.

Rousseau, D.M. (1989). Psychological and implied contracts in organizations. *Employee Responsibilities and Rights Journal*, 2, 121–139.

Scarborough, W. (2018). What the data says about women in management between 1980 and 2010. *Harvard Business Review*, 23 February 2018. Internet Version. https://hbr.org/2018/02/what-the-data-says-about-women-in-management-between-1980-and-2010

Schwab, K. (2016). *The Fourth Industrial Revolution*. World Economic Forum, Geneva. Crown Publishing Group. New York:

Segers, J., Vloeberghs, D., Henderichx, E. and Inceoglu, I. (2011). Structuring and understanding the coaching industry: The coaching cube. *Academy of Management, Learning and Education*, 10(2), 204–221.

Sherman, S. and Freas, A. (2004). The wild west of coaching. *Harvard Business Review*, November 2004 Issue. Internet Version. https://hbr.org/2004/11/ the-wild-west-of-executive-coaching?referral=03759&cm_vc=rr_item_page. bottom

Towler, J. (2005). *A Grounded Theory Study of Organisational Supervision of Counsellors: The Influence of the Invisible Client*. PhD. Thesis, University of Surrey, Guildford.

Ulrich, D. and Brockbank, W. (2008). The business partner model 10 years on—Lessons learned. *HR Magazine*, 25 November. www.hrmagazine.co.uk/article-details/the-business-partner-model-10-years-on-lessons-learned (accessed 30 October 2019).

Walsh, C.E. (1993). What caused the 1990–1991 recession (PDF). *Economic Review*, 2. Federal Reserve Bank of San Francisco.

Whitmore, J. (1992). *Coaching for Performance: A Practical Guide to Growing Your Own Skills*. San Diego, CA: Pfeiffer.

Internet Accessed

I.C.F. (2016). *Global Coaching Study*. https://coachfederation.org/app/uploads/2 017/12/2016ICFGlobalCoachingStudy_ExecutiveSummary-2.pdf (accessed 14 October 2019).
www.lifecoachingprofessionally.com/history-of-life-coaching.html (accessed 7 October 2019).
www.sherpacoaching.com/pdf_files/2019_Executive_Coaching_Survey_Sum mary_Report.pdf (accessed 15 October 2019).

Part II
Coaching in Practice
Tensions and Dilemmas in
Gaining Entry to the Field and
Practising as a Credible Coach
in Different Contexts

4   Coaching Qualifications, Credentials, and Governance

Introduction

As coaching has gained momentum, a number of tensions have emerged with respect to the underpinning knowledge base and competencies of coaching practitioners and the legitimacy of the institutions and associations that accredit the growing number of coaching qualifications. From the user's perspective, this raises the question: 'How do organizations and individuals ensure that they are engaging a credible coach?' Previous work by the authors (Evans and Lines 2014) indicates that the issue of how to present oneself as a 'credible coach' is a source of tension for practising coaches too. Yet in other aligned professions, such as Practitioner Psychologists, there are clearer standards of proficiency, as well as registers that users can consult to identify a certified Practitioner Psychologist. In the UK, for example, users can consult registers of accredited programmes on the Health and Care Professions' (HCPC) website (www.hcpc-uk.org) and The British Psychological Society's (BPS) website (www.bps.org). In the U.S., users could consult the American Psychology Association's website (www.apa.org).

In this chapter we will focus on discussing these inter-related questions:

- Becoming a coach. What are the entry routes, opportunities and barriers?
- What is the unique knowledge base of coaching? How is that knowledge base developed? What is the difference between the knowledge and skills acquired on academic programmes versus those gained on professional training programmes. How are issues of qualification legitimacy and equivalence managed and regulated?
- How do we know if the knowledge base/qualification that a coach claims to have is credible?
- Coaching and professionalisation—where are we now? Where are we heading?
- Governance in coaching. What are the current models and differences?

- Coaching associations. Who are the key players? How did they emerge? Where do coaching associations get their authority from? Who is monitoring/regulating these associations?
- To what extent is there still evidence for the hegemony of U.S. credentialing?

Becoming a Coach: Coach Entry Routes, Knowledge, Skills, Competencies, and Qualifications

As the coaching industry has grown exponentially in recent years the interest in coaching as a specific career, or as an additional skill set to be acquired by those working in HRD, or in education, would appear to have grown too (Egan and Hamlin 2014; Gray et al. 2015; ICF 2016; Maltbia 2014; Segers et al. 2011). Yet with the myriad of coaching providers, and no independent monitoring of their offering, establishing the provenance of some coaching qualifications is problematic. Previous work has identified the issue of credentialing as an area that is problematic to those trying to gain entry to the field of coaching (Evans and Lines 2014) and for the purchasers of coaching services (Arnott and Sparrow 2004; Passmore and Fillery-Travis 2011).

A non-scientific search on Google using the question 'How do I become a coach?' immediately produced 798,000,000 results (completed 25/2/2019; 440,000,000 completed 1/8/2018) with links to coach training providers and associations, for a would be apprentice coach to plough through. A more focused search, 'How to become an accredited coach?', produced 17,100,000 results (25/2/2019). Whilst many of these results relate to coaching in the world of sport, a number of key coaching associations that also accredit coach training aligned to coaching in the workplace (i.e., executive coaches, managerial coaches, business coaches) appear at the top of the search results:

- ICF, founded in 1995 by Thomas Leonard, which promotes itself as The Gold Standard in Coaching (www.coachfederation.org)
- European Mentoring and Coaching Council, founded initially in 1992 as the European Mentoring Centre by, by David Megginson and David Clutterbuck. Became EMCC in 2002, led by 5 founders: David Megginson, David Clutterbuck, John Whitmore, Eric Parsloe and Julie Hay (www.emccouncil.org/about_emcc/history/timeline_2006_2016/)
- Worldwide Association of Business Coaches, founded in 1997, which promotes itself as leading global authority on business coaching (www.wabccoaches.com/).
- Association of Coaching, established in 2002, which promotes itself as the 'leading independent and not-for-profit professional body dedicated to promoting best practice and raising awareness and

standards of coaching worldwide.' The Association of Coaching publishes the journal *Coaching: An International Journal of Theory, Research and Practice* (www.associationforcoaching.com/).

- Institute of Coaching, founded in 2009, with a 'mandate to cultivate the scientific foundation and best practices in coaching' (https://instituteofcoaching.org/coaching-overview/becoming-a-coach). The Institute of Coaching works in partnership with the Coach Training Institute, which they claim is the 'largest in-person coach training school' (https://coactive.com/ee_newsletter/images/uploads/cti-ioc-flyer-2015f.pdf—accessed 1/8/2018). The Coach Training Institute's courses are ICF recognised (https://coactive.com/).
- Coaching and mentoring network, established in 1999 by Pauline Willis. The network is now owned and managed by Lauriate Ltd. (https://new.coachingnetwork.org.uk/about-the-network/ (accessed 1/8/2018). There is a disclaimer on their website 'Lauriate Ltd cannot be held liable for misrepresentations, negligence, breaches of contract, misconduct, or any claims made by or against the coaches or mentors in their individual or corporate capacity about' (https://new.coachingnetwork.org.uk/about-the-network/legal-information/-accessed 25/2/2019).
- International Coaching Community, founded in 2001 by Joseph O'Connor and Andrea Larges, claims to be one of the 'largest professional organizations for coaches.' It operates its own coaching methodology which was awarded the European Quality Award in 2001 (https://internationalcoachingcommunity.com/about-icc/)

Further research identifies a comparison of the differentiators of coaching accreditation and credentialing requirements by other coaching organisations provided by Coaching at Work (2013) that relate to different coaching practitioner level: foundation, practitioner, senior practitioner, and master coach (www.coaching-at-work.com/wp-content/uploads/2013/09/Accreditation-DIfferentiation-Chart-.pdf—accessed 23/3/2018). The comparator organisations, referred to as the 'contributing professional coaching bodies' included European Mentoring and Coaching Council (EMCC), Association of Coaching (AC), International Coach Federation (ICF) and Association for Professional Executive Education and Supervision (APECS) (www.apecs.org/apecs-accredited-executive-coach-category-description). What is interesting to note here is that it appears that it is not until an individual aspires to become a Master Coach that some of these associations specify the type of coach training and associated knowledge; for two of the associations qualifications at Postgraduate level are specified. Novice coaches (and indeed purchasers) need to be aware of the difference between a programme of study and an individual being accredited: www.centreforcoaching.com/what-is-accreditation (last accessed 23/3/2018)

Given our interest in coaching from a global perspective, with a focus on the Asia Pacific and the Middle East, a Google search for 'How do I become a coach in Hong Kong?' produced 28,300,000 results (accessed 25/2/2019), many of the results again relate to sports coaching. Some the key providers that relate to coaching in the workplace include:

- Coach Training Honk Kong, founded in 2000, with a visions to 'vision to create a vibrant global community of coaches, and today is one of the worlds leading coach training schools.' (https://coach-campus.com/our-story/). They promote an integrated training model (https://coachcampus.com/coach-training/no-single-model/), which is certified by ICF.
- Hong Kong International Coaching Community, founded in (www.coachinghk.com/about-us/our-history).
- Coach Masters Academy, who offer an ICF approved coach certificate training (www.coachmastersacademy.com/events/news/icf-app roved-coaching-certificate-training-in-hong-kong).
- Schouten China University, founded in 1980, provides a Co-Active Coaching Certification Programme, certified by ICF (amongst other associations and institutions) (www.schoutenchina.com/cn-en/open-courses-overview/co-active-coaching-certification-program/).
- Asia Coaching and Mentoring Academy, founded in 2013, which also offers ICF certified programmes (http://coachmentor.asia/en/interCertification.php).
- Asia Pacific Coaching Alliance, unclear when founded, as the website does not state this information. It promotes its own trademarked coach certification programmes, but no mention of any external certification of its coaching programmes (www.apaccoaching.com/coach-training-amp-certification.html).
- Asia Pacific Alliance of Coaching - 'The Coaching Voice of Asia Pacific'—membership and networking, no mention of certification/accreditation (www.apacoaches.org/).

Repeating this same search, using the search term 'How do I become a coach in Dubai?' produced 17,800,000 results; again many of these results relate to coaching in the world of sport. We have selected programmes offered by organisations that relate more to coaching in organisations.

The Coaches Training Institute, founded in 2004, draws on co-active coaching model. It provides training at the Fundamental and Intermediate level. The training programmes are certified by ICF. (https://the-coachesdubai.com/about-cti/)

Coach Masters Academy, who offer ICF approved coach certificate training (www.coachmastersacademy.com/events/news/icf-approved-coaching-certificate-training-in-dubai).

Coach Training EDU, founded in 2009, with the aim 'To create a global community of coaches and professionals with thriving coaching careers that empower individuals to flourish' The training is certified by ICF (www.coachtrainingedu.com/).

Middlesex University, Dubai Campus, introduced an MA Education (Coaching and Mentoring) in 2014–2015. In addition to gaining a Master level qualification, participants can also participate in a three-day practical coach training programme, that leads to an EMCC recognised coach certification (www.mdx.ac.ae/courses/course-list/course-detail/ma-education-coaching-and-mentoring).

What these cursory internet searches reveal is a confusing picture of coach training and coach certification programmes; an observation also made by others (Bachkirova and Lawton-Smith 2015). Several metaphors come to mind when trying to make sense of this confusing picture: a labyrinth (a term that has been applied to the careers of female leaders—see Eagly and Carli 2007); a minefield, or 'fish market.' This latter metaphor was one used by one of our participants in the Asia Pacific region. What was meant here was with lots of coaching providers, each offering the same sort of fish and you do not know where to shop you might buy fish that is not right for what you want to cook. As you explore, interrogate, and interpret the websites of these coach training organisations and their offerings, you are left with a confusing message regarding the status and hierarchy of the different certifications: ICF, Institute of Leadership and Management (ILM), International Society for Qualified Coaches (ISQC), Association of Coaching (AofC), and EMCC. Thus in this increasingly online global world it would appear relatively easy to promote one's coach training business through web based technologies and indeed provide a sense that this is part of a bigger business/industry. As Swan (2017) points out from her in-depth single case analysis of one coaching organisation that provides coaching specifically for women. As Swan (2017) points out, analysing service offerings from websites is complex:

> Webpages are distinct 'hybrid' genres with digital, verbal, aural, kinetic and visual meaning-making modes that have particular affordances. These modes work independently but also make meaning potential through interacting in combinations.
>
> (Swan 2017: 280)

The point that Swan (2017: 281) appears to be making here is that these webpages are a representation of the world of coaching that create 'imagined interactions between represented coach and viewer'; they are not representative of the actual experience of coaching. As someone who may not have experienced coaching before then the reality of the coaching experience may not reflect their imagined experience from the narrative presented by coaches on websites in relation to the models and competencies that underpin their services. In this next section we debate some of the tensions associated with identifying and specifying caching competencies.

Coaching Competencies

The use of competencies as a way of assessing and developing individual performance has been a feature of organisations' human resource management approaches for over 30 years (Boyatzis 2008; Heinsman et al. 2007). Boyatzis (2008: 5) claims that it was David McClelland (1973) who first conceptualised competencies as a 'critical differentiator of performance.' Whilst there is no single definition of competencies, from a review of different definitions there appears to be the notion that competencies relate to the behaviours, or behavioural repertoires, associated with superior performance in a specific job. McClelland and Boyatzis (1980: 369) define competencies in a broad way, positioning competencies as encompassing 'a generic body of knowledge, motives, traits, self-images, social roles, and skills that are causally related to superior or effective performance in the job.' Woodruffe (1993: 29) defines competency as 'the set behaviour patterns that the incumbent needs to bring to a position in order to perform its tasks and functions with competence . . . competencies are behavioural repertoires that some people carry out better than others.' Yet Kurz and Bartram (2002) argue that 'a competency is not the behavior or performance itself, but the repertoire of capabilities, activities, processes and response available that enable a range of work demands to be met more effectively by some people than by others' (Kurz and Bartram 2002, in Heinsman et al. 2007: 413). In other words competencies are seen as a constellation of characteristics associated with the individual that results in effective performance. Within that constellation of characteristics, the underlying motives and values of individual can be a significant differentiator between superior and average performers (Heinsman et al. 2007: 424).

Drawing on a definition of competency by Besson & Hassadj (1999), Barosa-Periera (2014: 101) refers to competency as 'the individual's ability to apply acquired knowledge (qualification) and professional experiences into action that will lead to performance and results throughout different professional situations that he or she may encounter.' In this definition, Barosa-Periera (2014) alludes to competencies, particularly those associated with professionals, as a concept that has generic applicability irrespective of context. Yet as Woodruffe (1993) points out, tensions arise when organisations attempt to utilise generic lists of competencies, where it is assumed these are associated with high performance, but there is a general lack of transparency, and rigour around how a set of competencies have been derived. As we are living a more global, and multicultural society, it has been argued that competency frameworks, especially those aligned to professionals in developmental and therapeutic roles, should reflect cultural diversity (Barosa-Periera 2014; Collins and Arthur 2010); without this then the approach will continue to operate from an ethnocentric perspective. As we discuss later in this chapter, one of the dominant competency frameworks applied to coach certification appears to have been developed exclusively with Western coaching practitioners:

> The committee was made up of the founders or senior faculty of eight of the existing coach training schools visible at the time, all based in the United States. From this committee came the list of the 11 core competencies published on the ICF website in March 1999.
> (Barosa-Periera 2014: 103).

However, as Woodruff (1993) points out, organisations often confuse the terms competency (an attribute of the individual) with competence (an attribute associated with a specific job role). Confounding these two terms he suggests results in problems when attempting to operationalise competencies through for example selection and development processes. This particular tension that Woodruff (1993) refers to is something that we return to later in this chapter when analysing the similarities and differences in the competencies that Coaching Associations adopt as a basis of their coach certification and credentialing processes. However one of the differences in the way that competencies are used by Coaching Associations is that these are not assessed through assessment centres, as is often the case in selection and/or development approaches utilised within organisations, but instead through the submission of a portfolio of evidence put together by individual practitioners.

In an introductory paper in a special issue of *Competencies in the 21st Century* that discusses the design and teaching methods to develop managerial competencies, Boyatzis (2008: 6) refers to the construction of competencies as 'requiring both action (i.e., a set of alternative behaviours) and intent.' Intent in this context relates to the intended outcomes of the individual behaviours. These could be person-centric (i.e. posing questions aimed at understanding another person's perspective on a particular situation), or associated with use of power and influence, in other words where the intent behind a particular behaviour is to control others. Boyatzis (2008: 7) suggests that outstanding performers, whether these are managers or professionals, need to demonstrate three threshold clusters of behaviours (e.g., expertise and experience, knowledge, basic cognitive competencies), plus three further clusters of competencies that that enable distinctions to be made between average and outstanding performers. These additional clusters of behaviours include cognitive competencies (e.g., systems thinking), emotional intelligence competencies (e.g., self-awareness and self-management), and social intelligence competencies (e.g., empathy and relationship management). Drawing on the work of other authors who have written about competencies and performance (such as Luthans et al. 1988; Howard and Bray 1988; Campbell et al. 1970), Boyatzis (2008: 8) argues that these three additional clusters of competencies apply equally to high performers, irrespective of country contexts.

Having discussed some generic tensions relating to the use of competencies and competency frameworks, we now move on to an analysis of the competencies specified by Coaching Associations. Given the numerous Coaching Associations that exist, we have selected four of the better known (though arguably Western centric) Coaching Associations as the basis for our analysis. These include International Coach Federation, European Coaching and Mentoring Council, Association of Coaching, and the World Association of Business Coaching. In Table 4.1, we provide a summary of the specific competencies that each of these associations expect coaches to demonstrate to gain certification of their association. As a comparator we have included proficiency standards from the British Psychological Society's Practice Guidelines (BPS 2017), given the rise in the number of practising Coaching Psychologists. Although a Special Group of Coaching Practice was established within the BPS in 2002 (Palmer and Whybrow 2005), Coaching Psychologists are not yet included as one of the nine protected Practitioner Psychologist titles listed by the UK Health & Care Professions Council (HCPC) (www.hcpc-uk. org). We assume therefore that practising Coaching Psychologists adhere to the generic BPS Practice Guidelines.

Applying the definitions of competencies set out previously in particular the notion of competencies being associated with individual behaviours aligned with intent (McClelland and Boyatzis 1980; Boyatzis 2008), an initial observation of the competencies listed in Table xx is that these do not appear to match this conceptualisation of competencies. Some of these competencies, for example, *Establishing the Coaching Agreement* (ICF), *Establishing the Coaching Agreement and Outcomes* (AC), *Managing the Contract* (EMCC), *Planning and Goal Setting* (ICF), *Creating the Foundations for Business Coaching* (WABC), *Designing Strategies for Action* (AC), and *Coach as Leader and Developer of Own Business* (WABC), seem to relate more to coaching processes rather than the actual behaviours of coaches.

Other competencies, however, emphasise the knowledge base that coaches need to draw on to perform effectively. For example, *Use of Models and Techniques* (EMCC), *Working with the organisational context* (AC), *Understand leadership issues* (AC), and *Business and Leadership Coaching Capabilities* (WABC), which includes references to 'thorough knowledge of the world of executive leaders and executive development' and knowledge of systems thinking; although it would seem that these knowledge areas apply more if working as an Executive Coach.

Table 4.1 Comparison of Coaching Competencies (Data gathered February 2019 from each Association's websites)

	ICF www.icf.com	EMCC (2015) www.emccouncil.org	Association of Coaching (2012) www.associationforcoaching.com	World Association of Business Coaching (2007) www.wabccoaches.com	BPS Practice Guidelines - (includes SGCP, founded in 2002) www.bps.org.uk
1	**Setting the Foundations** *Meeting Ethical Guidelines & Professional Standards:* understanding coaching ethics and applying appropriately in coaching situations.	*Understanding Self:* demonstrates awareness of own values and beliefs and how these affect their practice, clients, and sponsoring organisation.	*Meeting Ethical, legal and professional guidelines:* follows AOC's professional standards and codes of conduct, including the Global Code of Ethics for Coaches, Mentors, and Supervisors.	**Self-Management– Knowing Oneself and Self-Mastery** **Knowing Yourself– Self-Insight and Understanding:** a high degree of awareness of what is important to you and the contribution you want to make–your values, purpose, and vision.	*Ethical values:* respect, competence, responsibility, and integrity.
2	*Establishing the Coaching Agreement:* understanding what is required in a coaching interaction and coming to an agreement with the client about the coaching process and relationship.	*Commitment to Self-Development:* improves standard of own practice and reputation of profession.	*Establishing the coaching agreement and outcomes:* clearly explains the coaching process and own coaching approach, models, and techniques.	**Acknowledging Your Strengths and Development Needs:** realistic perception of own strengths and development needs and showing commitment to continuous learning and self-development.	*Assessment and establishment of agreement with client:* derived through the theory and practice of academic and applied psychology; structured assessment strategies.

(Continued)

Table 4.1 (Continued)

	ICF www.icf.com	EMCC (2015) www.emccouncil.org	Association of Coaching (2012) www.associationfor coaching.com	World Association of Business Coaching (2007) www.wabccoaches.com	BPS Practice Guidelines - (includes SGCP, founded in 2002) www.bps.org.uk
3	Co-Creating the Relationship *Establishing Trust and Intimacy with the Client:* creating a safe environment to build ongoing mutual respect and trust.	*Managing the Contract:* establishes the expectations and boundaries of the coaching/ mentoring contract with the client and sponsors where appropriate.	*Establishing a trust-based relationship with clients:* accepts the client 'as is' and believes in the clients potential and capability.	*Self-Mastery—Managing Your Thoughts, Feelings and Behaviours in Ways that Promote Behavior Contributing to Career and Organisation Success:* self-regulation of reactions and emotions constructively; integrity and ethical course of action; self-responsibility; adaptability and flexibility in applying change.	*Formulation of client needs and problems:* uses psychological theory and research to provide a framework for describing a client's needs; draws on a number of models to meet needs and support decision-making.
4	*Coaching Presence:* being fully conscious with clients and employing a style that is open and flexible.	*Building the Relationship:* skilfully builds and maintains an effective relationship with the client and sponsors where appropriate.	*Managing self and maintaining coaching presence:* pays close attention to the client, staying fully present; stays aligned to personal values whilst reflecting the values of the client.	Core Coaching Skill-Base *Creating the Foundations for Business Coaching:* working within established ethical guidelines and professional standards; effective client contracting.	*Intervention or implementation of solutions:* draws on psychological models/ approaches to facilitate change, solve problems.

5	Communicating effectively **Active listening:** focusing on what the client is saying, understanding the meaning of what is said, supporting the client's self-expression.	*Enabling Insight and Learning:* works with client and sponsor to bring in insight and learning.	*Communicating effectively:* demonstrates effective listening and clarifying skills differences between what is said and what is left unsaid.	*Developing the Business Coaching Relationship:* establishing trust and respect and rapport.	*Evaluation and reflection of outcomes:* evaluation to help measure the effective of interventions, to help provide interpretations not predict future behaviours.
6	**Powerful Questioning:** asking questions that reveal the information needed to benefit the coaching relationship.	*Outcome and action orientated:* demonstrates approach and uses skills in supporting the client to make desired changes.	*Raising awareness and insight:* Asks question to challenge client's assumptions, elicit new insights; supports the client to generate options to achieve agreed outcomes.	*Promoting Client Understanding:* listening to understand; questioning effectively; facilitating depth of understanding.	*Communication through reporting:* integral to effective relationship with clients.
7	**Direct Communication:** using language that has the greatest positive impact on the client.	*Use of Models and Techniques:* applies models and tools, techniques, and ideas beyond the core communication skills and bring about insights and learnings.	*Designing strategies and actions:* supports the client to meet their outcomes; inspires the client to identify and implement self-directed learning opportunities.	*Facilitating the Personal Transformation:* promoting action; focusing on goal; building resiliency and managing termination of coaching relationship.	*Audit and research:* monitoring of protocols; research to ensure and maintain the evidence-base of psychology.

(Continued)

Table 4.1 (Continued)

	ICF www.icf.com	EMCC (2015) www.emccouncil.org	Association of Coaching (2012) www.associationfor coaching.com	World Association of Business Coaching (2007) www.wabccoaches.com	BPS Practice Guidelines - (includes SGCP, founded in 2002) www.bps.org.uk
8	**Facilitating Learning and Results** **Creating Awareness:** integrating and evaluating multiple sources of information to help he client gain self-awareness and achieve agreed outcomes.	*Evaluation of Results*: gathers information on the effectiveness of own practice and contributes to a culture of evaluation of outcomes.	*Maintaining forward momentum and evaluation:* maintains an outcomes- focused approach; asks powerful questions to move the client forward; discourages dependency on the coach.	*Professional development:* seek out client feedback on performance to develop your practice; recognise own limitations as a coach; use supervision to maintain and improve coaching skills.	
9	*Designing Actions:* creating opportunities for clients' ongoing learning during coaching that lead to agreed coaching outcomes.		*Undertaking continuous coach development:* regularly asks client for feedback; acts on own critical reflection and client feedback to improve coaching practice; participates in regular coaching supervision to reflect on and improve practice.	**Business and Leadership Coaching Capabilities** *Alignment: Understanding the business and displaying a strong grounding in business knowledge and competencies; demonstrating proficiency in systems thinking; aligning coaching initiatives with the business.*	

		For Executive Coaches	
10	*Planning & Goal Setting:* developing and effective coaching plan with the client.	*Working with the organisational context:* takes a systemic approach to coaching the client, encompassing the complexities of multiple stakeholders, different perspectives, and conflicting priorities.	**Leadership Knowledge and Credibility:** acting as a strong an influential role model; possess working knowledge of the world of executive leaders and leadership development; displays highly developed communication and interpersonal competences.
11	*Managing Progress & Accountability:* holding attention on what is important to the client, ensuring responsibility for action lies with the client.	*Understand leadership issues:* identifies ways of, and opportunities for, developing leadership behaviours and attributes through coaching.	**Coach as Leader and Developer of Own Business:** creating and managing business relationships; collaborating with other coaches; developing self in a business capacity.
12		*Working in partnership with the organisation:* designs an effective coaching contract. Commercial agreement and working alliance with the client, line manager, and coaching sponsor(s) within organisational parameters for coaching.	**Creating and Maintaining Partnerships with all Stakeholders in the Business** Coaching Process: proactively develops a network of relationships and strategic partnerships within the organisation; involves HR and other stakeholders.

(Continued)

Table 4.1 (Continued)

ICF www.icf.com	EMCC (2015) www.emccouncil.org	Association of Coaching (2012) www.associationfor coaching.com	World Association of Business Coaching (2007) www.wabccoaches.com	BPS Practice Guidelines - (includes SGCP, founded in 2002) www.bps.org.uk
			Understanding Organisational Behaviour and Organisational Development Principles: knows how to facilitate the creation of a vision and clarification of direction; knows how to facilitate the development of strategies for leading and managing organisational change. **Assessment: assessing the client;** *assessing the individual and organisational benefits of business coaching.* **Respect for and Knowledge about Multicultural Issues and Diversity: help the** client to recognise the value of diversity, and	

to maximise the benefits of racial and cultural differences in ways that improve outcomes; **understands potential preferences and biases associated with your own racial and cultural identity, and how these might enhance or impede delivery of services.**

In contrast knowledge is a key feature of the list of practice guidelines specified by the BPS where the underpinning knowledge required by psychologists is specified in five out of their seven practice guidelines.

The WABC list of competencies refers to the knowledge that coaches need with respect to diversity and multiculturalism; knowledge that is not explicitly referred to in the competencies of other Coaching Associations despite their International reach and the growing evidence of the importance of coaches demonstrating cultural awareness and sensitivity. Plaister-Ten (2013: 65) points to the importance of executive coaches, in particular, developing knowledge of cultural theory so they are better prepared to coach clients with 'complex cultural profiles' as a result of the effects of globalisation. Equally the number of people pursuing a boundaryless career, which can result in the notion of 'cosmopolitan identities' (Daskalaki 2012: 432), is also likely to present challenges to be considered within coaching dialogues. The importance of cultural sensitivity is also recognised in other therapeutic professions. A conceptual paper by Collins and Arthur (2010) that explored the historical bases of the competencies required by counselling practitioners proposed three 'culture-infused competencies' (Collins and Arthur 2010: 210). These include: *cultural awareness of self* (which would include awareness of differences between own cultural identities and those of others), *cultural awareness of other: understanding the worldview of the client* (which includes awareness of the socio-political influences that affects clients), and *culturally sensitive working alliances* (which includes taking into account and working sensitively with different cultural identities). Having conceptualised some of the additional competencies required by counselling practitioners Collins and Arthur (2010) have subsequently embedded these into the graduate education programmes in two Universities in Canada. Barosa-Periera (2014: 109) also suggests that the education and training of coaches operating in a global world should include developing cultural awareness and sensitivity. There seems to be some synergies here with Collins and Arthur's (2010) conceptualisation of the competencies required by Counsellors and the cluster of competencies that high performing professionals more generally typically demonstrate, such as emotional intelligence and social intelligence (Boyatzis 2008), although Boyatzis is not explicit in his work about the importance of cultural competences.

Other associations representing aligned professions, for example the International Council for Coaching Excellence (ICCE) (www.icce.ws/), which represents the interests of coaches. The ICCE provide an International Sport Coaching Framework (ISCF) that maps out the competences needed to be considered an effective sports coach; a role which the ICCE acknowledge is a 'complex and dynamic activity.' The ISCF includes capabilities required to carry out the job of a coach, the values to guide actions and the knowledge base and competences required in a number of core functional areas. There are six functional areas in the framework: setting the vision and strategy, shaping the environment, building relationships, conducting practices and structure competitions, Read and react to the field and Learn and Reflect. The three key knowledge areas included in the formwork include: *professional knowledge* (e.g., governance in sport, stages of athletes development, and knowledge of sports science and related disciplines), *interpersonal knowledge* (e.g., social context of sport, relational and coaching methodologies), and *intrapersonal knowledge* (e.g., coaching philosophy, factors influencing lifelong learning).

As with other Coaching Association's competency frameworks (albeit outside the world of sport), the ISCF includes different levels of competency. However, a key difference is that these different levels of competency are aligned to different coaching roles, such as Coaching Assistant, Advanced Senior Coach, and Master Head Coach. The assumption, it would seem, is that different competencies need to be developed (and thus demonstrated) as the coach progresses (hierarchically) through their coaching career. Yet there does not appear to be the same notion of role progression for coaches operating outside the world of sport. This may be an artefact of the diversity of coaches' professional backgrounds and careers. However, in the field of organisational coaching there does appear to be an assumed hierarchy of coaches, with executive coaching being positioned as having greater influence and prestige, thus requiring coaches operating at different levels needing to demonstrate additional competencies (Ciporen 2015; Maltbia, Marsick and Ghosh 2014; Plaister-Ten 2013). One of our participants talked about coaching needing to be tailored to the different levels of complexity and challenges that managers and leaders face as they progress through their careers, recognising that the levels of complexity increases exponentially as individuals become more senior. In addition the inter-relational dynamics/issues that those in more senior roles face compared with those in more junior roles is likely to be different, thus requiring a different approach by coaches. In addition we suggest that there may be a hierarchy amongst coaches about how they construct a narrative around their skills, knowledge and experiences in order to command greater income, status, and prestige. As Mischler (1999: 19) points out 'Narratives are identity performances, we express, display, make claims for who we are—and who we would like to be—in the stories we tell and how we tell them.' Whilst it is difficult to establish the actual income derived from coaching, surveys by Coaching Associations such as ICF in the U.S. and the Asia Pacific Alliances of Coaching (APAC) and Coach Training providers, e.g., Sherpa Coaching, indicate that coaches charge different rates depending on the type and seniority of the coachee. APAC's 4th Asia Coaching Survey, published in 2016–2017, reports the hourly coaching rate for coaches in U.S. dollars and the rate ranges from less than $150, up to $750 (www.apacoaches.com). In addition APAC's 2016–2017 survey indicates that there appears to be a difference in the rates that coaches seem to charge for coaching in different countries that fall under the Asia Pacific region. Sherpa Coaching's 2018 Coaching Survey indicates that the hourly rate charged by Executive Coaches is $386 (an increase from the $350–$360 hourly rate that coaches indicated they charged in the previous three years (www.sherpacaoching.com).

From a review and synthesis of the literature of Executive Coaching competencies, Maltbia, Marsick and Ghosh (2014) identify four executive coaching roles that require six core coaching competencies. Two of these, clustered under the label *Co-creating the relationship*, include Social Competence and Emotional Competence; competencies also referred to in the work of Boyatzis (2008). Executive Coaching aside, there does appear to be an expectation in some Coaching Associations' competency framework that as individuals gain more experience of coaching and thus apply for certification at a higher level that individual coaches will present different types of evidence to support their ability to perform a competency at a higher. In their Core Competencies Specification ICF specify the criteria by which 'applicants will NOT receive a passing score' for each of their three certification levels (ACC, PCC and MCC) (icf.to/CoreCompetencies); thus, an indication, we assume, of where individuals are not considered to be performing competently at a particular level.

The competency approach within the field of Human Resource Development more generally is not without its critics. One criticism is how competencies are often presented as objective scientific instruments, when arguably they are social constructions. In other words the meaning associated with a particular concept needs to be interpreted within a context given that the meaning associated with a particular phenomenon is embodied within the language and actions of the various social actors associated with that phenomenon (see Denzin and Lincoln 1998). From empirical research into the history and implementation of a competency based management development approach within a single multinational organisation, Finch-Lees, Mabey and Liefooghe (2005: 1200) point out: 'Of relevance here is the way in which the [xxx] documentation endows the capabilities with an aura of scientific objectivity, effectively obscuring the socially constructed nature of knowledge.' By knowledge here they are referring to the knowledge component of competency frameworks, something that Alvesson and Willmott (2002) argue that, along with skills, are means of regulating our identities: 'knowledge defines the knower: what one is capable of doing (or expected to be able to do) frames who one "is"' (Alvesson and Willmott 2002, in Finch-Lees, Mabey and Liefooghe 2005: 1200). If we adopt an interpretive, as opposed to a functionalist perspective, on competencies then in some contexts these can be helpful to individuals as a way to

> initiate and structure a narrative about performance or develop-
> ment . . . it allows you to air your view as to why you think you are
> one particular thing or the other and then for your boss to come back
> and say well have you thought of this or that?
>
> (Finch-Lees, Mabey and Liefooghe 2005: 1211)

The more observant reader will have noticed the shift in terminol-ogy in the quotations taken from Finch-Lees, Mabey and Liefooghe's (2005) work; namely the reference to the term capabilities as opposed to competencies, which reflects a shift in discourse within the organisation that their research was based. The authors draw on the work of Bolton et al. (1999), who distinguish capability from competency as 'competen-cies are concerned with the ability to demonstrate now what has already been acquired, while capability is concerned as much with future poten-tial as with immediate needs' (Finch-Lees, Mabey and Liefooghe 2005: 1186). There are some similarities here with how Robeyns (2005) refers to capability, although her perspective of capability has been influenced by the work of Sen (1993): 'The capability approach is a broad norma-tive framework for the evaluation and assessment of individual wellbe-ing . . . the core characteristic of the capability approach is its focus on what people are effectively able to do and to be' (Robeyns 2005: 94). Robeyns (2005: 96) suggest then that the capability approach is mainly a framework of thought 'a mode of thinking about normative issues; hence a paradigm—loosely defined—that can be used for a wide range of evaluative purposes.' A key difference between these two perspectives of capability though is how Finch-Lees, Mabey and Liefooghe (2005), based on their research, suggest that there is an assumed causal relation-ship between capabilities (or competencies), and individual and organi-sational performance, and that that this can be measured in an objective way. However, capability from an HR practice perspective is something other than a loosely defined paradigm; instead it is something that is enshrined in a procedure which can be applied consistently and fairly:

> Capability covers the employee's *ability* to do the job and unlike
> misconduct does not depend on any "fault" on the part of the
> employee . . . Feedback should be constructive, with the emphasis on
> finding ways for the employee to improve and for the improvement
> to be sustained. This could include providing timely appropriate
> and relevant staff development, training, mentoring and coaching.
> It should be tempered by explicit acknowledgement of achievements
> and positive contributions.
>
> (Extract from the Capability Procedure from the
> University of Roehampton)

What isn't clear from this particular procedure is what type of coaching might be needed, or indeed who might be best placed to provide such coaching.

A similar critique of the use of competency-based frameworks is present in a conceptual paper by Bachkirova and Lawton Smith (2015) that discusses a number of issues with competency-based approaches for assessing and accrediting coaches by Coaching Associations. A key argument in their paper is that 'competency approaches potentially oversimplify coaching practice and therefore misrepresent it' (Bachkirova and Lawton Smith 2015: 130). Evidence for this assertion they suggest comes from a grounded theory investigation by Griffiths and Campbell (2008) that involved analysing ICF competencies, which concluded that some competencies specified by ICF are not sufficiently differentiated. So, for example, *Coaching Presence* (a sub-component of competency 4 in Table 4.1) is arguably the same, or a component of *Active Listening* (a sub-component of competency 5 in Table 4.1); given the descriptors of 'being fully conscious with clients' (Presence) and 'focusing on what the client is saying' (Active listening). Thus where competency-based frameworks are based on a simple binary approach, i.e., where a behaviour is either present or not present, with little consideration to wider contextualisation, makes it difficult to differentiate between average and excellent performance. Yet in a dyadic client-coach relationship the question of who decides what might be classified as excellent performance is, we would argue, highly subjective. Each coachee is likely to have a different perception of what excellence looks like to them. This is likely to vary depending on a range of factors: previous exposure to coaching and other individualised learner-centric relationships; expected outcomes from a coaching intervention and how these have been defined; the level of agency (or locus of control) that an individual feels s/he has. Of course the coachee is not the only stakeholder in this debate. Organisations, who are likely to be the commissioners of coaching services, will also have a perspective on what constitutes coaching excellence. Individual coaches too will also have their perspective, which invariably will be informed by their specific coach educational background and professional experiences, not necessarily just in coaching.

In a conceptual paper by Drake (2011), in which he too argues that debates around coaching excellence need to go beyond 'traditional notions of competencies,' he refers to the concept of Mastery, which he defines as the combination of Artistry, Knowledge, and Evidence. Here, then, Drake (2011) is drawing on references to traditional craft workers, where there is a distinctive relationship between the materials, the maker and the tools deployed in their work. Transferring the concept of Mastery to coaching, Drake suggests this requires coaches to develop an ability to

> blend science-based evidence and practice based evidence in a given moment [which] requires a mastery of what one needs to know (and why) and a grasp of the situational subtleties to know how to use

what one knows to help clients achieve their goals and how to make sense of and articulate what transpires along the way.

(Drake 2011: 143)

Drake argues that coaches need to develop four types of knowledge: Foundational, Personal, Contextual, and Professional. He suggests that Foundational and Professional Knowledge 'inform coaches acuity of attention' (Drake 2011: 145). Whilst we can see a link here with competencies such as *Coaching Presence* and *Active Listening* in Coaching Associations competency-frameworks, what Drake (2011) is describing here is something that goes far deeper:

> The Mastery Window aligns well with this typology [of knowledge] but does so with an emphasis on the phronetic concern for power and praxis. Through it we can see that coaches need to continually develop across the four domains of knowledge and, in doing so, enhance their *Awareness* of what is going on (in themselves, their clients, their conversation and their environment); their sense of what to pay *Attention* to; their ability to effectively *Adapt*; and their *Accountability* for their work and their actions.
>
> Drake (2011: 146)

Mastery, Drake (2011) argues, is something that takes time to develop and perfect; thus behaviour that we would expect to see in 'advanced coaches' who after years of experience 'have a wider field of *awareness* . . . know where to focus their *attention* based on patterns they can recognise . . . and can adapt their approaches based on years of experimenting with theories in action across a diverse range of clients' (Drake 2011: 146). Yet coaches, unlike skilled Craft Artisans, tend to have a diverse portfolio of roles, which raises a question as to the timescale by which they may be perceived as Masters (and not in a way that is narrowly defined by specifying coaching hours). Again if we consider the concept of how the word mastery might be understood in different contexts, then it may be understood as 'comprehensive knowledge, or skill in a particular field' or 'control or superiority over someone or something.' This latter definition is not something that would be congruent with the philosophy of coaching referred to in Chapter 2.

Drake (2011: 152), based on his dual-roles as a coach and a coach educator, suggests that coach education in the future will need to reflect a range of changing knowledge needs:

Personal knowledge: with an emphasis on the emotional, physical and spiritual development needs to sustain oneself in an increasingly complex world.

Foundational knowledge: that will address the increasing demands from clients for more specialised knowledge.

Professional knowledge: where there is a growing expectation of peer and professional supervision to gain feedback in order to be better able to respond to emergent client needs.

Contextual knowledge: including increasing integration of coaching principles and practices of how business is expected to be carried out; thus where coaching becomes embedded into the essence of organisational life.

We can see similarities here in Drake's proposition regarding the knowledge needed by coaches and Heron's (1996) work on the types of knowledge needed when conducting cooperative inquiry research. Based on an assumption that coaching is a relational process where both parties in the relationship have equal power, then we could assume that coaches (and indeed coach educators) will have an understanding of Heron's (1996) four domains of knowledge:

Experiential knowing: being present, by direct face-to-face contact with a person. Knowing through the immediacy of perceiving through empathy and resonance. The outcome (or product as Heron refers to) is developing the quality of the relationship.

Presentational knowing: relates to the subjective-objective reality relating to non-discursive symbolism, such as the use of metaphor, analogies and storytelling deployed in the inquiry dialogue.

Propositional knowing: which relates to knowing about. In the context of research this would constitute knowledge of the underlying theories associated with the phenomenon under investigation.

Practical knowing: which relates to knowing how, so the range of skills and competencies associated with the inquiry process.

Heron (1996: 42) argues that there is

an up-hierarchy of knowledge proceeding from the ground of experiential knowledge, through presentational knowledge and propositional knowledge to the fulfilment of all these in practical knowledge . . . each later form of knowledge and the canons f validity that go with it are grounded on the earlier forms.

Implicit within this hierarchy of knowing is the notion of agency: 'the self as knowing subject is in and for the self as agent' (Macmurray 1957, in Heron 1996: 42). Heron (1996: 48) suggests that is where practical knowing (associated with the action paradox) is the primary intended outcome of the inquiry, then this is more likely to result in a higher-quality inquiry: 'when you main concern is to cultivate excellent practice with a domain, your learning about it is deeper.' As already discussed previously, coach competency frameworks are not explicit about the knowledge that coaches need to demonstrate, rather it is implicit in some of the competency descriptors. This is something we further in the next section, where we review and discuss different types of coach education and training.

Coach Education and Training Programmes: Public vs Private Providers

In this section we discuss the syllabus and knowledge base of different coaching programmes. If coaching is to become a recognised profession in its own right, then, as with other professions, we assume that it should have its own unique body of knowledge which then underpins the education and training of coaching professionals. Yet as indicated at the start of this chapter there appear to be thousands of coach training and educational programmes, offered by numerous providers. These training and/ or educational programmes range from as little as three days to one-two years, depending on the type of programme and provider (university, or private training organisation). These myriad of programmes are offered in traditional classroom settings, online, or a combination of approaches. The diversity of coach training/educational offerings raises a question regarding the equivalence and status of these programme offerings and how these fit with coaching programme accreditation and individual coach certification; both of which are key concepts associated with professionalisation as we discuss in more depth later in this chapter. Professional work is typically associated with the application of theoretical and scientific knowledge (Dent et al. 2016), that enables professionals to demonstrate an evidence-based approach to their practice. Thus as others point out the route to professional status invariably involves a qualification from a university, which gives the qualification obtained a particular status (Bachkirova and Lawton Smith 2015; Dent et al. 2016; Gray 2011), followed in many instances with a period of structured and supervised training (Scholarios and Lockyer 1999: 142), for example as in medicine, nursing, clinical psychology, and psychotherapy.

Our aim in this section is to analyse the maze of coach training/education offerings from the perspective of individuals seeking to invest in their own personal and career development. Specific questions include:

• To what extent do coaching programme providers provide sufficient detail about the underpinning philosophies and learning methods for individual to decide which programme best fits their needs?
• How portable are the various qualifications/certifications across geographic boundaries?

Whilst it is difficult to establish a definitive list of private coach training providers, it relatively more straight forward to gain a list of coaching qualifications offered by universities. We thus start our analysis with the similarities and differences in Masters level coaching programmes. We begin with the UK context, one that both authors are most familiar with, before moving on to discuss coaching programmes offered in universities in other countries, e.g., Singapore, Hong Kong, Australia, and the U.S.

As universities are state regulated institutions that are expected to adhere to rigorous quality codes when designing and maintaining their programs, we assume that these would offer a more robust and credible educational offering. In the UK, for example, the Quality Assurance Agency (QAA) *'is a key reference point for UK higher education, protecting the public and student interest, and championing UK higher education's world-leading reputation for quality. It enables providers to understand what is expected of them and what to expect from each other'* (www.qaa.ac.uk/quality-code). The QAA specifies a set of benchmark statements that apply to Masters level programmes, which sets the expectations relating to the knowledge, understanding and skills that an individual completing a programme at this level should be able to demonstrate. For example graduates completing a Type 1 Specialist Masters (which would include those completing a coaching Masters) should be able to:

> demonstrate deep knowledge and understanding of the specialist subject area while placing that subject within a wider organisational and contextual framework. They will understand current issues and thinking along with techniques applicable to research in the subject area. Graduates will have both theoretical and applied perspectives and will be able to apply a range of specialist skills to the organisations (and their context) in which they as specialists may operate.
>
> (QAA 2015: 9)

In addition to the QAA, another UK institution that ensures equivalency of academic, vocational, and professional qualifications is NARIC, which is a national Agency managed by the Department for Education on behalf of the government. NARIC is responsible for

> for providing information, advice and opinion on academic, vocational and professional qualifications and skills from all over the world . . . we provide the only official source of information on international education and training systems and wide-ranging international qualifications and skills attained from outside the UK.
>
> (www.naric.ork.uk)

NARIC's Code of Practice state states that its operational model is

> based on the evaluation of learning outcomes achieved through all paths and progression routes. This approach makes it possible to

recognise not only the various "national awards" with their differing entry points and purposes but also international qualifications such as joint diplomas, which vary significantly from system-specific national awards.

(www.naric.ork.uk)

Other countries have similar governance systems in place to ensure the quality of higher education programmes. In the U.S., for example, there is government accreditation of Master's level education, which has a similar role and status as the QAA in the UK (https://www2.ed.gov/admins/finaid/accred/accreditation_pg6.html#RegionalInstitutional).

Additionally. within the U.S. there is a separate independent Membership Association, the Graduate School Alliance for Education in Education (GSAEC), established in 2004, that defines its mission as 'To define, advance and sustain professional coach education globally by establishing and advocating standards that shape the academic discipline of coaching and coach education . . . Championing, promoting and amplifying the voice of professional coach education' (http://gsaec.org/about-gsaec-2/). Whilst not an accrediting body per se, the GSAEC offer member institutions the opportunity for 'qualified graduate-level programs to undergo a Peer Review based on a comprehensive set of academic standards developed by GSAEC, grounded in current theory and research' (http://gsaec.org/academic-program-guidelines/). GSAEC's academic programme standards include 20 standards, grouped under four sections: Organizational, Program, Engagement and Growth, and Quality and Sustainability (Maltbia, Marsick and Ghosh 2014: 176). The evidence base that GSAEC would appear to draw on to inform its work on advising on the academic discipline of coaching include a range of coaching and coaching psychology journals, listed on their website (http://gsaec.org/research-and-scholarship/journals-and-academic-resources/). What isn't clear from GSAEC's website though is what the jurisdiction is that GSAEC operates under to legitimise its authority as an advisor on the academic discipline of coaching and coach education. In addition the reach of GSAEC is also difficult to establish from its website, as only 13 institutional members are listed (http://gsaec.org/gsaec-institutional-members/).

In addition to completing a recognised qualification from a state regulated Higher Education institution, it is also possible for those seeking to enter into a particular professional to gain additional professional certification that enables them to specify additional post-nominals, where thy have complete a programme of study that has been accredited by a particular professional body. Accreditation is the formal recognition by an independent body, generally known as an accreditation body, that a certification body operates according to international standards." (ISO, no date). As an example, in the UK, HR professionals who have completed an HRM Masters that is accredited by the

Chartered Institute of Personnel Development (CIPD) are able to use the post-nominals Assoc CIPD; another artefact of their professionalism. However, given that there is no single institution that represents and regulates coaching in the UK and there are limited Universities offering coaching qualifications at Masters level where individuals can also gain certification from a particular Coaching Association (see Table 4.2). The situation is quite different where individuals complete a training programme, as opposed to a University level qualification, from a coach training provider that has been accredited by a Coaching Association e.g., ICF, EMCC, AC.

Within the UK Higher Education system, in addition to the knowledge and skills expectations being regulated through subject benchmark statements, the number of learning hours is also specified by the qualifications framework; students are expected to complete ten hours of directed study time for every ten credit module studied. Thus, for a full Master's degree this would equate to 1800 hours of directed study. The point that we are making here is that the learning that takes place in a Higher Education institution is highly regulated, structured, with defined learning outcomes and hours; this information is made clear to prospective students to make it easier for them to compare University programmes.

Yet if we compare the learning hours required to gain certification from one of the three more widely known coaching associates we find that this differs quite significantly from those completed on a Master's programme. A comparison by EMCC (2015: 3) of the coach training hours required by ICF UK, EMCC, and AC indicates a wide range of training hours: 20 hours at L1 (Foundation Coach) up to 1800 hours at L4 (Master Coach). Within this range, though, there are quite significant differences. For example, ICF UK require 200 coach training for Master Coach, AC require 80 coach training hours and EMCC require 1800 (540 of these need to be classified as practice hours). The 1800 coach training hours is more closely aligned to the expected learning hours on a Master's programme. Yet in addition to the expected Coach Training hours, each of these coaching associations require evidence of coach experience hours. At Master Coach level, this varies from 500 (EMCC), 1500 (AC) and 2500 (ICF). Yet what isn't clear from EMCC's (2015) Coach Accreditation/Credentialing Assessment comparison is what specific knowledge and skills are expected from the coach training. We can deduce that there is some expectation around be able to demonstrate knowledge and skills in: coaching methodologies, personal coaching approach, and self-reflection from this comparison, although evidence of self-reflection does not appear to be something that is required by ICF (EMCC 2015: 4).

Table 4.2 Comparison of Coaching Programmes Offered by UK Higher Education Institutions

	Institution	Programme Offering	Aims/Theoretical position/Syllabus	Affiliation/Certification
1	Birkbeck, University of London	MSc Career Management and Coaching	Programme aims to equip coaches, consultants and HR professionals to work with groups and individuals at a relational depth in organisations, as career coaches, coaches or consultants. It promotes critical engagement with evaluating theory, research and practice in these fields. Modules: Career Coaching Skills 1; Career Counselling and Coaching; Introduction to Coaching; Coaching; Life Career Development Research Methods; Career Coaching Skills 2; Consultancy and Professional Practice; Understanding Organizations and Change; Research project (Org Psychology). http://www.bbk.ac.uk/study/2019/postgraduate/programmes/TMSCOACG_C/	Learning outcomes derived from ICF, EMCC and Special Group of Coaching Psychology at the British Psychological Society (SPCP-BPS) competency frameworks.
		PGCert in Coaching (new in 2014-15)	This PGCert provides a progressive re-think of the way skills, practice and theory are viewed, analysed, and delivered in this field. The programme is broad enough to allow newcomers to the field an overview of the dominant coaching paradigms. Modules: Coaching portfolio (develops reflexive coaching, uses auto-ethnography as a methodology); Introduction to coaching (theory and practice); The Coaching Context (coaching techniques, systemic, organisational and political dimensions of coaching, ethics). http://www.bbk.ac.uk/study/2019/postgraduate/programmes/TPCCOACH_C/	

(Continued)

Table 4.2 (Continued)

	Institution	Programme Offering	Aims/Theoretical position/Syllabus	Affiliation/Certification
2	DeMontfort University	PGCert Professional Coaching	Programme brings together professional coaching practice, academic research and incorporating experienced coaching practitioners' own insights. Modules: Coaching Fundamentals, Coaching Exploration and Discovery and Organizational Coaching. https://www.dmu.ac.uk/study/courses/postgraduate-courses/postgraduate-certificate-in-professional-coaching/postgraduate-certificate-in-professional-coaching.aspx	Programme ensures required supervision to apply for Foundation Executive Coach level with the **Association for Coaching** – additional charge for this.
3	Goldsmiths, University of London	PGCert Psychological Coaching	Coaching element of programme based on Acceptance and Commitment Training (ACT) theory; an evidence-based, cognitive-behaviour therapy. Leadership development training based on Transformational Leadership theory. Modules: Introduction to Coaching Theory and Skills; Consolidating Basic CBT Skills Through Practice; Intermediate Coaching Theory and Skills, Effective Coaching at Work. https://www.gold.ac.uk/pg/pgcert-coaching/ https://www.gold.ac.uk/media/course-finder/programmespecifications/postgraduate-certificate-in-coaching.pdf	
4	Heriot-Watt	MSc Business Psychology with Coaching (Dubai campus only) + PgCert and PgDip	Programme aims to provide students with an in-depth understanding of psychological aspects of coaching such as productivity, resilience and optimal wellbeing; all areas considered key to coaching effectiveness. Modules - S1: Coaching Psychology; Social and Organisational Change; Organisational Culture; Intercultural Communication in the Workplace. Modules - S2: Coaching Psychology Practice; Diversity; Leadership; Research Methods + Dissertation. https://www.hw.ac.uk/study/uk/postgraduate/business-psychology.htm	ICF

5	Leeds Beckett University	MA Executive and Business Coaching	Programme explores key management concepts, theories and models used in coaching and mentoring. Students learn to critique and enhance their professional coaching skills through reflexive practice and action learning. Students learn to use their skill set and experience as a catalyst for positive change in the workplace. https://courses.leedsbeckett.ac.uk/executivebusinesscoaching_ma/ https://courses.leedsbeckett.ac.uk/coaching-mentoring-for-education/
6	Liverpool John Moores	PGCert in Advanced Educational Practice – Mentoring and Coaching (Taught). Can progress to MA Advanced Education Practice.	Programme aims to: Extend knowledge base in the area of Mentoring and Coaching in Education through critical engagement with current Education theory, research and practice and develop critical mentoring and coaching practice through reflection on and engagement with this knowledge base within their professional settings. https://prodcat.ljmu.ac.uk/Specifications/ECL/22769/2000002797/22_10_2015/version_02_01/22769-2000002797.pdf
7	Manchester Metropolitan University	MA Coaching and Mentoring	Programme aims to: develop an understanding of the theories behind coaching and mentoring; critically reflect on approaches as a mentor or coach and apply and evaluate new ideas to practice. Modules include: Dissertation; mapping the territory: critical concepts and issues; research and practice; shaping the future; specialist supported project: coaching and mentoring https://www2.mmu.ac.uk/study/postgraduate/course/ma-coaching-and-mentoring/

Table 4.2 (Continued)

	Institution	Programme Offering	Aims/Theoretical position/Syllabus	Affiliation/Certification
8	Middlesex	MA Existential Coaching	Programme draws on psychotherapeutic literature and existential philosophy aimed at teaching coaches to work in a holistic way with clients. Teaching and learning methods aimed at encouraging trainees to go much further than applying coaching frameworks or tools. https://www.nspc.org.uk/courses/ma-in-existential-coaching/ https://www.nspc.org.uk/accreditation/academic-accreditation.html	Non-compulsory practical 3 day certified coaching programme delivered by 'The Performance Coach' certified by EMCC.
		MA Education (Coaching and Mentoring) - Dubai	Aimed at providing the knowledge to introduce a coaching culture in schools. Programme provides a comprehensive analysis of common core principles in the fields of coaching and mentoring, encouraging students to develop and pursue their own personal and professional research interests. On completion of the programme graduates likely to benefit from increasing career opportunities within the Gulf Region. Modules: Developing Effective Teaching and Learning; Developing Effective Coaching and Mentoring and Dissertation https://www.mdx.ac.ae/courses/course-list/course-detail/ma-education-coaching-and-mentoring	ILM L3 Coaching qualification
9	Newman University Birmingham	MA Mentoring and Coaching (Education)	Then main focus on this programme is developing a mentoring and coaching culture within educational establishments. https://digital.ucas.com/courses/details?coursePrimaryId=79c1590b-de3d-615c-c782-96b07e110bd48&academicYearId=2019	

10	Northumbria University	MA Coaching (can apply for PGCert and PGDip as separate awards)	Programme philosophy: Coaching as a Development Approach. Students learn to integrate prior work and life experiences with the theoretical concepts underpinning coaching practice. Modules: Understanding coaching (reflective practice integral); Psychological dimensions of coaching practice (psychometric, critical reflection, action learning); Professional coaching practice; The coaching organization (relevance of coaching and organizational performance); Management Investigation (60 credits). northumbria/courses/master-of-arts-coaching-dtpcag6/	Coaching Practice opportunities. Develop a practice portfolio that could be submitted to AC, ICF, EMCC
		Coaching Postgraduate Diploma	Aimed at people who have completed a foundational coaching programme – a practising coach, with a PGCert from another University or ILM L7 qualification. Learning approach is student-centred, with an emphasis on students experimenting and reflecting on own practice as a coach. Underpinning theories and philosophies include: positive psychology, psychodynamic theory, transactional analysis, mindfulness and the application of latest research from neuroscience. https://www.northumbria.ac.uk/study-at-northumbria/courses/coaching-dtpcah6/	
		Postgraduate Certificate in Coaching	Modules: Understanding Coaching (coaching as a process, differences between mentoring, coaching and counselling) and Psychological Approaches to Coaching. https://www.northumbria.ac.uk/study-at-northumbria/courses/postgraduate-certificate-coaching-dtpcaj6/	

(Continued)

Table 4.2 (Continued)

	Institution	Programme Offering	Aims/Theoretical position/Syllabus	Affiliation/Certification
11	University of Nottingham (formerly offered through North Notts College)	PGCert Mentoring and Coaching Teachers (Can progress to MA Education)	Programme aimed at experienced teachers who have a mentoring role. Modules: Mentoring beginning teachers and Practice based enquiry. https://www.nottingham.ac.uk/pgstudy/courses/education/mentoring-and-coaching-teachers-pgcert.aspx	
12	Oxford Brookes University (with CIPD)	PGCert and PGDip Coaching and Mentoring Practice	Programme aimed at internal or, external coaches, consultants, mentor co-ordinators, coaching psychologists, counsellors, managers, human resources development or leadership professionals from the voluntary, public and private sectors. PGCert: Coaching and mentoring practice fundamentals; Transformational learning and adult development; Psychotherapeutic Dimensions of Coaching. PGDip: Advanced Coaching and Mentoring Practice + choice of 2 modules from: Psychological Perspectives on the Self; Coaching and Mentoring in Organisations; Positive Psychology; Independent Study and Research in Coaching and Mentoring. https://www.prospects.ac.uk/universities/oxford-brookes-university-3930/business-school-11700/courses/coaching-and-mentoring-practice-23402?keyword=coaching%20and%20mentoring&featuredCourses=&qualifications=21366&size=408&page=0	
13	Plymouth Marjon University	PGCert Coaching and Mentoring	Programme offers a study route to enable students to develop practical skills in coaching and/or mentoring and an understanding of the theoretical perspectives that underpin good coaching practice. Modules: Advanced coaching and mentoring (30 credits) and Coaching and mentoring in practice (30 credits). https://www.marjon.ac.uk/courses/mentoring/	

				EMCC (Senior Practitioner level)
		MA Education – Coaching, Mentoring and Leadership	Need to have completed PGCert before starting programme. The course ethos is informed by a renowned student-centred approach focusing on developing and enhancing professionals' practice through a critical and reflective action research methodology. Modules: Advanced coaching and mentoring; Coaching and mentoring in practice; Leadership in Learning & Educational Contexts; Leadership in Context; Independent supported study; Dissertation. https://www.marjon.ac.uk/courses/ma-education-coaching-mentoring-leadership/	
14	Sheffield Hallam University	MSc Coaching and Mentoring	Specialist part-time course aimed a diverse group of practitioners: HR, OD, change and strategic leaders and consultants; developmental consultants or trainers managers, executives and directors. The MSc stage enables students to become an ethical and critically reflexive practitioner, capable of operating effectively as a coach or mentor in a range of different contexts. Modules: Coaching and mentoring: skills; Coaching and mentoring: psychology; Coaching and mentoring: leadership and change; Coaching and mentoring: supervision; Coaching and mentoring: scheme design and evaluation; Team coaching; Advanced practitioner inquiry; Dissertation https://www.shu.ac.uk/about-us/academic-departments/sheffield-business-school/business-specialisms/coaching-and-mentoring	
15	University College Cork	MA Psychology – Applied Psychology (Positive and Coaching Psychology)	This programme brings together the fields of Positive and Coaching Psychology. Modules: Positive Psychology and Coaching; Wellness Coaching; Ethics and Supervision; Positive Organisational Psychology; Private Practice; Coaching Skills; Evidence Based Coaching; Positive Psychology in Group Settings; Research Methods and Data Analysis for Coaching Psychology. https://www.ucc.ie/en/ckd02/	

Table 4.2 (Continued)

	Institution	Programme Offering	Aims/Theoretical position/Syllabus	Affiliation/Certification
16	University of Chester	PGCert Coaching and Mentoring	This programme combines the theoretical and practical aspects of coaching and mentoring that can be applied in educational settings. Modules: Introduction to the skills, principles and practice of effective mentoring/coaching; developing client knowledge, skills and expertise through effective dialogue; co-ordinating mentoring and coaching programmes, https://www1.chester.ac.uk/study/postgraduate/coaching-and-mentoring/201809	
		MA Business and Personal Coaching (work based and integrative studies)	A negotiated work-based learning suite of prestigious university awards that enable practitioners to get credit for, and substantially build, their expertise - without disruption to their work commitments. https://www.prospects.ac.uk/universities/university-of-chester-3706/centre-for-work-related-studies-17265/courses/business-and-personal-coaching-work-based-and-integrative-studies-49989?keyword=coaching%20and%20mentoring&featuredCourses=&qualifications=21366&-size=40&page=0	
17	University of Cumbria	MSc Coaching and Mentoring, (+ PGDip and PGCert)	This programme is aimed at individuals wishing to enter professional coaching and mentoring, or existing professional coaches who want to extend their knowledge and practice to Master's level. It draws on transformative learning to cover the underlying principles and key theories of coaching and mentoring at Executive Level. It includes: the key contemporary theories related to coaching and mentoring; supervision; attaining professional standards; ethics and ethical coaching practice and transformative reflection.	

			Modules: Coaching and mentoring; coaching supervision; transformative reflection/professional identity; research methods; extending professional competence; attaining professional standards in coaching and mentoring; coaching and mentoring dissertation. https://digital.ucas.com/courses/details?coursePrimaryId=0230ba75-81f2-4340-a267-c7f143f935eb&academicYearId=2019	
18	University of Derby	MA Careers Education and Coaching	This programme is aimed at achieving high professional standards in career coaching given the affiliation with the Career Development Institute. Modules: Career guidance/Coaching Theory, Policy and Practice; Framework for Professional Practice; Developing Working Relationships with Clients; Using Career and Labour Market Information; Partnership Working; Research Methods, Independent Study. https://www.derby.ac.uk/postgraduate/education-courses/careers-education-coaching-ma/	Career Development Institute
		MA Education: Leadership Coaching and Mentoring	This programme aims to provide an integral and essential step to establishing the professional credibility and status of coaching and mentoring. The emphasis is on coaching and mentoring as the enabler of learning, together with encouraging reflective practice aligned with wider professional and organisational needs. PGCert modules: Crafting your Masters' Study + Pathway (Leader as Coach and Mentor; Principles and Practices of Coaching and Mentoring) + option (Independent Study). PGDip modules: Evidence Based Practice + Pathway (Leader as Coach and Mentor; Principles and Practices of Coaching and Mentoring) + option (Independent Study). https://www.derby.ac.uk/postgraduate/education-courses/education-coaching-mentoring-ma/	Association of Coaching

(Continued)

Table 4.2 (Continued)

	Institution	Programme Offering	Aims/Theoretical position/Syllabus	Affiliation/Certification
19	University of East London	MSc Integrative Counselling and Coaching	This programme offers professional training for those who aim to integrate various counselling approaches and coaching in their one-to-one practice.	Able to apply for BACP membership after completing programme – 3 years duration.
			Modules: Year 1: Core counselling theory and practice (30 credits); counselling application (30 credits).	
			Year 2: Evidence-based coaching as a part of integrative practice (30 credits); personal consultancy: an integrative framework for counselling and coaching (30 credits).	
			Year 3: Research methods and dissertation 1 (30 credits); research methods and dissertation2 (30 credits).	
			Placement hours (100); supervision integral to the programme learning.	
		MSc Applied Positive Psychology and Coaching Psychology	This programme equips students with the knowledge, skills, and confidence to help people and organisations to flourish.	
			Modules: Developing a professional coaching practice; Research Methods and Dissertation_2; Coaching in Professional Contexts; The search for something higher; Multi-dimensional flourishing; Research Methods and Dissertation_2; The Practice of Evidence-based Coaching; Perspectives on wellbeing	
			https://www.postgraduatesearch.com/university-of-east-london/52344374/postgraduate-course.htm	
20	University of Gloucester	PGCert Coaching and Mentoring (Can progress to an MEd on completion)	This programme aims to help students develop a deeper understanding of the personal, social and organisational learning processes that occur when mentoring and coaching are used competently. It develop the high level abilities of synthesis, analysis and critical evaluation of learning theories, coaching philosophies and models.	
			Modules: Advanced Practice in Coaching and Mentoring – Part 1 and 2	
			http://progspecs.glos.ac.uk/Live/15-16/EME/001%20PG%20 Cert%20Coaching%20and%20Mentoring.pdf	

(Continued)

21	University of Huddersfield	MA Education (Mentoring and Coaching)	This programme aims to help students explore the role of mentoring and coaching and its role in supporting personal development in organisations. It addresses the roles of mentors and coaches and their ethical and professional responsibilities. It provides the opportunity for students to develop an understanding of critical reflection. Core modules: Mentoring and Coaching, Methods of Enquiry, Dissertation. Choice of 17 optional modules: https://digital.ucas.com/courses/details?CoursePrimaryId=fb75f19c-0997-4ad8-958f-4c33 90ca6372&CourseOptionId=93431b46-4004-4712-9441- a7722f477859	Fits with EMCC QA Framework
22	University of Portsmouth	PGCert, PGDip and MSc Coaching and Development (Part-time) – work-based learning. Year for each level.	The programme is aimed at leaders, managers and training professionals who want to develop their skills, knowledge and understanding in the rapidly developing field of coaching. PGCert modules include: Foundation coaching skills; creating insights; applied positive psychology in coaching; coaching leaders. PGDip: transformational coaching; coaching within organisations; coaching teams and groups; coaching mastery. http://www2.port.ac.uk/courses/business-and-management/msc-coaching-and-development/	Programme delivered in partnership with The Performance Coach Leadership

Table 4.2 (Continued)

	Institution	Programme Offering	Aims/Theoretical position/Syllabus	Affiliation/Certification
23	University of Reading (Henley)	Henley Professional Certificate in Executive Coaching	This programme focuses on the organisational context for coaching. It provides students with the opportunity to carry out an original piece of practitioner research in the field. The Professional Certificate in Coaching forms part of the programme but it can be taken independently.	ICF, AC, EMCC Offered in South Africa, Germany and Finland
			Modules: Self-awareness as a coach (what is coaching, who am I as a coach; my personal coaching style; GROW model refresh); Tools and techniques (psychological models; coaching approaches; reflective practice); Integration (solutions-focused; ethics, supervision; integration).	
			https://www.henley.ac.uk/executive-education/course/the-professional-certificate-in-coaching	
		MSc Coaching and Behavioural Change	Modules: Neuro-linguistic Programming for Behavioural Change, Advanced Coaching Practice, Group Dynamics and Systems Thinking, Becoming a Reflective Practitioner	
			https://www.henley.ac.uk/executive-education/course/msc-in-coaching-behavioural-change	
24	University of Warwick	MA Career Development and Coaching	This MA is approved by the Career Development Institute (CDI) as meeting the qualification requirement for the UK Register of Career Development Professionals.	Career Development Institute (CDI)
		PG Diploma in Coaching	Diploma in Coaching, that covers a range of theoretical perspectives: person centred; gestalt; neuroscience and coaching; cognitive behavioural; appreciative inquiry	
			http://www2.warwick.ac.uk/study/cll/courses/professionaldevelopment/coaching/coachingdiploma/	

25	University of West of England	PGCert Leadership and Management (Coaching and Mentoring)	This programme is designed to meet the needs of busy professionals who wish to develop their knowledge and skills in both coaching and mentoring and leadership and management. Modules: Leading and managing people; personal mastery in leadership; coaching and mentoring; group facilitation. https://courses.uwe.ac.uk/Z20000066/certificate-in-executive-coaching-and-mentoring-ilm-level-7	ILM
26	University of West of Scotland	PGCert Mentoring and Coaching (online)	This Postgraduate Certificate Coaching and Mentoring programme is aimed at a diverse range of people from various sector organisations (public, private and voluntary) who may have responsibility for training and development and OD. Modules: Situated professional learning; Critical self-evaluation and development; Contextualising coaching and mentoring. https://www.postgraduatesearch.com/university-of-the-west-of-scotland/5632168688/postgraduate-course.htm	Accreditation: General Teaching Council for Scotland
27	University of Wolverhampton	MA Coaching and Mentoring (PGCert and PGDip options)	This programme aims to develop a critical understanding of the concepts and theoretical frameworks that underpin coaching practice. Students have the opportunity to engage in evidence-based discussions, as well discussions on applying theory into practice. Modules: Reflective Practitioner; Developing Coaching and Mentoring Practice; Principles and Theories in Relation to Coaching and Mentoring; Advanced Studies in Developing Your Coaching and Mentoring Practice; Designing and Delivering and Evaluating Coaching and Mentoring; Exploring Different Coaching and Mentoring Practices; Independent Business Analysis Project https://www.postgraduatesearch.com/university-of-wolverhampton/5715367878/postgraduate-course.htm	With Full MSc can apply for individual accreditation with EMCC at Master Practitioner level

(Continued)

Table 4.2 (Continued)

	Institution	Programme Offering	Aims/Theoretical position/Syllabus	Affiliation/Certification
28	UCLAN	Certificate Management Coaching Skills (Delivered over 6 weeks).	This programme aims to develop managers' knowledge and practice of the role of coaching as a management competence. It enables participants to equip themselves as an effective coach by: differentiating coaching from other helping skills and introducing essential coaching skills and models. Topics covered: Coaching and Management styles; Coaching models and theories; Types of coaching; Coaching principles and skills; Coaching conversations. https://www.uclan.ac.uk/courses/cert_certificate_management_coaching_skills.php	
29	Y0rk St John	PGCert Coaching and Mentoring	This programme aims to develop critically reflective coaching and mentoring practitioners, capable of working in a variety of settings. Students are encouraged to use their professional work context to practice and develop their skills. Typical modules: Coaching and Mentoring Skills and Technique; Coaching and Mentoring, Management and Leadership, Designing and Operating Coaching and Mentoring Schemes. https://www.yorksj.ac.uk/media/content-assets/registry/programme-specifications/postgraduate/business/1718/PGCert-Coaching-and-Mentoring.pdf	

Postgraduate Coaching Programmes Offered by UK Universities

The list of Postgraduate Coaching programmes set out in Table 4.2 has been compiled from the UCAS Postgraduate directory during the period January to March 2019 (www.ucas.com/postgraduate).

In our initial search for coaching qualifications on UCAS Life Coaching appeared at the top of a Google search as Figure 4.1 indicates, followed by Sports Coaching, although Life Coaching is not yet offered as a Master's level qualification.

A more detailed search for Postgraduate coaching programmes on UCAS (for 2019–20) identified that there are 82 Postgraduate coaching programmes (ranging from Postgraduate Certificate, Postgraduate Diploma to full Masters) offered by 45 UK Universities[1]. A large number of these coaching programmes related to areas of coaching that are not the main focus of our enquiry, e.g., Sport, Music, or Drama, and thus have been excluded from our analysis in this section.

Table 4.2 lists 29 UK Higher Education institutions that offer a combination of Postgraduate Certificate, Postgraduate Diploma and Masters in coaching. These programme offerings are aimed at different target audiences: experienced coaches, individuals aiming to get into coaching, HR, HRD, and Organisational Development professionals, managers, as well as educationalists. Seven out the 29 institutions listed in Table 4.2 seem to focus on coaching within an educational context. In addition, three of the institutions specifically mentioned that their programmes were delivered in different countries, either in the Middle East (Dubai), or in Hong Kong. This an important point, given our interest in the status of

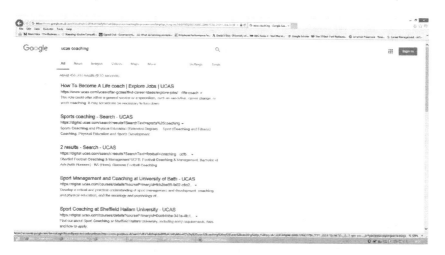

Figure 4.1 UCAS Search for Coaching Programmes (UK)

coaching in non-Western contexts. Later in this section we discuss coach education and training provision in other countries, e.g., Asia Pacific and Middle East.

What the data in Table 4.2 suggests is that there appears to be an interest in gaining a Postgraduate qualification in coaching, given the number of institutions that now provide a Postgraduate Certificate in Coaching, either instead of, or in addition to, offering a full Masters qualification. Fifteen of the 29 universities in Table 4.2 offered a Post-graduate Certificate in Coaching. This may be a reflection of changing demand and/or supply for this type of learning and development experi-ence either amongst existing professionals, or those seeking to gain entry to the coaching profession. For new providers, launching a Postgraduate Certificate, as opposed to a full Master's, is a good way to test the market whilst keeping initial development costs low. However, given the call for more evidence-based coaching practice it is somewhat surprising (and perhaps concerning) that the level of interest in completing a full Master's programme is not as strong as that for completing an interim Postgradu-ate award; although the UK QAA Subject Statements reflect progression from Postgraduate Certificate to full Masters. Given that completing a Dissertation as part of a Master's requires completing an empirical piece of research, this is perhaps a limitation of coaches' education. None the less, this change in demand/supply for Postgraduate Certificate qualifica-tions is in keeping with the rising demand for postgraduate qualifications in certain disciplinary areas, such as in Biological Sciences (which encom-passes psychology based subjects) as Figure 4.2 indicates.

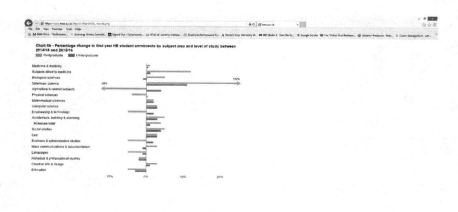

Figure 4.2 Changes in HE Student Enrolments, 2014/15 to 2015/16 (www.hesa. ac.uk)

It is not our intention to discuss in detail each of the coaching programmes listed in Table 4.2. Instead our aim is to offer some observations about: the level of information provided about the underpinning coaching philosophy and coaching models covered on the programme, as well as other underpinning theoretical frameworks, e.g., theories of adult learning, reflective practice, and reflexivity; differences and similarities in the core and optional modules on the programme; and emphasis between theory and practice and aligned to this whether any additional professsional certification with Coaching Associations or other Professional institutions is possible. This is the type of information we assume that purchasers of coaching pogrammes would want to know prior to making a decision about which programme to invest in.

In general, the level of detail provided by institutions about their coaching programmes was quite varied. Nine Universities made detailed programme specifications available through their website, making it easier to identifiy the expected knowledge, cognitive, and thinking skills, transferable skills and professional behaviors that would be acquired/developed in their programmes; these included Goldsmiths Univeristy of London, Heriot-Watt University, Liverpool John Moores, Oxford Brooks University, Sheffield Hallam University, University of East London, University of Gloucester, University of Portsmouth, and York St John University. Other universities provided an overview of the programme aims, core and optional modules, as well indicating who the programme is aimed at, i.e., those new to coaching, those with some experience, and those seeking to add coaching to an existing professional portfolio, such as those working in HR/HRD, or OD.

Underpinning Coaching Philosophies and Theories

Ten of the institutions listed in Table 4.2 refer explicitly to psychotherapuetic, or psychological, philosophies and theoretical perspectives in the programme overviews provided on their websites. Some examples include:

> Understand theories of human cognitive, emotional, behavioural, social and physiological functioning relevant to coaching, including, but not restricted to: goal setting theories; developmental theories; psychodynamic theories; group dynamics; abnormal behaviour; etc.
>
> (Birkbeck, University of London)

> Drawing on psychotherapeutic literature and on existential philosophy, we teach coaches to work in a holistic way, engaging with the unique world of each client. Existential coaches encourage clients to look at issues such as meaning, authenticity, freedom, choice and responsibility, and how these come into play in their lives.
>
> (Middlesex University)

Coaching as a Development Approach. On this part-time MA Coaching you will integrate your prior work and life experiences with the theoretical concepts underpinning coaching practice.

(Northumbria University)

Whilst other institutions indicate that coaching philosophies will be covered on their programmes, they are not explicit about what these are. In contrast, five institutions referred to theoretical underpinnings of transformational learning, or social and organisational learning (e.g., University of Cumbria, University of Gloucester, Northumbria Univeristy, Oxford Brookes University, and the University of West Scotland).

A focus on supporting coaches to develop as reflective practitioners was something that ten universities indicated would form a key part of the learning process on their programme. This we suggest is a critical pedagogical approach for coaching programmes, given the expectations for CPD and coach supervision by the different Coaching Associations (see EMCC 2015) and other associated professional bodies (e.g., the BPS, UK HCPC).

Similarities and Differences in the Core and Optional Modules on Univeristy Coaching Programmes

Perhaps unsurprisingly the range of modules offered on the various programme offerings varied considerably. These differences we assume is a factor of: who the programme is aimed at (e.g., those new to coaching, professionals looking to add coaching to their existing professional practice, leaders/managers in organisations); the underpinning philosophy (e.g., psychotherapeutic, psychological, organisational development); and the specialisms of key academics delivering on the programmes.

Over half of the Postgraduate Certificate programmes listed in Table 4.2 included a module that covered differences between coaching and mentoring, including the skills aspects of coaching and mentoring. Some programmes included modules that address the broader context within which coaching is delivered e.g., the Birkbeck University's PGCert includes a module on the Coaching Context, which they refer to as the organisational and political dimensions of coaching, including the ethical dimension and the University of the West of Scotland's PGCert offers a module on Contextualising Coaching and Mentoring. Several universities include a module on Co-ordinating mentoring and coaching programmes, so again would suggest more of a practice focus.

Only two universities offering a Postgraduate Certificate offer modules that appear to focus on the professional development needs of coaches: Birkbeck University (coaching portfolio—which focuses on reflexivity using an auto-ethnographic approach) and the University of West of Scotland (critical self-evaluation and development). Two universities though do refer to developing 'reflective coaching and mentoring practitioners' (University of Reading and York St John).

Accrediation by Coaching Associations

As Table 4.2 indicates only a small number (eight) of institutions mentioned whether their programmes were accredited by any of the Coaching Associations referred to earlier in this chapter. In some instances, intsitutiosn indicated that particinats would be able to apply for individual certifcation after succesfully completing the programme, or could take part in additional training that would help achieve certfication. This lack of professional accreditation of univeristy coaching programmes could be due to the insufficient emphasis on coaching practice within the curricula, one of the criteria used by Coaching Associations when certifying individual practitioners (see EMCC 2015). As mentioned earlier in ths chapter, some authors are critical of how, in the emerging coaching profession, unlike in other professions, a university qualification in coaching is not deemed essential:

> in fact it has become increasingly difficult for universities to gain accreditation for postgraduate qualifications by professional bodies because the accreditation ststems are modelled on short trianing programmeswitha focus on developing skills and completing coaching hours [*thus a proxy for competence*].
>
> (Bachkirova and Lawton Smith 2015: 125)

(NB. Text in italics is our addition, not that included in the original authors' work).

Partnership Approach to Offering Coaching Programmes

Even where Universities may not be offering a coaching programme directly themselves, then they may accredit the training delivered by other private providers. For example the University of Sussex validates a Postgraduate Certificate in Coaching delivered by Roffey Park, a leadership and organisational development institute, based in Sussex. The programme

> Combines the practical application of coaching in organisational settings (across sectors) with the academic rigour of up-to-date coaching theory. . . . It is more advanced than the first-step coach training providers, by taking into account the basic coach competencies (accredited by ICF, AC or EMCC), but going beyond "the toolkit"

into developing a signature coaching presence and stance for each participant.

(www.roffeypark.com/wp-content/uploads2/
Coaching-4-page-flyer.pdf)

I-Coach Academy—set up in 2001 by Prof. Mike van Oudtshoorn—offers different levels of coaching programmes—foundation and certificate, which can lead to Master's in Professional Coaching validated by Middlesex University—Alison Whybrow and David Megginson on the faculty.

> I-coach offers accredited programmes with routes to Masters and Doctorate Qualifications from the Institute for Work Based Learning at Middlesex University, UK. All I-coach pathways are also professionally accredited by the European Mentoring and Coaching Council (EMCC). On successful completion of the Mastery in Professional Coaching module you will graduate with an I-coach academy certificate with EMCC EQA award at Master Practitioner and a certificate of credit from Middlesex University for 60 post graduate level credits. The full qualification pathway is accredited by the EMCC at Master Practitioner in its EQA framework whilst the completion of the Mastery module alone will award Senior Practitioner level.

(www.i-coachacademy.com)

Coaching and Professionalisation—Current Debates

As coaching has now become a global phenomenon, in this section we take a more critical look at the institutions and institutional actors who are staking a claim for coaching to become recognised and accepted as a profession. Whilst gaining a definitive list of coaching institutes and associations is difficult, some of the more established associations include: Association of Coaching, European Mentoring & Coaching Council, International Coach Federation (ICF), and Institute of Coaching (Gray, Garvey and Lane 2016). More recently, coaching as specialist sub-division in the field of psychology has emerged (Grant 2006). In the UK, this has led to a special interest group—Coaching Psychology—within the British Psychological Society (BPS 2002; Palmer and Whybrow 2005). A development which as stated on the coaching special interest section of the BPS website was 'a response to concerns about untrained or poorly trained coaches, and the related need to promote improved standards of practice for the benefit of the profession of coaching, coaches, their clients and the public at large.' Drawing boundaries around a particular grouping of professionals is one of the stages in the professionalisation journey, as will be discussed later in this chapter. Specialist coaching psychology groups have been established in other parts of the world too, e.g., Australia, Denmark, Israel, and South Africa according to Grant (2006).

Although each of these associations can be observed as active in exercising their agency to stake a claim for the professionalisation of coaching, as Gray (2011: 5) points out coaching 'is a long way from meeting even the basic requirements of a true profession because it lacks a holistic theoretical framework derived from a sound empirical base and a unique body of knowledge.' In this chapter we focus on how one specific coaching institution, ICF, have/are mobilising their resources in pursuit of professionalisation.

What we are observing is a number of governance structures implemented by different coaching institutes and associations, aimed at staking a claim as the legitimate authority of the professionalisation of coaching, globally. In addition to the coaching associations mentioned previously, other organisations appear to be exercising their agency to become recognised as the legitimate regulator of coaching and mentoring services. One such organisation, the International Regulator of Coaching and Mentoring Services (www.ircm-register.org/), claims to be regulated by the Regulator of Community Interest Companies, appointed by the UK Department for Business, Energy & Industrial Strategy. Yet the provenance of this organisation and the Directors is far from transparent. We suggest that this is problematic for users of coaching services given that professional standards, coach qualifications, and affiliations are one of the many criteria used by organisations when selecting coaches (Arnott and Sparrow 2004; Brennan 2008; CIPD 2004). But as others suggest it is questionable whether those who practise coaching can claim a unique identity and body of expert knowledge (Gray 2006; Hamlin, Ellinger and Beattie 2008), criteria that typically differentiate professional occupations from other occupational groups (Elliott 1972; Wilensky 1964).

A key concern, given the focus global focus of this book, is surfacing tensions/questions on how coaching and professionalisation is perceived and positioned in non-western contexts. The origins of coaching within the Western tradition are heavily influenced by the language, metaphors, and ideas embedded in the professional sporting arena. Thus coaching, positioned as a process for increasing performance, has been at the forefront in the early years of the emergence of this type of occupational activity. However, conversations with coaches practicing in Asian society indicate that their original founders (pioneers) saw coaching as an educational tool, intended to aid and empower different communities, and to work with disadvantaged groups of society. Yet, we suggest, the 'profession' of coaching changed from a community social change orientation with the shift in emphasis on the coaching of business executives, where the intention of the 'game' changed from personal and social change to the notion of coaching as a business.

The thinking behind these early coaching initiatives was to assist behavioural change and community cohesion. Through the lens of institutional theory we expose how coaching as a social and cultural system is shaping the cultural norms and behaviours of the organisations and societies within which it now operates. We thus build on and extend the work of others (Mook 2007; Nangalia and Nangalia 2010) who suggest that coaching should be culturally congruent. Yet if the dominant players in the race for professionalisation originates in the West, dominated by Western notions of competencies and capabilities (Bachkirova and Lawton Smith 2015), this then has implications for coaching delivered in different cultural contexts. For example how might the concept of competency assessment associated with high performance fit in cultural contexts, such as the Middle East, where selection for employment is not necessarily associated with performance but social ties and connections? This is a question that we return to in Chapter 5.

Thus now that coaching has become a global phenomenon more strategic governance issues are surfacing, providing this disparate and highly segmented service with fresh challenges and the need for higher order thinking. In this next section we apply resource mobilisation theory to analyse how ICF has become a dominant organisation in the coaching world with regard to coach credentialing.

All Routes Point to ICF: A Resource Mobilisation Analysis of How ICF Has Shaped Its Legitimacy as the Global Voice on Coaching and Credentialing

ICF, founded in 1995 by Thomas Leonard, has established itself as 'the most recognized international association representing the coaching profession' (Williams no date: 38). Information provided on ICF's website indicates that the association, and its members, are working 'toward the common goal of enhancing awareness of coaching, upholding the integrity of the profession, and continually educating themselves with the newest research and practices.' The ICF website observes the historical contribution that Thomas Leonard made towards the inception of ICF, as an organisation, and Leonard as a pioneer in coaching. Leonard has been cited as pivotal in the transmission of coaching via a number of different channels, such as virtual programmes that people could subscribe to via the internet through a new business, Coach University. This medium allowed thousands of people worldwide to connect with the principles of coaching and begin to use coaching as a method of working one-to-one with people in organisations and businesses. However, Leonard was a firm advocate of teaching coaching to everyone who was interested, as he believed that anyone could be a coach if they acquire the skills and develop the practice.

When ICF was first established the focus and objectives seem more aligned to what is now called 'Life Coaching,' with a focus on supporting individuals who want to alter their personal and possibly their professional lives. Yet life coaching now does not necessarily hold the same status as other forms of coaching; life coaches are categorised as semi-professionals and could be considered a form of precarious worker 'Most life coaches work as independent contractors who lack an institutionalized system of social relations and must rely on their own abilities to secure employment. . . . Workers in such positions may arrive there by choice, others by necessity' (George 2013: 180). ICF has moved on from their primary focus of Life Coaching towards a broader perspective of coaching that embraces executive coaching as well as personal coaching.

The most recent ICF Global Coaching Study (ICF 2016), run in collaboration with PricewaterhouseCoopers LLP, indicates that there are currently approximately 53,300 professional coach practitioners worldwide: 35% of these are from Western Europe; 33% from North America; and 7% from Asia (ICF 2016). These figures represent an increase from the 2012 ICF Global Coaching Study, where the reported estimated number of coaches worldwide was 18,000 (Lodwick and Haslett 2012). ICF indicate that coaches now operate across different 'coaching continuum' (ICF 2016: 7): external coach practitioner; Internal coach practitioner; external and internal coach practitioner; human resource talent developer/manager using coaching skills; and manager/leader using coaching skills. However, it should be noted that participants who completed ICF's Global Coaching Study self-identify as a professional coach. Yet within ICF's membership base there would appear to be distinct categories of membership, only 20,000 of ICF's members, out of a potential 53,000 coach practitioners, are defined as 'credential-holder members' (http://coachfederation.org/prdetail.cfm?ItemNumber=4347). The significance of the distinction between 'credential-holder' and 'non credential-holder' categories is one that requires further investigation. Why might individuals want to become a member of a particular coaching association, but not seek to gain the credentials that they offer?

ICF's prominence has grown through a number of strategies (see Table 4.1). These include: establishing a strong chapter-based membership structure in a number of countries; the credentialing of individual coaches; accreditation of coach training programmes provided by institutes/associations across the globe and more recently the strategic alliance with two European coaching associations, the Association for Coaching (AC) and the European Coaching and Mentoring Council (EMCC), in 2012. The press release issued to signal this alliance stressed

> The creation of this Alliance is a step forward in achieving ICFs goals of advancing the coaching profession and being in service of humanity flourishing. . . . It is important that the coaching and mentoring bodies speak with a unified voice. The profession, the coaches, and the purchasers of coaching will benefit from that.

Sustainability of the profession of coaching was also stressed in this press release.

As ICF developed across the U.S., growing chapters in other countries and then across Asia, the focus became one of training and developing people as coaches and then offering them programmes where ICF recognised their qualifications and would credential them as professional coaches. This created a dichotomy with the original ideas of Leonard, who was not necessarily against credentialing coaches but was more in favour of a loose federation of interested people who could continue to learn from and with each other in an informal peer community of practice.

One coaching practitioner that we spoke to informally about our work suggested that

> He [Leonard] had not intended the ICF to become a regulatory agency. He intentionally selected the word "Federation" because it meant "uniting in a league". Leonard had a much broader vision for the ICF as a 'Portal' for coaches around the world. In its early development he made it clear that he thought coaching was too young, too new and too full of potential to regulate and define standards before it had time to evolve and mature. He didn't want coaching to be restricted, put in a box and defined too soon.

However, as ICF is now over 20 years old, these arguments might not hold now, and coaching seems to be on the threshold of change both in the way in which it is developing and its position in the world. This is not a new phenomenon, in that the schism between the founder of modern nursing, Florence Nightingale and Mrs. Bedford-Fenwick is very similar. Nightingale was convinced that as long as people were trained in some way as nurses then they could develop their skills through on-the-job experience. Nightingale was responsible for the first secular-nurse training school at St. Thomas' Hospital in London and is responsible for much of the thinking behind the philosophy and early practice of nursing. Bedford-Fenwick, on the other hand, supported the recognition of nursing as a profession and lobbied Parliament in the UK to introduce laws and regulation governing the training and development of professionalised nurses. We can put these differences in perspective as part of the journey towards professionalisation of any emerging field of practice. However, in the case of medicine and nursing, the links between government regulation and the setup of official training and development 'schools' has played an important part in the development of professional credibility. Coaching on the other hand is not tied into government regulations or official training 'schools,' thus it depends on the services of organisations such as ICF, EMCC, and WABC, to support the development of future coaches.

Although ICF originated in the U.S., where interestingly coaching is not recognised as a profession by the U.S. Labour Department (Bennett 2006), the majority of its current membership is not in the U.S. Since 2002 to 2016, ICF's membership in Asia has been growing. The inaugural meeting of the Singapore ICF chapter, one of the earliest chapters in Asia, was held in 2002; this was organised by a Singaporean National, who went on to become the first Singapore ICF Chapter President. ICF Singapore became a Chartered Chapter in 2003, at which point membership was up to 39. By 2007 membership had increased to 74, by 2011 membership had increased to 234 and by 2016 membership had grown to 368; 179 (49%) of these members held an ICF credential. So they are able to call themselves an Associate Certified Coach, Professional Certified Coach, and Master Professional Coach (www.icfsingapore.org/our-history.html). The reasons for the growth in coaching professionals in Asia is not something that is discussed on ICF's website. However, other work (Nangalia and Nangalia 2010) suggests that this growth may be due to the number of MNCs who are developing their operations in Asia.

The growth in the reach of coaching's rise in Asia is not without its problems. Whilst the dominance of Western ideas in coaching appears to have been accepted in some parts of Asia, informal conversations by one of the authors with coaches in Singapore identified that ideas, concepts, and metaphors that are commonly used in coaching are primarily Western in origin and focus on sporting examples, creating a clash with some of the social norms in Asia. The emphasis of rationality of thinking in the West and the more traditional Eastern focus on Zen, Taoism, and Buddhist ideas may not correspond or be in synchrony when coaches are practicing their craft. The collision of the principles of coaching from the original position of asking Socratic questions and the tradition of being an Elder/Mentor in the community seems to be at odds with cultural norms and expectations. An observation shared by others running coaching businesses in other Asian contexts, such as in India (Nangalia and Nangalia 2010). We suggest that the discourse and dialogue between different cultural and social groups requires all coaches to review their practice within a global paradigm and be prepared to alter or change coaching to fit with the diversity of people's traditions and the impact of social norms. The impact that coaching is making on global cultures can be seen as Western centric. Gilmartin (2009) refers to three waves of colonialism that moved across the world over several centuries of commercial advancement. The Western organisations that are promoting coaching may inadvertently be creating a fourth wave of colonialism by maintaining coaching as a mainly Western framework that is not in harmony with the requirements of different cultures and communities. This rather quiet form of colonialism can go unnoticed until Western approaches to coaching has become the dominant form of behaviour and culture change in Asia.

Analysing ICF's Status Through a Social Mobilisation Theoretical Lens

In this next section we draw on social mobilisation theory as the theoretical lens for our analysis of how ICF has mobilised its power to position itself as the dominant coaching association and voice in the professionalisation discourse. Social mobilisation theory is an established sociological theory for understanding and analysing 'noninstitutionalised collective actions consciously orientated towards social change' (Jenkins 1983: 529). Such change could encompass movements that reflect either personal change (e.g., sects, cults, communes), or institutional change (e.g., legal reforms). Whilst it could be argued that coaching is not a social movement per se, as Wilensky (1964: 144) points out, first teachers, or pioneers, of specialism act as 'enthusiastic leaders of a movement . . . or protagonists of some new technique' who then go on to push to build a professional association. Recent developments in social mobilisation theory however (i.e., resource mobilisation theory) situates social movement within an institutionalised context. Resource mobilisation theorists, according to Jenkins (1983: 529), position social movement as 'extensions of institutionalised actions' aimed at: altering social structures; the organisation of unorganised groups against institutional elites, or the mobilisation of social groups to represent the interests of excluded groups. As McCarthy and Wolfson (1996) point out resources are key to social movements and the mobilisation of change. These resources include people, money, and legitimacy, which are mobilised through three distinct ways: agency, strategy, and organisation. Agency, as Caldwell (2005: 111) points out, is a key factor, given that agency encompasses 'modes of enactment in practice that mix intentionality and moral action, power and knowledge.' Yet, as Caldwell (2005: 111) points out, change agents (who use their agency to enable some form of change) are not necessarily 'unbiased facilitators' or independent of making 'value judgements.'

Our argument is that given ICF's strategies, and organisational structure (i.e., chapter based organisational structure), it has similar characteristics to other social movement structures. A movement that uses its collective agency to maintain its legitimacy as 'the leading global organisation dedicated to advancing the coaching profession' (http://coachfederation.org/about/?navItemNumber=557/). Despite being a relatively young institutional body—first established in 1995—ICF has already staked a claim as the only globally recognised independent credentialing programme for coach practitioners, who have met stringent education and experience. Yet the results of the latest ICF Global Coaching Study (ICF 2016) indicates that the credentialing of coach practitioners is still problematic; whilst 51% of coaches (from 15,380 survey respondents) indicated that they hold an ICF credential, a large number of survey respondents engaged in coaching were unsure if they had a coaching certification/credential.

Table 4.3 maps out the strategies, organising structures and modes of agency deployed by ICF to build and maintain its dominant voice in the professionalisation of coaching. The data we present aligns with what Wilensky (1964: 146) observed in his research on how professions come into being

> the early masters of the technique or adherents of the movement become concerned about standards of training and practice . . . the teachers and activists then achieve success in promoting more effective organization, first local, then national. . . . Toward the end, legal protection of the monopoly of skill appears.

The data we present in Table 4.1 is consistent with this pattern. Moreover the notion of the 'ideology of professionalism' (Evetts 2011: 411) that encompasses the building of a strong occupational identity, collegiality through organising structures, a strong sense of importance and contribution, as well as the guardians of ethics and standards, can be identified in our analysis of ICF's strategy, organisation, and agency.

We have drawn on resource mobilisation theory as an analytical framework to map out and analyse the routes and mobilising power structures of one of the larger coaching associations, International Coach Federation, that is dominating the movement towards the professionalisation of coaching. Our aim is to expose the hegemony of this particular coaching association which we suggest is grounded in a Western philosophy of coaching.

The shift from an informal network of coaching practitioners towards professionalisation is an important step in the history of coaching. As discussed previously, ICF, EMCC, and the Association of Coaching have formed an alliance to create the Global Coaching and Mentoring Alliance (2012), enabling them to use their individual and collective agency to stake a claim for coaching to become recognised as a profession. Laudable as this claim might be we feel that there is a need for further questioning of the legitimacy of this claim. In this section we draw on literature on the sociology of the professions and institutional theory to assess to what extent coaching could be considered en route to professionalisation.

Drawing on the work of Freidson (2001), Muzio, Kirkpatrick and Kipping (2011) define professionalism as a 'analytical category delineating a distinctive way of organizing work,' where those employed in such work 'retains control over its work, its organisation, execution and legitimate evaluation' (p. 806). Professionals and professional institutions are perceived as playing a key role in advising and shaping business practice (Muzio, Brock and Suddaby 2013). However, as the economic, social, legal, and political context within which professional associations

Table 4.3 Resource Mobilisation Analysis of ICF

Features of resource mobilisation	Evidence	Sources
Agency	Founder: Thomas Leonard who founded International Coach Federation (ICF) in 1995, is acknowledged as one of the coaching pioneers active in staking a claim for coaching as a profession. Mobilised support of other 'coaching pioneers'—to build ICF into the organisation it is today. ICF promotes itself as the world's voice on coaching. It represents the voice of around 53,300 coaches worldwide.	http://coachfederation.org ICF (2016); Brennan (2008)
	Meso: ICF Global Board of Directors, consisting of 9 people, uses its collective agency to select and appoint future Directors. Criteria for appointment published on ICF's website.	http://coachfederation.org/about/landing.cfm?ItemNumber=3152&navItemNumber=3154
	Members of ICF Global Board of Directors use their collective agency to promote and maintain legitimacy through ensuring the self-regulatory oversight of coaching standards, certification and credentials. But there does not appear to be any independent scrutiny of these accredited coaching programmes.	Williams (no date); George (2013); Bachkirova and Lawton Smith (2015)
	Individual Global Board Directors promote the aims, status and institutional credibility through targeted practitioner-focused publications and conference presentations. Carefully crafted and monitored media messages—tracked by ICF itself.	Brennan (2008); Mook (2007); Williams (no date);
	Setting and promoting own research agenda, including the publication of research that indicates the value of coaching to organisations.	Bono et al. (2009); Brennan (2008)
	Micro: Local chapters run by volunteers. Global Communities of Practice (CPS), aimed at sharing best practice and tools amongst members to enhance their professional development. CPS's are designed to promote active participation from members; although the website does not elaborate on what this looks like in practice.	

Strategy	Maintains its dominant position in the field of coaching through a combination of certification of individual coaches and accreditation of coach training delivered by training providers/institutes across the globe. Some examples include: Global Coach Trust (India) and Coaching Supervision Academy (UK), Coach Masters academy (Dubai)	https://globalcoachtrust.org/about/ http://coachingsupervisionacademy.com/the-csa-way/ [accessed 18/2/2017] www.coachmastersacademy.com/events/news/icf-approved-coaching-certificate-training-in-dubai [accessed 1/4/2107]. Stern and Stout-Rostron (2013)
	Coach education, training and certification based on specific ontological and theoretical perspective—but what is this and how transparent is it? As with other coaching institutions, the research that underpins their coach education and training is prescriptive—focus on sharing of 'best practice'	
	Growth through partnership with other Coaching Organisations (e.g., Association of Coaching, EMCC) in 2012 as the Global Coaching & Mentoring Alliance.	www.streetinsider.com/ [accessed 4/2/2017]
	Mobilising the global coaching community through ICF Converge 2017. An event described as "a dynamic global event designed to strengthen connections within the coaching community and offer cutting-edge learning opportunities around topics including the art and practice of coaching, building a thriving coaching business, cultivating strong coaching cultures in organizations, coaching science, and the future of coaching and of the workforce.'	http://brand-manual.webflow.io/style-guide [accessed 4/2/2017]
	Controlling the format and branding of communications through a Style Guide for Members—unified voice, enhance professionalism and credibility.	
	Rebranding the ICF website in 2017, which further promotes the global nature of ICF's reach: highlights chapters in 130 different locations and website content that can be accessed through 100 different languages enabled through the use of Google translate.	https://coachfederation.org/blog/welcome-new-coachfederation-org
Organisation	Macro: ICF Board of Directors. The organisation has its own governance structure—ICF Regulatory Committee—whose role is to preserve the integrity of the coaching profession.	http://coachfederation.org/about/landing.cfm?ItemNumber=3152&navItemNumber=3154
	Members of the ICF Board of Directors are expected to have 'Familiarity with research/innovation in the application of science, practice and education.'	http://coachfederation.org/landing.cfm?ItemNumber=2108&navItemNumber=4353

(Continued)

Table 4.3 (Continued)

Features of resource mobilisation	Evidence	Sources
	Different types of membership: 'credential-holder members' and ordinary members.	ICF Singapore Chapter www.icfsingapore.org/our-history.html
	Micro: Two organisational structures operate at the micro level.	ICF Honk Kong Chapter www.icfsingapore.org/; www.icfhk.org/the-board.html
	Local ICF Chapters. These structures are run by volunteers and provide opportunities for members to meet with fellow coaches and 'get more involved with ICF'. Although it does not say on ICF's website what this involvement consists of. Each Chapter has its own Board structure, drawn from elected members, ratified by a Nominations Committee. Board members can serve for a maximum of 4 years in office.	ICF Dubai Chapter www.linkedin.com/company/international-coach-federation—dubai-chapter. 1588 followers in February 2019.
	ICF Global Communities of Practice (CPs). These structures are intended to provide a platform for sharing best practice, tools and trends in the coaching world. Each CP is managed by volunteer co-leaders. CPs are expected to promote active participation amongst members.	UK Chapters. Coaches have the opportunity to connect with 2,089 members and a network of over 25,000 coaches across 136 countries www.coachfederation.org.uk/
	Local volunteer groups are expected to 'contribute to effective and efficient decision-making and aligned to the organization's strategic objectives.'	http://coachfederation.org/about/landing.cfm?ItemNumber=823&navItemNumber=616
	This includes running special events to promote the benefits of coaching during International Coaching Week; an initiative started by ICF in 1999.	www.fredericknewspost.com/news/economy_and_business/growing-profession-helps-coach-people-toward-their-goals/article_2c8c533f-8f74-5cbd-9f57–4ecb4b9c2b15.html https://coachfederation.org/events/international-coaching-week

operate is continually changing, this surfaces a question as to how collective agency is deployed to 'disrupt, maintain, or create institutions' (Muzio, Brock and Suddaby 2013: 700)? But how do professions as institutions gain their legitimacy? Institutional theory is a theoretical lens that has been applied to examine the nature of institutional agency more broadly (DiMaggio and Powell 1983; Greenwood and Hinings 1996; Scott 2008) and more specifically to the emergence, status and agency of the professions (Scott 2008), including professions, such as management consultancy (Muzio, Kirkpatrick and Kipping 2011) and management education (Masrani, Williams and McKiernan 2011).

We believe Scott's (2008) notion of institutional theory, where organisations are crafted as agentic social and cultural systems, is of relevance to our analysis of the professionalisation of coaching. Scott refers to the 'three pillars of institutions.' For those not familiar with Scott's three pillars, we briefly outline here what these are. The first pillar is the regulatory element, where institutional legitimacy is based on regulatory rules, with agreed rules, norms, and legal sanctions. The second pillar is the normative element, where the basis of order is binding expectations and where the basis of legitimacy is governed and operated morally through certification and accreditation. The third pillar is the cultural-cognitive element, where the basis of order is through constitutive schema that is culturally recognised and supported.

Professional occupations play a unique and distinctive role in society (Evetts 2011; Scott 2008; Wilensky 1964); they have become creators/agents of institutional frameworks. Yet Scott also points out that each profession differs in the way that they deploy elements of the three pillars of institutions. Some he suggests operate within the cultural-cognitive space, where the primary weapon consists of: a combination of ideas; control mechanisms, aligned to specific ontological frameworks; creating typologies, as well as creating principles or guidelines for action (2008: 100). As with other types of institutions, professions can exercise their agency through a combination of coercive, mimetic, and cognitive-cultural mechanisms to bring about institutional change. As Scott (2008: 1) observes, aligned to the growth of the professions is a parallel rise in the number of associations (not professional institutions per se) operating at national and international level aimed at establishing and controlling standards of practice. This would certainly appear to be the case within the field of coaching with many associations emerging since the mid-1990s established by what is often referred to as pioneers of coaching (Brennan 2008) and/or internationally recognised coaching practitioners and researchers (Stern and Stout-Rostron 2013). As Scott (2008) cautions, these associations can have more freedom to pursue voluntary and co-operative approaches to standard setting. In doing so, associations ensure compliance not necessarily through 'mutually reinforcing obligations' but through the 'power of templates' and 'scripts for action' (Scott: 58). As Bachkirova and Lawton

Smith (2015: 126) suggest, early pioneers of coaching associations have 'a vested interest in keeping the established system of accreditation once created, because everyone's status and living depends on it.' Something which arguably serves the best interest of extant coaching associations, since they are less exposed to scrutiny by external regulators. This tension is apparent from our observations and analysis of the current debates within and across different coaching associations.

Furthermore, there is the issue of the inter-relationship between social actors, the professional body(ies) that they associate with, or aspire to associate with, and the contexts within which they aim to practise. In the opening article of a special edition on professions and institutional change in the *Journal of Management Studies*, Muzio, Brock, and Suddaby (2013) surface three tensions that resonate for us with the arguments presented in this paper. First it is noted that new professionalisation projects (coaching being a case in point, as is the case with Human Resource Development) enfold within organisational boundaries and succeed by 'solving core problems for their employers and colonizing enclaves and key positions in the organizational hierarchies' (Muzio, Brock, and Suddaby 2013: 710). A second set of observations relate to the establishment of professional institutions themselves

> when a new institution is in the process of being constructed, the taken-for-granted assumptions and normative values, which tend to mask both reflexivity and agency, are temporarily removed and, for a short period of time, actors engage directly and transparently in the task of institutional creation.
>
> (709)

Thus as occupations pursue their professionalisation projects they redraw the boundaries and the rules governing their and contiguous fields to protect their identity and status (Elliott 1972; Muzio, Brock and Suddaby 2013; Wilensky 1964).

As coaching has emerged as an accepted development intervention, Muzio, Brock and Suddaby's (2013) observation of professions solving core problems for organisations would appear to fit with what coaching practitioners appear to offer. Yet coaches can be in an ambiguous position, compared to more established and related occupations, such as in HR or HRD professionals, since they may not be recognised as a distinctive occupational group and thus arguably not in a position to colonise enclaves and key positions. For some individuals coaching is an approach that is deployed as part of a broader repertoire of services offered to organisations. A further tension here, as George (2013) points out, is that of the coaching industry not having its own unified body of knowledge or methods, something that generally differentiates occupations classed as professions (Elliott 1972; Wilensky 1964). Yet as George (2013) suggests this looseness would appear to enable practising coaches to differentiate themselves and/or their offering from that of related occupations, such as consulting and therapy.

The role that professional associations (a particular form of institution) play in shaping a profession is an important one, given their 'symbolic status, their exertion of agency and influence of isomorphic pressure' (Masrani, Williams and McKiernan 2011: 384). As Scott (2008) points out isomorphism is the process that occurs where external factors (for example perceived threats) result in institutional agencies focusing their attention on coercive, normative and mimetic mechanisms, which over time result in emergence of a dominant mode of operation, reproduced through the discourse of best practice (Evans 2014; Masrani, Williams and McKiernan 2011). Through re-tracing the roots, mobilising structures, and resources deployed by ICF, we believe we have drawn attention to the hegemony of this institutional body.

Summary and Conclusion

From the literature sources drawn on in this chapter and in previous chapters, together with insights gained from conversations and interviews with coaching practitioners in non-Western contexts, we suggest that there is a polarisation of views about the current status of coaching and its movement towards professionalisation. The concept of professions and professionalisation is socio-cultural artefact. In other words it is work that is socially and culturally defined. Moreover, it is assumed that the professions hold a particular status in society given their specialist knowledge (theoretical and scientific). With this status comes particular expectations around governance, trust and integrity (Dent et al. 2016; Evetts 2011; Scott 2008; Wilensky 1964).

Currently coaching would appear to be largely a very personalised and individualised service, which arguably is congruent with the notion of the service ideal of the professions (Wilensky 1964). However as coaching is now perceived as a commercial commodity, in contrast to its historical roots as a socio-cultural learner-centred developmental approach, this has implications for upholding the integrity of the service ideal. Tensions could emerge then between the service ideal (typically associated with the professions) and the commercialisation of coaching.

Currently there appears to be a division between coaches who want training and development from credible providers, but not necessarily consider that coaching should go down the route of professionalisation. This may be a reflection of the context and/or type of coaching practice, e.g., coach practitioner, as opposed to managers using coaching skills as part of their managerial practice.

In conclusion we are left with two key question that it would seem still need considering. First, to what extent it is necessary and/or feasible for there to be a truly global governance of coaching in the light of different and diverse country and regional cultures, each with their own governance structures for recognising and managing professionals? Second, what are the implications of ICF the current dominant voice in the coaching professionalisation discourse continuing to dominate this discourse as coaching evolves around the world?

References

Alvesson, M. and Willmott, H. (2002). Identity regulation as organizational control: Producing the appropriate individual. *Journal of Management Studies*, 39(5), 619–644.

APAC. (2016). *4th Asia Coaching Benchmark*. www.apacoaches.org/resources/country-regional-coaching-survey/ (accessed 25 March 2019).

Arnott, J. and Sparrow, J. (2004). *The Coaching Study 2004*. Birmingham: University of Central England.

Bachkirova, T. and Lawton Smith, C. (2015). From competencies to capabilities in the assessment and accreditation of coaches. *Internal Journal of Evidence Bases Coaching and Mentoring*, 13(2), 123–140.

Barosa-Periera, A. (2014). Building cultural competencies in coaching: Essay for the first steps. *Journal of Psychological Issues in Organizational Culture*, 5(2), 98–112.

Bennett, J.L. (2006). An agenda for coaching-related research: A challenge for researchers. *Consulting Psychology Journal: Practice and Research*, 55(4), 240–249.

Besson, D. and Hassadj, S. (1999). *D´evelopper ou recruter les Comp´etences? Les start´egies am´ericainesdegestiondescompetences*. Paris, France: L'Harmattan.

Bolton, A., Brown, R.B. and McCartney, S. (1999). The capacity spiral: Four weddings and a funeral. *Journal of Vocational Education and Training*, 51(4), 585–605.

Bono, J.E., Purvanova, R.K., Towler, A.J. and Peterson, D.B. (2009). A survey of executive coaching practitioners. *Personnel Psychology*, 62, 261–404.

Boyatzis, R.E. (2008). Competencies in the 21st century. *Journal of Management Development*, 27(1), 5–12.

BPS. (2002). *Special Group in Coaching Psychology*. https://www1.bps.org.uk/networks-and-communities/member-microsite/special-group-coaching-psychology (accessed 23 March 2018).

BPS. (2017). *Practice Guidelines* (Third edition). August 2017. British Psychological Society.

Brennan, D. (2008). Coaching in the US: Trends and challenges. *Coaching: An International Journal of Theory, Research and Practice*, 1(2), 186–191.

Brennan, D. and Williams, P. (2005). *Coaching Professionalism, the ICF, and You*. www.cce-global.org/Assets/BCC/Resources/TheCoachingProfessionGrowsUp.pdf (accessed 4 March 2017).

Caldwell, R. (2005). Things fall apart? Discourses on agency and change in organizations. *Human Relations*, 58(1), 83–114.

Campbell, J.P., Dunnette, M.D., Lawler, E.E. III and Weick, K.E. Jr. (1970). *Managerial Behavior, Performance, and Effectiveness*. New York: McGraw-Hill.

CIPD. (2004). *Coaching and Buying Coaching Services—A CIPD Guide*. London: CIPD.

Ciporen, R. (2015). The emerging field of executive and organizational coaching: An overview. *New Directions for Adult and Continuing Education*, 148, Winter.

Collins, S. and Arthur, N. (2010). Culture-infused counselling: A fresh look at a classic framework of multicultural counselling competencies. *Counselling Psychology Quarterly*, 23(2), 203–216.

Daskalaki, M. (2012). Personal narratives and cosmopolitan identities: An autobiographical approach. *Journal of Management Inquiry*, 21(4), 430–441.

Dent, M., Bourgeault, I.L., Denis, J.L. and Kuhlmann, E. (2016). *The Routledge Companion to the Professions and Professionalism*. Oxon: Routledge.

Denzin, N.K. and Lincoln, Y.S. (Eds.). (1998). *The Landscape of Qualitative Research: Theories and Issues*. London: Sage Publications.

DiMaggio, P.J. and Powell, W.W. (1983). The iron cage revisited: Institutional isomorphism and collective rationality in organizational fields. *American Sociological Review*, 48, 147–160.

Drake, D.B. (2011). What do coaches need to know? Using the mastery window to assess and develop expertise. *Coaching: An International Journal of Theory, Research and Practice*, 4(2), 138–155.

Eagly, A.H. and Carli, L.L. (2007). *Through the Labyrinth: The Truth About How Women Become Leaders*. Boston, MA: Harvard Business School Publishing.

Egan, T. and Hamlin, R.G. (2014). Coaching, HRD, and relational richness: Putting the pieces together. *Advances in Developing Human Resources*, 16(2), 242–247.

Elliott, P. (1972). *The Sociology of the Professions*. London: Palgrave Macmillan.

EMCC. (2015). *Coach Accreditation/Credentialing Requirements: Comparison Chart*. https://emcc1.app.box.com/s/ryvg44bshj9vcig0ee69gxp7cejngs3b (accessed 4 April 2019).

Evans, C. and Lines, D. (2014). 'Which hat do I say I'm wearing?' Identity work of independent coaching practitioners. *European Journal of Training and Development*, 38(8), 764–779.

Evetts, J. (2011). A new professionalism? Challenges and opportunities. *Current Sociology*, 59(4), 406–422.

Evetts, J. (2012). Professionalism: Value and ideology. *Sociopedia.isa*, 1–20.

Finch-Lees, T., Mabey, C. and Leifooghe, A. (2005). 'In the name of capability': A critical discursive evaluation of competency-based management development. *Human Relations*, 58(9), 1185–1222.

Freidson E. (2001). *Professionalism: The Third Logic*. Cambridge: Polity.

George, M. (2013). Seeking legitimacy: The professionalization of life coaching. *Sociological Inquiry*, 83(2), 179–208.

Gilmartin, M. (2009). Colonialism/imperialism. In, *Key Concepts in Political Geography*. London: Sage Publications, pp. 115–123.

Global Coaching Mentoring Alliance (GMCA). 21 November 2012. *GMCA Press Releases*. https://www.emccouncil.org/about_emcc/gcma/ (accessed 26 February 2020).

Grant, A.M. (2006). A personal perspective on professional coaching and the development of coaching psychology. *International Coaching Psychology Review*, 1(1), 12–22.

Gray, D.E. (2006). Executive coaching: Towards a dynamic alliance of psychotherapy and transformative learning processes. *Management Learning*, 37(4), 475–497.

Gray, D.E. (2011). Journeys towards the professionalisation of coaching: Dilemmas, dialogues and decisions along the global pathway. *Coaching: An International Journal of Theory, Research and Practice*, 4(1), 4–19.

Gray, D.E., Garvey, B. and Lane, D.A. (2016). *A Critical Introduction to Coaching and Mentoring*. London: Sage Publications.

Gray, D.E., Saunders, M.N.K., Curnow, B. and Farrant, C. (2015). *Coaching and Emerging Profession—Or Just a Spanner in the HRD Toolbox?* UFHD 2015 Conference Proceedings.

Greenwood, R. and Hinings, C.R. (1996). Understanding radical organizational change: Bringing together the old and the new institutionalism. *Academy of Management Review*, 21(4), 1022–1054.

Griffiths, K.E. and Campbell, M.A. (2008). Regulating the regulators: Paving the way for international, evidence-based coaching standards. *International Journal of Evidence Based Coaching and Mentoring*, 6(1), 19–31.

Hamlin, R.G., Ellinger, A.D. and Beattie, R.S. (2008). The emergent 'coaching industry': A wake-up call for HRD professionals. *Human Resource Development International*, 11(3), 287–305.

HCPC. (2018). *Professions and Protected Titles*. www.hcpc-uk.org/about-us/who-we-regulate/the-professions/ (accessed 4 March 2018).

Heinsman, J., de Hoogh, A.H.B., Koopman, P.L. and van Muijen, J.J. (2007). Competencies Through the eyes of psychologists: A closer look at assessing competencies. *International Journal of Selection and Assessment*, 14(5), 412–427.

Heron, J. (1996). Quality as primacy of the practical. *Qualitative Inquiry*, 2(1), 41–56.

HESA. (2019). *Percentage Changes in First Year HR Student Enrolments by Subject and Level of Study*. www.hesa.ac.uk/files/sfr-files/sfr242_chart5b.png (accessed 1 April 2019).

Howard, A. and Bray, D. (1988). *Managerial Lives in Transition: Advancing Age and Changing Times*. New York: Guilford Press.

ICCE. (2012). *International Sport Coaching Framework*. www.icce.ws/_assets/files/news/ISCF_1_aug_2012.pdf (accessed 9 March 2019).

ICF. (2016). *2016 ICF Global Coaching Study: Executive Summary*. www.coachfederation.org/files/FileDownloads/2016ICFGlobalCoachingStudy_ExecutiveSummary.pdf (accessed 18 November 2016).

i-Coach. (2018). *Coaching Programmes*. www.i-coachacademy.com/coaching-programmes/masters-in-professional-coaching/#1542209509991-b1909a85-601e) (accessed 9 March 2019).

ISO. (no date). *The Facts About Certification*. www.iso.org/certification.html (accessed 4 April 2018).

Jenkins, J.C. (1983). Resource mobilization theory and the study of social movements. *Annual Review of Sociology*, 9, 527–553.

Kurz, R. and Bartram, D. (2002). Competency and individual performance: Modelling the world of work. In, Robertson, I.T., Callinan, M. and Bartram, D. (Eds.) *Organizational Effectiveness: The Role of Psychology*. Chichester, UK: John Wiley & Sons, 227–255.

Lodwick, D. and Haslett, T. (2012). *The Paradigm Thinking Behind the Actions of the International Coach Federation and Some Implications for the Future of Coaching.* ANZAM 2012 Conference. www.anzam.org/wp-content/uploads/pdf-manager/363_ANZAM-2012-350.PDF (accessed 28 January 2017).

Luthans, F., Hodgetts, R.M. and Rosenkrantz, S.A. (1988). *Real Managers.* Cambridge, MA: Ballinger Press.

Macmurray, J. (1957). *The Self as Agent.* London: Faber & Faber.

Maltbia, T.E., Marsick, V.J. and Ghosh, R. (2014). Executive and organizational coaching: A review of insights from literature to inform HRD practice. *Advances in Developing Human Resources,* 16(2), 161–183.

Masrani, S., Williams, A.P.O. and McKiernan, P. (2011). Management education in the UK: The roles of the British academy of management and the association of business schools. *British Journal of Management,* 22(3), 382–400.

McCarthy, J.D. and Wolfson, M. (1996). Resource mobilization by local social movement organizations: Agency, strategy, and organization in the movement against drinking and driving. *American Sociological Review,* 61, 1070–1088.

McClelland, D.C. and Boyatzis, R.E. (1980). Opportunities for counselors from the competency assessment movement. *The Personnel and Guidance Journal,* 368–372, January.

McClelland, D.C. (1973). Testing for competence rather than intelligence. *American Psychologist, l.,* 28(1), 1–40.

Mischler, E.G. (1999). Storylines. In, *Craftartists' Narratives of Identity.* Cambridge, MA: Harvard University Press.

Mook, M.N. (2007). Does coaching need regulation or recognition? In, Gray, D.E. (2010). Journeys towards the professionalisation of coaching: Dilemmas, dialogues and decisions along the global pathway. *Coaching: An International Journal of Theory, Research and Practice,* 4(1), 4–19.

Muzio, D., Brock, D.M. and Suddaby, R. (2013). Professions and institutional change: Towards an institutional sociology of the professions. *Journal of Management Studies,* 50(5), 699–721.

Muzio, D., Kirkpatrick, I. and Kipping, M. (2011). Professional, organizations and the state: Applying the sociology of the professions to the case of management consultancy. *Current Sociology,* 59(6), 805–824.

Nangalia, L. and Nangalia, A. (2010). The coach in Asian social hierarchy on the coaching relationship. *International Journal of Evidence Based Coaching and Mentoring,* 8(1), 51–66.

Palmer, S. and Whybrow, A. (2005). The proposal to establish a special group in coaching psychology. *The Coaching Psychologist,* 1, July.

Passmore, J. and Fillery-Travis, A. (2011). A critical review of executive coaching research: A decade of progress and what's to come. *Coaching: An International Journal of Theory, Research and Practice,* 4, 70–88.

Plaister-Ten, J. (2013). Raising culturally-derived awareness and building culturally-appropriate responsibility: The development of the cross-cultural kaleidoscope. *International Journal of Evidence Based Coaching and Mentoring,* 11(2), 53–69.

QAA. (2015). *Subject Benchmark Statements: Master's Degrees in Business and Management.* www.qaa.ac.uk/docs/qaa/subject-benchmark-statements/sbs-business-and-management-15.pdf?sfvrsn=1997f681_16 (accessed 5 April 2019).

Robeyns, I. (2005). The capability approach: A theoretical survey. *Journal of Human Development*, 6(1), 93–114.

Scholarios, D. and Lockyer, C. (1999). Recruiting and selecting professionals: Context, qualities and methods. *International Journal of Selection and Assessment*, 7(3), 142–156.

Scott, W.R. (2008). *Institutions and Organizations*. Thousand Oaks, CA: Sage Publications.

Segers, J., Vloeberghs, D., Henerickx, E. and Inceoglu, I. (2011). Structuring and understanding the coaching industry: The coaching cube. *Academy of Management Learning & Education*, 10(2), 203–221.

Sen, A. (1993). Capability and well-being. In, Nussbaum, M. and Sen, A. (Eds.) *The Quality of Life*. Oxford: Clarendon Press.

SHERPA Coaching. (2018). *The 2018 Executive Coaching Survey*. www.sherpacoaching.com/pdf_files/2018_Executive_Coaching_Survey_Executive_Summary.pdf (accessed 2 April 2019).

Stern, L. and Stout-Rostron, S. (2013). What progress has been made in coaching research in relation to 16 ICRF focus areas from 2008 to 2012? *Coaching: An International Journal of Theory, Research and Practice*, 6(1), 72–96.

Swan, E. (2017). Postfeminist stylistics, work femininities and coaching: A multimodal study of a website. *Gender, Work and Organizations*, 24(3), 274–296.

Wilensky, H.L. (1964). The professionalization of everyone? *The American Journal of Sociology*, 70(2), 137–158.

Williams, P.W. (no date). The coaching profession grows up. *Choice*, 4(3). www.cce-global.org/Assets/BCC/Resources/TheCoachingProfessionGrowsUp.pdf (accessed 21 January 2017).

Woodruffe, C. (1993). What is meant by a competency? *Leadership & Organization Development Journal*, 34(1), 29–36.

5 Narratives of Coaching in Different Contexts

Introduction

In this chapter we will be presenting a number of vignettes drawn from narrative accounts of coaching interventions by practitioners working in different geographic and cultural contexts. Our accounts are drawn from two specific regions—the Middle East (with a particular focus on Dubai and Saudi Arabia) and Asia-Pacific (with a particular focus on Singapore, Hong Kong, and Thailand). We have focused on these regions as they have been described in the existing literature as having a distinctive economic, geo-political, and cultural heritage which presents particular challenges and opportunities for Human Resource Management and Human Resource Development (HRM/HRD) (see Budhwar, Varma and Patel 2016; Afiouni, Karam and El-Haj 2013). We discussed the relationship between coaching and HRD/HRM in Chapter 3, and will continue to build on this discussion. One of the foci of this chapter is a discussion about the implications of transplanting specific philosophies and metaphors of coaching into different national and cultural contexts without any deconstruction, or critical thought, about the nature of the culture in which they are being used.

We used the questions that follow as a template for developing and our vignettes, and the basis of the survey questions we asked our and participants'. The data obtained from the Middle East we from the literature and knowledgeable nationals based in the region. With regard to Asia-Pacific, we carried out a survey and then with both sets of data we analysed for themes and phenomena that formed the basis of our discussions.

- In their own words: What does coaching mean to them? How does this differ to the concept of mentoring? Within the cultures that coaches operate in, is there an easy translation of the term?
- When in a coaching dialogue: What is shaping, influencing the process of coaching in the moment? What influences their decisions during a coaching conversation? As a coach what do they think they are

doing when they are working with clients? How has their thinking and approach developed over time? What influences them outside of the coaching conversation when they are not coaching and will still influence their coaching practice?

- Do coaches adopt different philosophies when coaching male/female clients? This question may surface some useful insights for a critical commentary on the gendered nature of the dyadic coaching relationship.

- What level of national cultural understanding, or 'cultural filters' (Garvey, Stokes and Megginson 2018: 235) do coaches working with global clients need to develop? How do they develop this understanding? (I have added in this additional question from the proposal.)

- When working with clients in different regions, how do you adapt and/or work with indigenous constructs (e.g., *wasta*, Guanxi) or indigenous philosophies (e.g., qiye jituan)? (from Budhwar, Varma and Patel 2016: 316.)

- Avoiding ethnocentrism: How as a global coach do you adapt your philosophy and approach to meet the needs of different client groups from diverse cultural backgrounds?

Before we present our vignettes, we start with a discussion about some of the challenges associated with concepts, such as coaching, which may have a distinct meaning in different cultures from that where the initial concept originated and or/evolved given the differing socio-political contexts. This part of the discussion is based on information obtained from the Middle East and a sample of the current literature. We will continue this discussion in the summary at the end of this chapter. We consider there is more research work to be done to extrapolate and elaborate the points we have made and for HRM/HRD and coaching researchers to examine the assumptions that underpin global-professional practice in different and widely varied regions across the world. Coaching research, as with HRD research more generally especially in the global context, is still a developing field of scholarly activity (Ellinger and Kim 2014).

We will discuss another area of continuing interest the extent to which HRM/HRD practices are converging, or diverging, as ideas are transmitted from developed (i.e., the West) to emerging/developing economies. Other authors (Lee 2017; McLean 2017; Metcalf and Woodhams 2012) have debated some of the tensions with the notion of ethnocentricity, colonisation, and indigenisation within the field of HRD in particular. Garvey, Stokes and Megginson (2018: 280) have raised questions about the notion of a 'neofeudalistic discourse' within global firms, resulting in universalist HRM/HRD approaches that favour low cost, best-practice' approaches. They too question the role that professional associations play in reinforcing a neofeudalistic approach. In particular they question the role of ICF, as one of the major coaching associations, in influencing the notion of convergence in coaching philosophies and practices. This perspective of the status and impact of professional institutions is one that we have already discussed and critiqued in Chapter 4.

Situating Coaching Within a Broader HRM/HRD Base in Non-Western Contexts

Coaching as we have already discussed has become a key approach within HRD's broad repertoire of developmental approaches within different organisational contexts, especially in the Western world. There are, again as we have already discussed in previous chapters, different genres of coaching: Executive Coaching, Managerial Coaching; Life-Coaching; Career Coaching; and Transition Coaching.

However, as coaching as a scholarly field is still a developing, evidence to indicate either a convergence, or divergence of specific coaching genres in different geographical regions, is thus quite limited. This observation mirrors that of similar debates around convergence/divergence with the field of HRM/HRD (Brewster et al. 2016; Budhwar, Varmar and Patel 2016) with which arguably coaching is closely aligned. Budhwar, Varmar and Patel (2016) suggest that when making comparisons about HRM/HD approaches this needs to be considered through three distinct lenses: Macro (including the effects of globalisation, national business and culture, role of professional bodies), meso (including attention to sector specific challenges and opportunities, strategic alliances, specific HR challenges) and micro (including in the key actors/stakeholder involved in different practices and the way social capital works). We will discuss the wider aspects of the eco-system that may affect the work of a coach in Chapter 9.

In their paper debating the convergence-divergence binary in the Asia-Pacific region, Budhwar, Varmar and Patel (2016) surface several challenges at the meso-level. One key issue related to talent supply given the growing economic importance in this region. They suggest that the supply of talent is not keeping up with demand. Even where organisations are able to attract talent from other regions, then cultural integration can be problematic and requires a big investment in training. A second key issue is one of cronyism, defined as 'favouritism shown by a superior to his or her subordinate based on their personal relationship, rather than the latter's capability or qualification' (Budhwar, Varma and Patel 2016: 319). Cronyism is perhaps a similar tension to the concept of *wasta* (an Arabic word meaning nepotism, clout, or who you know), which brings challenges for internal recruitment and development in organisations in the Middle East; something we discuss later in this chapter. Whilst Budhwar, Varma and Patel (2016) do not refer specifically to coaching in their paper, it is clear that some of the challenges that HR faces in this region could (or would) be addressed through the use of coaching in

other contexts, where coaching is perceived as key to enhancing performance, particularly through the adoption of a goal-orientated approach
(David, Clutterbuck and Megginson 2014). The differences between goal
based coaching and process based coaching were discussed in Chapter 3.
We consider this to be an important debate as organisational sponsors
might 'measure' the effectiveness of coaching as an HRM/HRD intervention based on the attainment, or not, of goals that had been set during
the contracting meetings.

In a paper that presents a systematic literature review of the state of
HRM in the Middle East, Budhwar et al. (2018) suggests that there is
still a scarcity of insights into how HRM/HRD operates in this context.
They argue that the Middle East society is unique given a combination
of its complex socio-political situation, the unique nature of the workforce, i.e., tensions in balancing expertise provided by expatriates from
different countries with meeting the expectations from nationalisation/
localisation employment programmes (such as the Emirati programme
designed for citizens of the Emirates). These combined contextual factors
invariably seem to affect the performance standards and norms amongst
these distinct categories of employees. However, as we have stated earlier in this chapter there does need to be more social and professional
research into this as we are approaching this from a Western perspective
and may unconsciously be making assumptions about the norms of the
countries that make up what we call the Middle East. In addition cultural
factors and religious values equally inform how individuals behave and
perform in the workplace in this context (Budhwar et al. 2018; Noer,
Leupold and Vale 2007). And may be hidden from view inside a country
culture and potentially can create tensions within country nationals when
faced with models from a different persuasion.

Despite the paucity of extant literature on the current status of HRM/
HRD practice in the Middle East, as within the field of International
Human Resource Management (IHRM) more generally there is a growing interest in the extent to which emerging HRM practices in this region
and other regions are converging/diverging with each other. (Brewster
et al. 2016; Harzing and Pinnington 2015). As Harzing and Pinnington
(2015: 59) point out, there is an assumption that in the global business
world there is an 'optimal set of strategies, decisions and practices . . .
that promote greater homogenization. . . . HRM practices, especially
through MNCs, and their global as well as local effects, are likely to con-
verge towards an emerging global paradigm.' It is perhaps not surprising
that the U.S. is thus held as an exemplar, or model, of best practice. For
example in the context of coaching and as we discussed in Chapters 2 and
3, the emergence of coaching from a sports based paradigm in the U.S.
and the growth and global spread of the International Coaching Federation (ICF), there is a commonly accepted set of coaching competencies
that act as a template for any countries opening an ICF Chapter. The

reach and presence of ICF, as a global player suggests a dominance that does not appear to be replicated by other organisations concerned with coaching credentialing. We suggest that this might lead to convergence of coaching practice and possibly create areas of tension and conflict within countries that might not share the humanistic premises of coaching. We will return to this point in the summary of this chapter.

From their systematic literature review of the HRM research/trends in the Middle East, Budhwar et al. (2018) identify a number of factors that seem to suggest some evidence for convergence of HRM approaches: rise in the number of MNCs operating in this region, encouraged through Foreign Direct Investment funding; growth in global business schools, who convey specific types of knowledge and utilise Western texts and the relevance and weight attributed to the expertise of management expert/gurus from the West. They suggest too that as the United Arab Emirates (UAE) develops economically, particularly in new areas such as digital technologies, then the demand for a more strategic approach to HR is likely to emerge, and potentially the practice of coaching. Thus, one current area of interest, and one that mirrors developments in non-Western contexts, is the emphasis on building high-performance work places. Yet, as others point out (Brewster et al. 2016), cultural differences play a significant role when shaping performance management approaches in different countries. In the Middle East context in particular a combination of factors—sociocultural, religion (Islamic values), economic and localisation policies, and bureaucratic work structures (Afiouni, Karam and El-Hajj 2013)—make the implementation of performance management systems problematic. Within this context there is, thus, 'difficulty in understanding the underlying logics of performance management' (Brewster et al. 2016: 238).

We have seen from our earlier discussion, one of the primary drivers for the adoption of coaching in Western organisations in particular relates to the expectations around enhanced organisational and individual level performance (Ellinger et al. 2014: Garvey, Stokes and Megginson 2018; Whitmore 2017). Yet the concept of performance, as with the concept of coaching, we suggest, is context dependent. By this we mean that the practice needs to be understood and developed in a way that reflects the nuances of a particular sociocultural context. Given the tensions with how performance is conceptualised within the Middle Eastern context, as discussed previously, we suggest that this could have implications for how coaching is both enacted by coaches and accepted as providing value within the workplace.

As pointed out in the paper by Budhwar et al. (2018) the concept of *wasta* influences how individuals typically gain entry into organisations in the Middle East; drawing on the support of family connections (*wasta*), individuals thus bypass formal recruitment and selection processes within organisations. The route by which an individual gains entry into an organisation, i.e., not through any formal, rigorous and equi-table process may invariably affect their perception of how they then need to perform in that organisation: 'The detrimental outcomes of the practice of *wasta* include lack of competence, unprofessional behaviours, perceptions of ill-justice, resentment and risk of retaliation . . . unfair practices and impacts careers' (Budhwar et al. 2018: 18). Research by Al-Nasse and Behery (2015), involving 656 participants drawn from 29 different organisations, suggests that the interplay between national and organisation cultures in the United Arab Emirates has a negative effect on workplace behaviours, resulting in bullying and alienation. Their study investigated the impact of managerial coaching on trying to eliminate such behaviours, with varying degrees of success (need to expand on this point). One of the tensions that research like this surfaces is that of potential role conflict, i.e., line managers are appraisers of performance but are also expected to engage in managerial coaching to bring about performance enhancements amongst their team members (need to see if there is anything written about this already). Given the culturally ebbed notion of *wasta* within the Middle East, then this dynamic may have more nuanced performance implications.

Ghosh (2018) refers to some of the challenges in the knowledge base of mentors working in diversified mentoring relationships, e.g., different race, ethnicity, and cultural backgrounds. Drawing on Heron's (1992) theory of knowing: experiential, presentational, propositional, and prac-tical, Ghosh (2018) argues that in diversified mentoring relationships mentors need to be able to balance experiential knowing, i.e., knowing that is developed from, 'embodied resonance with a phenomenon' (160) with presentational knowledge, i.e., the ability to demonstrate affec-tive empathy in order to ensure an effective mentoring relationship. To develop presentational knowing skills mentors and mentees need to draw on techniques such as storytelling, visual/dramatic art, or metaphors). Yet this may not be easy, given that, as Ghosh points out, a 'diversified mentoring relationship are partnerships between two individuals who do not have equal privileges and social identities' (162). How might these same phenomena/observations apply to coaching relationships amongst coach and coachee who have different cultural backgrounds/experience?

Narratives From Singapore, Hong Kong, and Thailand

The process of ethnocentricity (McLean 2018) maintains the order and status of western models. The question that surfaces at this point is why Western models dominate. One part of the answer is that there are no non-Western models being developed. (We will return to this theme in the summary and discussion section at the end of this chapter.) And as a result, this section will discuss coaching from the perspectives of our participants in the mentioned countries, as we wanted to represent the voices, of Singapore, Hong Kong, and Thailand, rather than impose a Western centric perspective. We used a qualitative survey approach initially to the data gathering process and then used the answers of our participants to form a narrative about coaching in a specific part of Asia. This section, therefore, represents the actual words of our participants and compares them to generate a conversation, and in the summary a narrative of what might be happening in the countries listed previously. We have deliberately, and in accordance with the opening phases of grounded theory (Lines 2004: 65–96), left out the interweaving of the literature so that we do not obscure the thoughts and language of the participants. The full set of questions that we asked our participants, based on the questions in the opening section of this chapter, can be viewed in the appendices. We have therefore not reiterated them here in the main text for this chapter, rather giving space to the narratives as they were offered to us during our research for this book. First, we will report on the findings and identify the main themes. A narrative perspective of the participants' views and opinions will be discussed in the summary section at the end of the chapter.

We raised the question about coaching both from an etymological perspective in Chapter 2, and from a discussion about how the literature defines coaching in Chapter 3. In this chapter we are rendering the perspectives of our participants, drawn from Singapore, Hong Kong, and Thailand. The sample represented, individual coaches who are Singaporean nationals, Expatriates working in Singapore and Hong Kong, and Thailand, as well as coaches who are Hong Kong nationals. The expatriates are coaches who have been living and working in the region for many years, some up to 25 years. They were chosen because they have a good grasp of the culture, the dynamics of coaching in the region, and were in many cases fluent in the local languages. In addition, the majority of the participants were ICF credentialed. We also worked with a focus group of local coaches in Hong Kong who had diverse cultural backgrounds and in the main were citizens of Hong Kong. For purposes of clarity their words are identified with the letters (FG. We have therefore drawn on a sample of coaches who represent the cultural demographics of this region.

These coaching communities are, in comparison to the communities of North America, UK, and Europe, discrete and personally interconnected, and as a result we have not included biographical details in this section so that we can preserve the confidentiality and anonymity of the individuals who graciously gave their time and opinions to support our research, we have decided to label their answers as, e.g. (P1.

Coaching—Descriptions From the Field in Asia

We have sought the opinions of coaches in Asia to ascertain how they describe and perceive coaching so that we could develop an understanding the diversity of opinions and how they might see coaching differently to other parts of the world.

We did not anticipate that coaches would offer dictionary type definitions in answer to our questions rather they would use real world language to describe a key activity that is part of their portfolio of work. What coaching means to our participants reflects how coaching might be described to potential clients and when they might market themselves in networking conversations.

One of our participants described the process of asking the question, 'what is coaching? 'As a group question it generates confusion about the definitions and competition amongst the group about who has the right answer' (P1). There are individual variations in how our participants described coaching, everyone has a personal viewpoint, and this can lead to long discussions and debate without any real agreement being reached about common definitions.

> Coaching at a personal level, coaching is the art and science [theory] of helping people achieve positive changes in their thinking and behaviour—mainly through the process of asking the right questions. To unlock the client's potential and build on something that is already there.
>
> (P4)

Coaching as a blend of 'art and science' conveys the implication that there is more than just theory, there is a science of coaching, and is partly an 'art' (Cf. Chapter 4). This participant was referring to a recent neuroscience programme that he had attended. The science was drawn from neuroscience. This example illustrates how eclectic coaching is, as theories, ideas, and science are borrowed from diverse disciplines that are being claimed by coaches. (C.f. Chapter 3) The 'art' of coaching might have something to do with the style of the coach's interactions with their clients. The form and the structure of their work, which is influenced by the underlying model of coaching they use. We will discuss the 'art' of coaching in the section on the process of coaching.

According to another participant originally from Hong Kong, and now based in Shanghai, described the term coaching in the following manner.

> There is no unified Chinese translation for the word 'coach'. The most common ones are Jiao Lian or sports coach, Lao Shi or teacher, Gu Wen or consultant. These concepts are all associated with being an expert. Even, in the Chinese speaking world, we tend to associate the English word 'coach' as someone with subject matter expertise. Whereas the word facilitator does not have this inborn problem and people associate the term facilitator as not having subject matter expertise.
>
> (P9)

The associations in the previous terms colours the idea of being a coach, particularly in China, and this may be shared across Asia, with essential expertise and may begin to influence the manner or style in which a coach presents themselves to potential sponsors and the form they adopt when conducting a coaching session. We would need to conduct further research to verify if the term facilitator carries the cultural overlay, as described previously, in other countries and particularly in the 'Western world.' However, it introduces us to the possibility of a shift in the form of coaching as it enters countries and cultures that may not share a humanistic approach to learning and development. We will continue this discussion in the section on cultural influences.

The general theme of helping others and being alongside the client resonated across most of the participants' contributions, 'Coaching means helping others by being alongside them' (P7). Coaching is seen as a helping and a relational activity, engaging both the coach and the client. We will discuss the idea of 'helping' and 'being alongside' in a later section.

Other participants described coaching in the following manner. 'To me coaching means facilitating insights, learning and results' (P2). The link between coaching and facilitation is reflected across our participants' answers, '[Coaching] is facilitative rather than directive in nature.' The motivation of the coach to pursue coaching as a career is illustrated by 'Coaching means to me, finding fulfilment in helping others achieve their goals' (P4), the sense that coaching is a two-way process in which the coach finds satisfaction in their work whilst the client is achieving their goals. The participant continues with another aspect of what coaching means to them, 'unlocking a person's potential.' This implies that the person has the capacity to achieve their goals because they have 'hidden potential, locked inside them.'

The concept of 'empowerment' surfaced from our participants as support for the trust in the client's capacity to be self-determined. 'It's an empowering line of inquiry' (P3). We can see from the perspectives of our participants that coaching is an interactive relational process, with the distinct purpose of helping clients to unlock their hidden potential and achieve their goals. Whereas another participant saw the relationship as one that might last longer than the coaching sessions, [it is about] 'having a trusted companion with me in the flow of life.' Another proviso about the nature of the coaching relationship is the focus of coaching/; 'it is all about the coachee. The coach does not share [their] personal information [with the coachee]'. There is another aspect that reflects the client's involvement in the coaching process and one that might not be readily surfaced; the client 'needs to be willing to be coached' (FG). Whereas another participant's perception of coaching is more discrete: 'I view coaching as a skill set' (P3). The focus on skills seems to position coaching as another 'set of skills' that might be in addition to, and as an enhancement of, existing capabilities. This does not exclude the idea of coaching as a separate occupation but seems to align coaching with other professional skills. There is a sense that the direction of travel that resonate across the answers from our participants, towards a 'goal or outcome' and towards the more philosophical outcome of being a 'better form of themselves and to live their lives.'

Perspectives of Coaching and Mentoring

This section focuses on the differences between coaching and mentoring. We were interested in ascertaining if there seems to be any dissimilarity between the terms coaching and mentoring. We noticed that our participants positioned the mentor as the one who is the 'expert, with explicit recognition of the skills and expertise of the mentor' (P6). Other participants differentiate coaching from other forms of helping, e.g., mentoring, where the expectation is, 'more about sharing the [mentor's] experience . . . generally it is a more experienced person who shares their successes and failures with a less experienced person so they can learn. A mentor is a trusted friend and advisor' (P2). The sense of an experienced person sharing their learning with a less experienced person resonates across the answers of our participants, whereas 'coaching is for the coach to support clients towards transformation' (P5).

Another participant introduces the idea that the relationship between the mentor and the mentee is different to that of the relationship between the coach and their client. The participant's description uses a unique phrase to position the relationships. 'Mentoring involves experience sharing . . . therefore the relationship is less parallel.' However, according to (P9), 'mentors might use coaching techniques in the mentoring session.' This mingling of approaches within the same session might lead to confusion or could enhance the session. Whereas coaches, 'are empowering the relationship with mutual trust, [and] the relationship is more parallel' (P5). The use of the word 'less parallel' to describe an unequal mentoring relationship and 'parallel' to describe a possibly equal relationship in coaching, might indicate that in coaching the relationship is situated along twin tracks, the coach and the client are on parallel and yet separate paths, working together to help the client help themselves. The mentor, however, is on a different path to that of the mentee and will therefore be travelling in a different direction. There is a differentiation of the possible power dynamics between a mentor and mentee, whereas in coaching the implication is that the coach and the client are more equal in terms of power. Whether this is accurate across all coaching relationships is difficult to ascertain as we have mentioned, coaching remains a private activity, even if it is team coaching, these sessions are rarely recorded and disseminated.

However, the differentiation of mentoring from coaching is not necessarily so clear in Hong Kong, and possibly in other countries across Asia.

'Generally speaking I feel that mentoring and coaching get confused in Hong Kong and there are times that a [client] is really looking for a mentor to share and advise on "how to do it" with them.' This aspect may reflect the educational culture of Hong Kong where teachers are seen as experts in their subjects and a coach might be associated with the idea of being a 'teacher.' There does not appear to be a straightforward translation of the word coach into Mandarin or Cantonese, the two main languages in Hong Kong. As we noticed in the previous section one participant summarised the confusion in the following way. There is no word for coach in the Chinese language. In China, the most common translations for the term 'coaching' are, 'teacher' (*Lao Shi*), 'consultant' (*Gu Wen*), and 'sports coach' (*Jiao Liang*). The idea of being a teacher is that the teacher will impart knowledge and also be an expert in their subject. The underlying meaning here is also that of 'practice, and 'discipline,' where the teacher, or if we extend the use of the word, the coach, is expected to be an experienced person who has practised their profession and can present a sense of authority, expertise, and knowledge. If we compare this with the point about coaching being about, 'helping another person to find answers for their own challenges,' we then have a distinction that might not fit with the expectations in Asia. According to our participants, in Thailand, there is less familiarity with the term coach. Use of the word coach may produce a response of, 'ah, you are a teacher' or 'so you provide training' (P4). Singapore has a longer association with coaching, being the first place in Asia to create an ICF Chapter, and according to the website, 'The Inaugural Meeting for ICF Members was held on April 11, 2002' (www.icfsingapore.org/2-uncategorised/96-our-history.html).

There is, as we discussed in Chapter 3, the expectation that expertise is reinforced by the impact of coaching being a service. As a result the values of consumerism might predominate coaching and the phrase, 'I pay and therefore I deserve a solution to my problem,' (P9) According to our participants this is apparently the case in China the culture of which role models the values of consumerism. We will continue to explore this point in the section on 'cultural impact.'

Influences on the Process of Coaching

We have not attempted to describe what happens in the actual process of coaching. One of the reasons for this is encapsulated in the words of one of our participants. The 'explicit process of what exactly is happening in every moment of a coaching conversation remains unknown' (P6). This is mainly because coaching is often a private activity and is rarely recorded. The conversational details therefore remain between the coach and the client, and even if these are spoken about later the precise elements of the discussion are recalled and then re-interpreted. The shaping and influencing of the process appears to be affected by the following elements, e.g., the 'client's initial reactions during the contracting phase' (P6) and the clients; 'readiness to share what is important to them.' There are other factors during the process of contracting, including the activity, stakeholder, and sponsor contracting to ensure that the coach is clear about the objectives and purpose of the coaching assignment.

The precursors listed previously are part of the wider picture of the process of coaching for most of the participants, in this particular research;

> Coaching is a structured process of dialogue and reflection that enables a client [coachee] to expand their perceptions of a situation they are facing; widen their options for addressing that situation and expand their interpersonal relations repertoire as a result [of the coaching process].
>
> (P1)

There are several strands within the previous quote. With the idea of a 'structured process' and a sense of 'purpose,' rather than an unstructured free flow conversation, coaching would seem to have a form that can be identified as different from other types of conversation. The process at its core is 'dialogical and reflective' and 'enables the client' to 'expand perceptions,' 'widen options,' and 'expand their interpersonal repertoire.' The relationship between the coach and the coachee is inherent within the process. The idea that the coach is enabling the client, rather than disabling the client, seems obvious and yet is important to surface as a reminder of the underlying purpose and focus of coaching.

Another participant offered the following elements that coaching, 'goes beyond simple models, techniques and processes' (P6). And supports the idea that coaching is a process rather than a series of pre-ordered steps, or one where the coach slavishly follows a particular model from beginning to end, irrespective of the client's requirements. The process was also described as 'facilitating insights and possibilities to move the client into action and improve performance' (P2). This seems to provide the process of coaching with a sense of purpose and an expectation of an outcome. However, the outcome appears to be 'positive'; there is no room for what might seem to be a negative outcome. The intentions are clear that the outcome must lead to an improvement in their thinking, behaviour, and their performance. How and by whom the outcome is judged is not clear from our small-scale research because we did not ask that particular question. We surmise that there might be a tension here between the expectations of the organisational sponsor, the coaching client and the coach themselves. What might appear to have been a 'good session' from the perspective of the coach might not resonate with the client and vice versa. The organisational sponsor might be expecting changes that are observable and possibly measurable. Whereas the client might have benefited from the 'reflective moments' in the coaching session and the changes might be more internal rather than manifested externally. There is also a question of whether coaching is a 'process' based activity or is outcome based. These two aspects might influence the process of coaching and produce very different forms of coaching. This is an area for further research.

The elements of 'trust' surfaces in different ways, from our participants' accounts of their coaching the interaction between 'relationship' and 'trust' (P4), is an important influence on the coaching dialogue. In addition other aspects such as, the trust the coach has in their own skills and their own abilities to ask appropriate questions to stimulate action in their client. The trust the coach has in the 'process of coaching', and the trust the coach has in their client's ability to reflect and make the necessary changes that are required for a positive outcome to be realised and trust that the insights will materialise from within the client's own system. The implication is that the client 'knows best how to approach their life' (P4).

The idea that coaching is a personal activity is also described in the following way: 'To me coaching means helping others by being alongside them.' The meaning of coaching is described in personal and relational terms as 'being alongside the [client]' (P4). This does not answer the question of what happens during a coaching session and what influences the process. However, as (P6) identifies, part of this process is, 'providing them [the client] with that "much needed" space for [the] personal attention that supports them in their learning and development as both a professional and a private citizen.' This theme is developed by (P4), while 'at the same time, keeping the [clients] and eventually their organisation's desired outcomes in mind.' The primary influence appears to be the client's personal and professional agenda, the organisation's expectations may come along secondarily. This may inadvertently create tensions both within the coach and the client and the use of the coaching session. Our participants' indicated that 'contracting with the sponsors, and the client' is an essential aspect of coaching so that the purpose is clear.

The idea of 'gut feel' resonates throughout the answers of the participants (P4). Another participant (P7) describes it in the following way.

> My intuition guides me. I feel I am paying attention to almost everything as someone comes to the session. The way they are walking, sitting down, what they are saying [how] they are saying it, their body language, and the feeling that is arising within me. So often I will let my intuition and what is happening in my body guide my decisions on what I ask or say next [to my client].

The theme of 'personal attention' is implicit in the previous quote. An essential aspect of the coach's behaviour and demeanour is to somehow develop an atmosphere that has 'space' and the coach is paying attention to their client. And as (P4) continues there are a number of factors that might be competing for the coach's and the client's attention.

> Mine and the [clients] preparation for the session, our physical and mental condition on that day, and language capabilities, in the case of remote coaching, the quality of the internet or telephone connection. The environment, (quiet space, office environment, coffee shop . . .) and thus the presence or absence of distractions, my ability to be truly in the moment, my gut feel, my being okay with "not knowing", and trying to get results for the client. The initial goals and desired outcomes and the changes along the way.

(P1) highlights an

> integrated sense of what the client is saying, not saying, expressing verbally and through other channels, and what that is producing in me. [All of which] is moderated by the broader context of what the client is trying to do and what they are expressing in relation to that.

The myriad factors that the coach is somehow required to decipher and interpret all at the same time are influencing the process of coaching in an 'integrated' manner. And all of this can be 'sullied, by a desire to move the client from where they seem to be stuck, or to get some form of closure "before the session ends" ' (P1).

We can see that the interpretations of the influences on the process of coaching have a number of different dimensions. The personal perspective of coaching from the coaches' viewpoint and what they consider coaching to be appears to contain their personal beliefs about coaching as well as the role they are playing as a coach. Another and slightly different opinion represents coaching, 'as a skill set . . . helping another person to find answers for their own challenges.' We will discuss the process of helping in a later section. However, the fundamental aspect of the previous statement is reflected in other participants' answers as 'helping another person to find answers for their own challenges.' The primary strategy seems to be 'asking good questions'; implicit in this is the assumption that there are good and bad questions and the good ones are the ones that unlock potential. Supporting the questions is a belief that the person is capable of discovering their own answers.

Enabling and Helping the Client

We have separated out this particular section because it appears to offer us an insight into the kernel of coaching. From our participants' answers, it seems that the purpose and the focus of coaching seems to be embedded in the terms 'enabling' and 'helping' (P7). The idea of enabling the client is also represented in line with the idea of helping and neither of these terms is new. Using the words of (P1), 'helping [is described] as a sub-set of enabling,' 'helping connotes providing assistance to someone to help them overcome an obstacle to something they are trying to accomplish.' Another participant (P7) describes the term helping as, 'working and being alongside others to assist them in their desired outcome,' and '[This] may include doing the work.' This appears to be about the immediacy of the client's situation and introduces the idea of a beginning phase of the work being undertaken. This is described as 'the context [situation] may be immediate and require help and the intervention may also carry a longer term [aspect] of enabling' (P1). If we extend this idea of immediacy, the immediate situation might require help in the form of skills that can be applied to help with recovery from a situation, e.g., recovery from drowning, stress, or burnout. This sense of immediate support for the person might need to precede the process of coaching. Another participant (P6) begins to illustrate how these two terms might be used in an interchangeable manner: 'Coaching means helping [the client to] develop their potential.' There is therefore a blend of 'helping and enabling' that might circulate throughout the coaching assignment. In the section on cultural influences we uncover how the expectations of the clients and the sponsors might affect this relationship of 'helping and enabling.'

Developing our understanding of the 'enabling and helping' facets of the coaching process highlights particular skills and possible attitudes that coaches might need to learn. One respondent describes one aspect of this set of capabilities in the following way:

> At a more general level, and for how I practice, it is more about how the coach provides that 'quality of attention' that enables a 'momentary' fit between the client's, emotional-cognitive-sensing-interpersonal intelligences, that if it can be genuinely sustained can be translated into positive, 'tangible' learning and development outcomes.

There are many aspects here that require further scrutiny. The 'quality of attention' from a coach possibly linked with their attitude towards the coachee. And in addition, their skill set of, 'Listening, being curious, asking questions and through this process helping the other person to find some answers for their own challenges' (P3).

Enabling as a term has been described in terms of developing the client's future focused capabilities, 'suggests assistance that goes beyond an immediate goal-obstacle relationship. To future instances of situations that today or right now are obstacles' (P1). This includes the skills we mentioned in a previous section, as in 'coaching means bringing that quality of attention to enable learning and development' (P6). 'Creating a conducive environment and encouraging [the client] to move forward in their challenge or issue. Supporting and perhaps guiding them along the way, but not really doing the work for them.' (P7) continues with another slant on the concept of enabling,

> I feel that enabling is more empowering for both the giver and the receiver than helping. If I relate this to coaching . . . then I feel we are usually enabling others to move forward with more confidence that they have the resources within them.

However, the terms, 'helping' and 'enabling' surface the element of 'responsibility.' The implications in the previous sections are that it is the coach who provides the process that does the 'enabling' and the 'helping' of the client. And somehow the coach will 'unlock the client's potential.' (P6) identifies what they consider to be some of the responsibilities of the coach in the coaching relationship. 'my interpretation of the act of enabling and helping [focuses on the] set up [of the] power dynamics during and after the engagement.' (P6) lists a number of points for which the coach is responsible during the coaching assignment:

- Expectations
- Contracting
- Clarity and boundaries of the coach and the client
- Type of coaching partnership
- Perception of how we [the coach and the client] focus on moving forward
- Experiences and expertise along the spectrum of the coaching process
- Self-awareness and social awareness

These points appear at first to be self-explanatory and obvious and are also aspects covered in coaching competencies specified by Coaching Associations. They do form a pathway through the process of coaching that the coach and the client can use together to navigate the power dynamics of the relationship and the course of the coaching process. We could extrapolate this point to include the idea that these elements need to be an integral aspect of coach training and development. The idea of the power dynamics has been identified in a previous section by (P5). Their point was that the power dynamic in the relationship between a coach and a client was to be 'parallel' or equal. Power is shared and each person is responsible for different elements of the process, as in the points made by (P6) previously. It may be that less experienced coaches might be drawn into taking more responsibility for being helpful, and the more experienced might be more confident to expect the client to take this responsibility for themselves. (P2) describes how they felt at the beginning of their coaching career:

> I feel that when I started out as a coach I wanted to help others to solve their issues. I now realise that this puts me above the client and

that it is not about saving them or about me at all, but rather about letting them self-discover their unique purpose and unlimited potential, I am just there to help facilitate that process.

We will return to the theme of how power might influence the process of coaching in the section on cultural dimensions.

Reflections on Being a Coach

We were interested in developing our understanding of what coaches thought about and considered about their practice. They were open to identifying the influences on their decision making process during and after coaching their clients. Most of them saw the decisions they made during a coaching session as being influenced by several different factors. This ranged from direct observations of the client and of themselves. One of the participants described it in the following way.

> The client is the focus. What I hear, see and sense from the client.'(P5). The idea of, 'tuning into the client, their words, what is said, what isn't said, their body language, tone of voice, but also to myself, my feelings and intuition. At the highest level, I also need to be tuned into what is happening around us, e.g. any noise or activity that may influence or inform what is happening, [in our session].
>
> (P3)

This appears to identify the existence of a co-created relationship between, 'tuning into the client' and 'being aware of self' and the interference of outside stimuli that may trigger or inform the session. The idea of intuition or gut feel resonated across the participants' answers. No one described what they meant by intuition and it would be presumptuous of us to assume we know what they are describing. However, this seems to imply that the presence of the coach is important. We have not probed deeper into this aspect of being a coach, and consider that 'presence', is an important phenomena for further research, particularly in terms of what it might mean in different cultures. The awareness of self includes:

> What comes to [the] mind [of the coach] in the moment, moderated by [a consciousness of] the broader context of what the client is trying to do and what they are expressing in relation to [their issue].
>
> (P1)

The influence of intuition in the coaching process is another area for further research, along with how the thoughts and the imagination of the coach during and after coaching affect their interaction with the client. Another participant who, from a psychoanalytic perspective, considered the following to be important widened this point, 'one of the bigger challenges in coaching . . . interventions is to properly distinguish material arising from the client, from projections and countertransference reactions in ourselves' (P1). This surfaces the idea that 'gut feelings,' 'intuitions,' and the imagination of the coach may not be, of themselves, neutral and maybe part of deeper processes that require investigation and discussion between the coach and the client. This opens up a discussion that is outside the scope of this chapter about the levels at which coaching takes place, and the place of continuing to develop the coach's personal understanding about the often hidden processes within a coaching conversation.

The process of continuing to develop the coach's practice and skills was identified in the following quote:

> Without question the most valuable development tool in my own approach has been reflections on how the material I work on with my clients might relate to my own experience and difficulties. Accessing that has often required supervision, or at least the opportunity to share 'difficult cases' with other experienced coaches, to widen my own perspective on the situation, the client and my own agency in the case.
>
> (P1)

The coach requires the confidence to consult with 'other experienced coaches,' and similar to the work they undertake with their clients, 'to widen perspectives' and to examine their own 'agency' in the way the coaching sessions are progressing. This blend of working with others as a coach and then reflecting on their own practice is an important aspect of being a reflective practitioner who can learn from the experience of coaching and their awareness of themselves. Some of the participants mentioned that they used supervision to support their reflective practice.

The sense of knowing that one's work requires processing with others needs to be spotted by the practitioner, either at the time of the session or during personal reflection afterwards.

> Whether the outcome of the coaching session is "good" or "bad", I usually set some time aside to reflect or analyse what it was specifically that led to the outcome. Then I do my best to do more of what's working and eliminate or at least reduce what's not working.
>
> (P4)

This particular participant does not elaborate on the process he uses to reflect. However, he makes decisions to alter and change his interventions or style to prevent further occurrences of what he considers to be ineffective aspects of his practice. We discussed in an earlier section about who makes the judgements of what might be 'positive' or 'negative' outcomes. Here we have an insight into a coach who makes their own judgements.

And (P4) also asks the client for feedback. 'I will ask my client directly what we can do differently to enhance their coaching experience.' The inclusion of the client seems to indicate that this coach perceives the coach client relationship as dialogical, where they are both involved. (P3) described the influences in another form, identifying the activities of the clients, 'My clients taking action, trying new things or approaches and learning from [those experiences] feedback from clients, referrals, success stories form clients or peers. Continuing to develop, read and attending workshops.' The impact of clients' responses to the coaching process feeds back into the coach alongside continuous development in different forms.

The questions we asked did not identify the range, or type of clients with whom our participants worked. We were interested if differences in gender and differences in cultural background were taken into account during a coaching session. The differences in cultural background will be discussed in the next section as this also includes variation of national culture as well as culture of the client. (P6) identified that 'adapting coaching styles based on gender is subtle.' The changes may be less deliberate and more as illustrated by (P3), who said, 'Not deliberately, but I am sure I do at a subconscious level.' The assertions that alterations according to gender are more subtle and less conscious raise another area for more research about the gendered nature of coaching. Other participants were open about not taking gender into account. (P5) states that 'I don't differentiate by gender.' There were distinct categories of responses to this question, the ones who did not consciously take gender into account the others who considered they did subconsciously and those who after answering the question raised the following points. (P7) identified, 'not consciously. But this question has made me think that perhaps I could subconsciously be more "supportive" to female clients to encourage them to take on leadership roles.' The action of 'encouraging female clients to take on leadership roles' carries the implication that in that particular culture women might be cautious about putting themselves forward for leadership positions. One participant who is clearly male because of the way in which he answered this question raised a different point.

> Somehow I have a feeling that at times it is easier for me (as a man) to work with male clients. It might be easier for a man to relate to how another man "ticks", and I am aware that I might not understand very well how a woman may function differently from a man.
>
> (P4)

We do not know what information this participant was using to make that decision as it is not apparent from his answer. However, it is important to notice that coaches might require more preparation for the subtleties when coaching men and women. It is also important for the authors to reflect on this question and to surface the stereotypical manner of asking the question in a binary fashion, leaving out the array of people who might not identify themselves with these 'normal' labels and might require a coach who is comfortable and experienced in understanding the subtle and often overlooked aspects of gender in the process of coaching. This area of research is important as our understanding of gender broadens and the often-silent assumptions that are made are not surfaced early enough.

Cultural Differences That Might Affect Coaching in Asia

We were interested in this area of our inquiry as coaching has become a global intervention used in many different countries and diverse cultures. The participants who responded to this inquiry, as we outlined at the beginning of the narrative section, represented a wide range of cultures and coaching experience in Thailand, Hong Kong, and Singapore. The scene in Singapore, Hong Kong, and Thailand is a complex of expatriates from a wide variety of countries around the world who mainly work in multinational companies, with some permanent residents, with the right to work and live in the country until their P.R. permit expires, and country citizens. This creates a pluralistic society in which coaching takes place, demanding a high degree of sensitivity to how culture and societal norms affect the process of coaching. There is another layer added to this particularly in Singapore. One of our participants described in this manner. 'There isn't an indigenous construct of culture in Singapore since we are a nation of immigrants' (P7). The mix of ethnicity embraces many original cultures and the development of a Singaporean identity has been respectful of these differences. Coaching in Singapore is therefore a multicultural experience. (P7) continued:

> Perhaps a basic understanding of cultures is sufficient, e.g. the need for being seen as an individual in the American culture versus the need for group consensus in an Asian culture. The rest I feel will come up during the coaching conversation if it is important to the coachee.

The central premise of allowing the client to lead the coaching conversation and the coach following the clients agenda might appear to subsume the impact of knowledge of cultural differences. This is supported by (P3) who states that

> My clients come from a number of nationalities and cultures. I believe that [it is] more important than developing full cultural understanding, is [to have] the awareness that such filters do exist, on both sides, and to be openly curious about them. The client will say, and I can enquire and change if appropriate. Equally, I can and need to challenge my own filters regularly.

Another participant (P6) identified that, 'knowing cultural etiquette, is more valuable.' This raises the idea that knowing how to behave socially and relationally inside a culture might be more important than a deep understanding of the culture itself. (P1) extends this by adding that

> It has been vitally important to have people with whom I can discuss "what artefacts and behaviours" might mean in particular cultural contexts, to lessen the risk of culturally-framed and erroneous interpretations of the client's material.

The risks associated with not knowing or not having more informed people to draw upon are that the individual coach may accidently make interpretations of the client that do not fit or are accurate. (P3) offers another dimension: 'Sometimes understanding and being able to use local language expressions, anecdotes, or metaphors can be powerful.' The participants in this research were all able to speak more than three languages, in most cases; they used English as their business language and were able to converse in appropriate local languages. This surfaces another area of inquiry with the following question; what might be the impact of using English as a second language on the coach, the clients, and the coaching process? In the previous section we discussed how, e.g., Mandarin, does not have a direct translation for the word *coaching*, and as a result the coaching process might be somewhat different in China or other parts of Asia where national language does not embrace the concept, purpose, or focus of coaching. In addition, as (P2) identifies after several years of working in Hong Kong,

> The education system does impact to what level people have experience [of asking questions] and are able to self reflect and generate solutions for themselves . . . it is important that the coach meets the client where they are in that development and helps them to learn those skills [of self reflection] if they have not been cultivated before.

The structures and philosophies of National educational styles that do not foster the activity of asking questions and challenging authority figures, or thinking for oneself, may neglect the self-reflection skills that are necessary for clients to learn from the process of coaching. It seems that it is important; (P5) iterates, 'general cultural sensitivity is needed . . . keeping curious about the client . . . as many clients are multinational their culture may not be defined by a simple label.' Another aspect of cultures where power is invested within a hierarchical system is the conundrum of being coached in a certain manner to do something that is based on a Western model of society and then working within a formal system that does not support or understand the process and value of coaching. (P4) points out that senior leaders might 'struggle applying "coaching skills as a leader" [where] asking questions in order to encourage and empower people, . . . may be simply perceived as "not knowing", [which can be seen as] 'a weakness in a traditional leadership model.' This participant is talking about Thailand in particular; however, the notion of asking questions and inquiring into subjects by 'experts' can be seen as problematic as the expert is not valued or respected. If we extend this point further, we can envisage a situation where coaches might not be respected or seen as useful if they inquire or ask questions. The expert 'knows' what they are talking about and therefore to inquire seems to convey the impression that the expert 'does not know' and is therefore suspect.

Discussion of the Themes

In this section we do not intend to reiterate the previous in a shorter form. The intention of this part is to consider the themes that have been presented by our participants, using a critical analysis in order to raise further questions and areas for discussion. We will also consider those elements that appear to be missing from the narrative so far and to question some of the taken for granted aspects of coaching in Asia. We will also return to the literature at this point to illustrate some of our points.

The Development of Coaching

We can see from the previous discussion and the analysis so far that coaching is pluralistic and is in different phases of development in the countries from which we have obtained information. In Singapore coaching has been around for over 17 years and therefore has had a chance to situate itself within the business world and society in general. Hong Kong has a similar story and even though there may be 'confusion' about terms such as 'mentoring' and 'coaching,' the practice of coaching has insinuated itself into the business community, particularly the multinationals that operate in the city. How far coaching has been accepted in the wider society is an area for further inquiry, and this research has not focused on the degree that coaching has penetrated the wider local Cantonese communities. As a result of less familiarity with coaching some Asian countries' might expect 'wisdom and insights' from the coach because coaching identity is not clear yet in the Asian market or because the Asian market would be more aligned with mentoring services than with coaching services (Barosa-Periera 2014: 105). The development of a coaching identity might produce a hybrid of coaching for which, at the moment, we do not have a suitable term. This process might produce a divergence form the established Western centric version of coaching. How might coaching as an occupational group respond to the 'Asian hybrid coach'?

Thailand is a different story and is an example of the early development of coaching within a society. This country could serve as a research focus to examine the stages of development that coaching as an idea and concept, as a practice both within organisations and the local Thai communities, undertakes on it way towards an occupation or a set of skills that are utilised for people development. The U.A.E. is another example of a very different culture and societal structure that might produce a divergence in the form and process of coaching, especially as the form of mentoring for women; we do not know how mentoring works for the men within the society, and we have less information about the development of coaching. Budhwar et al. (2018) introduce the notion of 'Hybridisation' of HRM/HRD approaches in the Middle East rather than evidence of convergence. Something they attribute to the interplay of maintaining traditional Islamic values but at the same time the desire within organisations to adopt Western HR approaches that are generally perceived as more strategic. This is an example of history in the making, and by studying the emergence and divergence, and possible hybridisation of coaching in different countries, we might gather how Western ideas might morph across the world and how 'globalisation' can adapt to different cultures and societal mores.

The Cultural Aspects and Power Aspects of Coaching in an Asian Society

Coaching as we discussed in Chapters 2 and 3, lays claim to the principles of Humanistic Psychology as an underpinning to the practice of coaching. Many of the principles, e.g., that 'the individual has the resources within [themselves] for self-understanding, for altering [their] self-concept, changing [their] attitudes and self-directing [their] behaviour,' have been adopted and incorporated into the belief system of coaching as a process. However, as we discussed in Chapter 2, these ideas have a specifically Western historical context that may not have been enacted within Asia and the U.A.E. and as a result it could be construed that the approach of coaches to their work is 'affected' by these types of beliefs and may lead to the possibility of confusion, mainly because the society and country does not have a shared historical context.

This might be illustrated by the use of coaching language. We came across words and phrases that seem to fit with a humanistic perspective of human beings, e.g., 'being with the client,' 'walking beside them,' and 'being present'; these phrases mean something within the humanistic tradition but might require further translation into national languages and local dialects. We have seen how the word *coach* is not readily translated into, e.g., Mandarin, and this might lead to a divergence of practice away from the standardised expectations of established coach programmes. We do not consider that the participants were using inappropriate phrases or terms to describe their work, and as we indicated previously they tended to use their understanding of local languages to help translate the words they used. Many of them also followed the client and entered into a dialogue with the client to make sense of the language of coaching.

Grant (2017: 42), citing Willemyns, Gallois and Callen (2003), points out that the language of coaching can lead to 'power differentials, tend[ing] to lead to [the] creation of in-groups and out-groups.' The 'differential of power' that Grant (2017) is referring to has implications for coaching in countries where the culture is different and where English is often a second or third language. The translation of words between two or three languages might lead to some misunderstandings of meaning that are never clarified or surfaced. In addition the power base of the coach is increased as they have the language and the 'highly jargonised language' of the dominant West. We previously indicated, with the word 'coach,' that there are no direct translations into many of the Asian languages. If coaches use terms that are 'normal' and 'familiar' to them and do not pay attention to the way in which their clients might be making sense of them, they miss out on developing the high degree of empathy and rapport that is required for the coach to be effective. We are using this as an example of what might happen if attention is not paid to the 'normal' language in coaching. We do not assume that coaches do not know this but chose to bring it to the attention of the coaching communities around the world as part of growing awareness.

A question that arises at this point is; what happens if someone does not have the capacity to self-reflect, or even know that there is a process of self-reflection that is different to self-criticism? We discussed in the section on 'helping and enabling' that there might be a process of supporting the client to learn how to make the best use of the coaching process. The second overarching part of the process was to enable the clients to coach themselves. Heron (1989: 12, 22) describes this process as being divided into authoritative and facilitative; he validates the authoritative processes where the 'positive power of authentic' authority is exercised to help the client by 'guiding their behaviour, giving them instruction, raising their consciousness.' In coaching terms this would not be considered to be coaching and might be considered to be mentoring or even instruction. However, we argue that during the helping phase of coaching the client might not be in a position to help themselves. If the coach mainly operates from this position then they might not shift into the more facilitative coaching process of developing the clients 'autonomy' where 'the practitioner facilitates or [coaches] the client [into] deciding for themselves.' Heron (1989) continues with this perspective:

> Balancing authoritative and facilitative [coaching] interventions is all about the proper exercise of power: the practitioners power over the client, the power shred by the practitioner and client with each other, the autonomous power within the client.

The coach working in an Asian context might need to balance the authoritative and the facilitative aspects of coaching interventions as they are expected to be the 'expert' in a society that values 'expertise'; however, as we have discussed the blend of these approaches is important as the main purpose of coaching is to develop the client to become more self-governing and autonomous in making their own decisions and exercising choices. However, Brown (personal communications September 2019) points out that from a neuroscience perspective, 'the person cannot create new experiences that they have not previously encountered'; this raises another issue with the notion that the client has the internal resources with which they can resolve their own predicament. There are many beliefs and assumptions that are used in coaching that might need to be re-examined in the light of emerging new ideas, as we examine the implications of coaching practices,. The process of future proofing with the client will need to take into account that the coach might not be around for the client when a similar situation occurs, and the client will be thrown onto their own resources and manage themselves. Coaches might face a dilemma between retaining business and enabling the client to become autonomous and independent of their services. We discussed the tension between creating a viable coaching business and ethical practice in Chapter 3. We raise this here as it reinforces the purpose and focus of coaching.

Supervision—An Emerging System

One of our participants (P7), describes the influence of a supervisor on her practice: 'I sometimes wonder what my supervisor would say when I am in a coaching conversation.' This implies that there is a process of supervision supporting the practice of this particular participant. Other participants, i.e. (P1), mentioned that they found it helpful to access supervision when they wanted to discuss 'difficult cases.' We have here an emerging phenomenon that does not appear to be widespread in Asia. The place of supervision is gaining ground and the importance of 'being supervised' is being seen as an important and essential part of professional practice. Welch (Foreword of Clutterbuck, Whitaker and Lucas 2016: xiv) describes how 'the demands being made particularly on internal coaches' to 'cope with more clients, and in some cases, to share the content of coaching sessions' precipitate the need for 'high quality supervision . . . to resource . . . coaches in handling these demands professionally, whilst retaining client confidentiality.' This highlights some of the tensions and the difficulties that may affect the practice a coach in a society where power is invested in a formal hierarchy that may make demands on, particularly internal, coaches to break the rules of confidentiality. This is surfacing another area for more research that investigates the degree to which coaches are supervised and the extent to which they find this process helpful. In addition, we surmise that the potential and actual client of coaching services might be less open to discussing their situation if they are concerned with how the conversation may be presented to others, including their manager. This seems to be a key part of the contracting conversations that the coach, the client, and the organisational sponsor will require prior to the start of any coaching engagement.

Missing Voices and Asian Centric Literature

McLean (2018) makes the point that the voices in different areas of the world are not heard because of the national language and how this might interfere with the speaking and writing processes. He continues with the theme that the main voices are from the West and these dominate conferences, articles, and books. Some practitioners struggle with the practice of writing using their own language. We consider this applies equally within the West as well as other parts of the world. The process of writing is something that practitioners do above their 'day jobs' of building a coaching business and coaching clients. The practitioner who is working in a second or third language may not have the confidence to begin to write and fear that others will denigrate their efforts.

Thackray (2016, 2017) offers a process whereby coaches across Asia can submit blogs on a regular basis and these can then be used to develop ideas about practice, which are then self-published in books for distribution across the region. Thackray (personal conversation 2018) is providing a potential route to publication that can support the differences that are found in Asia. Lam (2016) describes the introduction of coaching into Hong Kong, a former British colony; she supports the idea of ethnocentricity: 'coaching has largely been driven by Western thinking and business practice.' She continues her article with an in-depth analysis of coaching in Hong Kong. It is outside the scope of this particular study to describe her work in detail; however, she provides a rich study of the emergence of coaching in Hong Kong, and her work continues to examine 'if the Western technique of coaching is being accepted by the local Chinese coaches and their clients.' Lam (2016) wrote this article whilst she was working at Hong Kong University. It could be construed that academics are in a privileged position, where writing and being published is concerned, as it is part of their 'day job.' We look forward to reading the results of Thackray's, and Lam's work as they take forward to ideas about coaching in Asia and how local coaches accept or alter the nature of coaching. Again this is history in the making and an indication that research and ideas are being questioned below the radar of the main publications.

Summary

This chapter has drawn on several vignettes from narrative accounts of coaching interventions by practitioners working in the Middle East and Asia Pacific. We have discussed the impact and consequences of situating coaching within a broader HRM/HRD base in non-Western contexts, and the ethnocentric processes that maintain the order and status of Western models. Thus, we extended out discussions as to why there do not seem to be any Middle Eastern or Asian models or theories being developed. We identified how these voices from diverse areas of the globe are missing from the main narrative of coaching. We discussed the impact of English as a second or third language on this process. In addition we examined the linguistic implications of transferring words like coaching into cultures and languages where there is no similar tradition of coaching or direct translation of the word and meaning of being a coach or the terms used in coaching. We argued that this creates confusion as to the process of coaching as it morphs into different cultural and business environments with long standing traditions and beliefs that might conflict with the spirit of coaching. We utilised the coaches' answers to our inquires to describe coaching from their perspectives and practices. Terms such as enabling and helping were critically examined top uncover the impact of these on the practice of coaching. We developed understanding of what coach's thought about and considered about their practice and examined the cultural and power differences that influence and affect caching in Asia. We challenged the jargon of Western models and how this could maintain the power base of the coach. We identified how supervision in Asia is an emerging practice with less established systems than possibly in the West.

References

Afiouni, F., Karam, C.M. and El-Hajj, H. (2013). The HR value proposition model in the Arab Middle East: Identifying the contours of an Arab Middle Eastern HR model. *The International Journal of Human Resource Management*, 24(10), 1895–1932.

Al-Nasse, A. and Behery, M. (2015). Examining the relationship between organizational coaching and workplace counterproductive behaviours in the United Arab Emirates. *International Journal of Organisational Analysis*, 23(3), 378–403.

Barosa-Periera, A. (2014). Building cultural competencies in coaching: Essay for the first steps. *Journal of Psychological Issues in Organizational Culture*, 5(2), 98–112.

Brewster, C., Houldsworth, E., Sparrow, P. and Vernon, G. (2016). *International Human Resource Management*. London: Kogan Page.

Budhwar, P., Periera, V., Mellahi, K. and Singh, S.K. (2018). The state of HRM in the Middle East: Challenges and future research agenda. *Asia Pacific Journal of Management*. https://doi.org/10.1007/s10490-018-9587-7.

Budhwar, P., Varma, A. and Patel, C. (2016). Convergence-divergence of HRM in the Asia-Pacific: Context-specific analysis and future research agenda. *Human Resource Management Review*, 26, 311–326.

Clutterbuck, D., Whitaker, C. and Lucas, M. (2016). *Coaching Supervision—A Practical Guide for Supervisors*. London: Routledge, Taylor & Francis Group.

David, S. Clutterbuck, D. and Megginson, D. (2014). Goal orientation in coaching differs according to region, experience and education. *International Journal of Evidence Based Coaching and Mentoring*, 12(2), 134–144.

Ellinger, A.D. and Kim, S. (2014). Coaching and human resource development: Examining relevant theories, coaching genres, and scales to advance research and practice. *Advances in Developing Human Resources*, 16(2), 127–138.

Garvey, B., Stokes, P. and Megginson, D. (2018). *Coaching and Mentoring: Theory and Practice*. London: Sage Publications.

Ghosh, R. (2018). Diversified mentoring relationship: Contested space for mutual learning? *Human Resource Development International*, 21(3), 159–162.

Grant, A.M. (2017). The third 'generation' of workplace coaching: Creating a culture of quality conversations. *Coaching: An International Journal of Theory, Research and Practice*, 10(1), 37–53. Routledge a Taylor & Francis Group.

Harzing, A-W. and Pinnington, A.H. (2015). *International Human Resource Management*. London: Sage Publications.

Heron, J. (1989). *Six Category Intervention Analysis* (Third Edition). Guildford: Human Potential Resource Group, Department of Educational Studies, University of Surrey.

Heron, J. (1992) Feeling and Personhood – Psychology in Another Key. Sage Publications. London

Lam, P. (2016). Chinese culture and coaching in Hong Kong. *International Journal of Evidence Based Coaching and Mentoring*, 14(1), February. Full text archive. http://ijebcm.brookes.ac.uk.

Lee, M. (2017). HRDI, colonization, and post-truth politics. *Human Resource Development International*, 20(5), 350–360.

Lines, D.P. (2004). *A Grounded Theory Study of How Individuals Work Their Way Towards the Executive Company Director Position: Balancing Visibility and Exposure Within U.K. Corporations*. Submitted for the degree of Doctor of Philosophy. Department of Education, School of Arts, University of Surrey, Guildford.

McLean, G.N. (2017). *The Case of the Misguided Researcher: A Fairy Tale of Ethnocentricity (Evil Witch) Versus Indigenization (Good Witch)*. UFHRD International Conference, Portugal, 8 June.

Metcalf, B.D. and Woodhams, C. (2012). Introduction: New directions in gender, diversity and organization theorizing—Re-imagining feminist post-colonialism, transnationalism and geographies of power. *International Journal of Management Reviews*, 14, 123–140.

Noer, D.M., Leupold, C.R. and Vale, M. (2007). An analysis of Saudi Arabian and U.S. managerial coaching behaviours. *Journal of Managerial Issues*, XiX(2), 271–287, Summer.

Thackray, Y. (Ed.). (2016). *Translating Coaching Codes of Practice—Insights form the Leading Edges of Everyday Practitioners*. London: Blogpress Publishing.

Thackray, Y. (Ed.). (2017). *Translating Coaching Codes of Practice—Leading the Way into the Personal Knowledge Bases of Everyday Practitioners*. London: Blogpress Publishing.

Whitmore, J. (2017). *Coaching for Performance*. Boston, MA: Nicholas Brealey Publishing.

Willemyns, M. Gallois, C. and Callan, V. J. (2003) The International Journal of Human Resource Management. Vol. 14. (1) 117-127. Taylor-Francis Group (Published online 24 June 2010) https://doi.org/10.1080/09585190210158547

6 Narratives of Being a Customer and Consumer of Coaching

Introduction

In Chapter 5 we provided narrative accounts from coaching practitioners working in the Asia Pacific region. These accounts provided insights into how these coach practitioners understand and define coaching within the context of the specific culture that they are practising in. These accounts also provided insights into how coaching is differentiated from other development approaches, for example mentoring. In this chapter we provide narrative accounts of how commissioners of coaching and coaches themselves understand coaching and why they engage with coaching as a development process. It is hoped that the narrative accounts in this chapter will complement those in Chapter 5, given that they offer insights from different stakeholder perspectives. In presenting these accounts we are mindful that these are limited to some extent by language differences; something that we identified as a tension in Chapter 5, given that some of the concepts that we are exploring have different meanings.

The narrative accounts presented in this chapter are from our participants who are Hong Kong nationals, or Singaporean nationals, but working in multinational organisations (see Chapter 1 for more details about our participants). To maintain the confidentiality of our participants we do not refer to them by name in the accounts that follow, nor do we make explicit reference to nationality in specific narratives.

The chapter is set out in two parts. The first part focuses on narrative accounts from the customer/purchaser perspective. The second part focuses on the coachees' experience of being coached. We treat these stakeholders as separate entities given that coachees' may not necessarily be the commissioners of coaching in an organisational setting.

Part 1 contains narrative accounts from individuals who commission coaching within an organisation. The questions we asked the commissioning participants (who we refer to as CP xx) were:

- How do you define coaching in your organisation?
- Why do you use coaching as an intervention in your organisation?
- What kind of situation/s stimulate you to make the decision to use a coaching approach?

- What other criteria influences your decision to adopt a coaching approach to developing people within your organisation?
- What other approaches might you use as well as coaching to develop individuals?
- How do you take into account the differing requirements of, e.g., executives, female leaders, and leaders from different cultures and ethnic groups?
- How do you integrate coaching into other development approaches?
- Do you integrate technology-mediated interventions, as an alternative approach to delivering coaching, if so how might you do this?

Part 2 contains narrative accounts from individuals who have nagged in a coaching relationship, together with our interpretations of these narrative accounts. The questions we asked our coachee participants (who we refer to as Cxx) were:

- Why did you choose to be coached?
- What were your assumptions of the value of coaching? Did these assumptions change over time?
- What worked for you in your coaching conversations?
- What worked less well for you in your coaching conversations?
- To what extent did your coach understand the cultural context in which you are working and/or developing?
- What, if anything, got in the way of your learning and development outside the coaching situation?

Narratives from Commissioners of Coaching

We discussed in Chapter 3 how the proliferation of coaching, as a favoured intervention in the personal and professional development of individuals within both private and public sector organisations, has evolved particularly within the U.S. and European context. Our aim in this chapter is to provide insights into commissioners of coaching in the Singapore and Hong Kong understand coaching and the rationale for introducing coaching into their organisation.

How Coaching is Conceptualised by Commissioners of Coaching

Our accounts indicate that the commissioners of coaching, and possibly the organisations that they work in, do not have a unifying definition of coaching and in some cases the boundaries between mentoring and coaching seem quite fluid. One participant commented,

> I don't think we have a standard definition of coaching which we publish; however, we do use GROW (Goal, Reality, Options and

Will) as the standard framework for coaching conversations. It is considered as an imperative for all our People Leader.

(CP1)

Yet for another participant it seems that the adoption of coaching is something that has evolved over time, as a logical development of adopting mentoring in the organisation:

> We have nurtured the coaching culture at our workplace. Mentoring program has been implementing for 3 to 4 years. The purpose of this program is a more experienced employee to have a thorough knowledge of the company, a mentor will sometimes need to teach, to motivate and to offer feedback to help mentee to reach their goals such as career growth, interpersonal skills. . . . Currently we rolled out a buddy program, the purpose of this program is to help our new employee adapt to our company culture and working environment quickly. We assigned old employees as an ambassador to help new employees feel comfortable to ask questions about the company procedures and culture. It creates a cross departmental interaction opportunities and networking.
>
> (CP2)

Whilst CP2 refers to nurturing a coaching culture, they do not elaborate on the differences between coaching and mentoring. However, we get a sense of how important coaching has become with regard to the development of organisational leaders. The reference to the use of the GROW model (Whitmore 2017) in the first account—'It [GROW] is considered an imperative for all of our People Leaders'—gives a clear sense of this association between leadership performance and coaching. This statement surfaces several questions for us about the expectations of leaders even in organisations in the Asia Pacific region. What we seem to be observing here is an example of a specific coaching model, one developed in the West, being adopted in a different cultural context. What we don't know, as our participant did not elaborate on this, is whether there had been any form of adaptation to ensure the GROW model is more readily understood in this cultural contexts. In other words in the Asia-Pacific region (where our participants are based) how do individuals come to understand and make sense of a model like GROW? To what extend might individuals feel comfortable in setting goals that could be perceived as more individualistic, which potentially could conflict with a more collective way of behaving? What we seem to have here in this particular narrative is an example of Ethnocentrism, as opposed to Polycentrism, i.e., the recognition that as people in different cultures differ, thus an argument for adapting organisational procedures and processes (Perlmutter 1996). We suggest that this could be an example of convergence of a coaching practice, even though the field of coaching is still evolving and is conceptualised in different ways, as discussed in Chapter 5.

Despite the mandate to adopt the GROW model in CP2's organisation, the individual seems to be referring to what we understand as adopting more of an affiliation with the notion of coaching as a social process (Shoukry and Cox 2018). Note the contrast in language used by this participant 'We have nurtured a coaching culture.' However, although participant CP2 refers to the term coaching, what he seems to be describing is more what might be considered traditional mentoring, given the reference to older employees acting as ambassadors, who can teach and guide more junior employees. The term *ambassador* then is perhaps more associated with mentoring. In a predominately Asian context it is more acceptable, as senior figures can have their say in how new employees are inducted and how they are brought into contact with the overarching culture of the firm. It is possible that the introduction of coaching, into a predominately hierarchical culture, might be in conflict with the influence of senior people who are still exerting significant power within the organisation. The association of 'older employees' with the introduction of coaching into an organisation that has not previously had coaching as an intervention can also be seen as an important and acceptable step in bringing the experienced older leader into future development regimes within the organisation. The use of the term *ambassador* may also be a reflection of the extent to which coaching has evolved, or understood, in different cultural contexts given as discussed in Chapter 5 there is no literal translation for the word coaching in the Chinese language.

One of our other participants, who is from the Middle East, commented that: 'In public and private sector organizations in Saudi then they use the term mentor (where we would use coach). Mentoring is a relational concept, where the role of the mentor is that of helping mentees to develop/progress into leadership roles' (CP3). This same participant raised another important consideration in the adoption of mentoring, which she referred to as the ethics of mentoring, for example how a male mentor might effectively support female leaders in understanding and developing their career in a culture where women do not have access to the same opportunities as men. She commented how in Saudi Arabia male family members act as informal mentors to female family members, offering careers advice. This observation raises a couple of couple of unanswered questions for us. First, can coaching become a significant force in organisational change where those in positions of power are so family centred? Second, to what extent might male leaders, from outside the family, demonstrate some form of bias, conscious or unconscious, with regard to how women are supported to develop their careers.

What we observe here in these accounts is difficulties in defining and understanding the terms mentoring and coaching amongst those who have responsibility for planning, organising, and encouraging the take up of these developmental approaches. Whilst we recognise that this may be as a result of language differences in different national cultures, the believes (and values) that coaches personally ascribe to coaching and mentoring are another factor that need to be considered here:

> A mentor is someone who allows you to see the higher part of your-self when sometimes it becomes hidden to your own view . . . men-toring is one of the best ways to assist others in identifying their true spikes . . . mentoring only works when both parties are getting something meaningful out of the relationship . . . the mentor is just as enriched by the ongoing relationship as the mentee.
>
> (Carayol 2017: 139, 155, 278)

This quote from Carayol (2017), who coaches leaders in multinational organisations from his UK base, suggests a particular coaching philoso-phy. So for coaching to be successful the relationship between the coach and the coachee needs to be founded on the notion of reciprocity. Phrases like 'A mentor is someone who allows you' and 'mentoring only works when both parties get something meaningful out of the relationship', stand out in stark contrast to the comment by CP2 of 'It [GROW] is considered an imperative for all of our People Leaders.' Although not mentioned explicitly we might interpret this comment as an approach to coaching that is perhaps not founded on the notion of reciprocity but instead gives a sense of the power dynamics at play where an organisa-tion is prescriptive about the coaching approach that is adopted.

Rationale for Adopting Coaching Within the Organisation

From the narrative accounts from our commissioners of coaching we get a clear sense of the performance enhancing expectations from the adop-tion of coaching. The two quotations that follow indicate a number of expected outcomes from coaching, organisational and individual:

> We, as an organisation, are working towards using coaching as an intervention to support our leaders perform, help manage transitions in their career, and unlock their potential to grow both personally and professionally.
>
> (CP1)

As participant CP1 further elaborates, the adoption of coaching is intended to 'enhance and accelerate a performance mindset.' Yet there appears to be a recognition that coaching also needs to have a personal growth focus: 'provide guidance to senior leaders for transitioning to more complex roles and assignments and tailored coaching agenda to develop impact with stakeholders' (CP1*)*.

This reference to personal development is also mentioned in the rationale for why participant CP2's organisation has introduced coaching: 'One-on-one coaching can speed up our staff learning curve such as identifying each individual development needs, planning development activities and support personal problem-solving. It is an effective way to improve specific skills, building a personal awareness and increasing engagement' (CP2).

Whilst there is a clear performance expectation in the previous accounts, possible attributed to participants assumptions about the evidence base that coaching enhances performance 'All empirical evidence suggests the benefits of coaching' (CP1), there would seem to be a sense of the importance of mutuality of benefits associates with coaching. In other words for coaching to be accepted, coaching needs to be perceived as bringing personal benefits to individual leaders, in addition to supporting organisational transformational change. The importance of acknowledging that coaching needs to support individuals develop their self (personal) awareness is a theme that we identified in the personal narratives of why individuals choose to be coached (see Section 6.3).

One other point that we feel is important to draw attention to, is the comment by CP2 about 'one-on-one coaching'. As we discuss in Chapter 7, in order to make coaching accessible to a wider group of people in the organisation there are signs that organisations, especially in the U.S. and UK, are adopting AI enabled coaching tools either to replace of complement face-to-face coaching. One of our participants (CP1) did however refer to how this is something that his organisation plan to consider in the future, they 'plan to pilot scalable coaching based on video chats and online chat app, which is then processed by artificial intelligence tools to provide patterns and specific coaching guidance.'

Specific Triggers for Utilising Coaching

The responses to our question around specific triggers for adopting coaching in participants' organisations provided similar reasons to those commented on in the rationale for adopting caching in the previous section. As participant CP2 explained there was a clear link with supporting organisational change at a given point in time: 'We adopt executive coaching in order to support our organizational change in 2019.'

However this participant then went on to describe several other triggers (or critical incidents) for adopting coaching, which were either organisational or individually focused:

> Support individual and organizational change performance. Provide adequate support to enable personal transformation and career role transition. Support the development of future leaders for the organization via enhanced ability for strategic thinking, providing vision

and direction, accelerating change, energizing people, teamwork and influencing, delivering results, valuing all people and developing people; address a specific problem area or challenge.

(CP2)

This particular narrative surfaces several questions for us around organisational priorities and resources for coaching. Who decides and reviews priorities for coaching? When and how does the budget get established? Who is accountable for ensuring the expected outcomes are achieved? Given that coaching conversations take place within a relationship of expectations around confidentiality and trust (as discussed in Chapter 5), how do organisations evaluate the outcomes of coaching? The comment by one of the participants (CP1) that

> There is no one-size-fits-all strategy [in organization]. It all depends on the need of the hour and cost budgets. As a basic guiding principle, we encourage all to take charge of their own development and leverage the relevant development opportunities that work for them.

Yet this same philosophy of encouraging ownership of one's own development would appear to differ in different organisational contexts. Participant CP2, for example, spoke of how initially they (by this we assume the commissioners, or possibly senior leaders) identified the development needs: 'When we started the coaching, we would identify the development needs and the improvement areas for each individual.' This comment surfaces a number of questions for us. Is this a normal way of approaching coaching in organisations that are new to adopting coaching as a way enhancing performance? Or might this approach be a reflection of the power dynamics that exist in specific cultures, so what Hofstede and Hofstede (2005) defines as power-distance?

This same participant (CP1) referred to a multiple of triggers for adopting coaching: 'Promotions, role change, talent development and acceleration, specific request for help.' This situation surfaces a question for us around the alignment of coaching as a process, with other Human Resource Management/Human Resource Development (HRM/HRD) policies and processes. Despite the reference by participant CP1 of the growing empirical evidence base that coaching is performance enhancing, we suggest a similar caution here to claims around the benefits of high performance, or best-practice high-commitment, models of HRM (Guest 2011). As Guest (2011) points out despite over 20 years of research we do not have a definitive answer about the relationship between HRM and performance. Given the complex nature of HRM and the different contexts within which HRM is applied, we thus need to be cautious about making claims around the performance enhancing nature of specific, or bundles of, HRM/HRD approaches. Guest (2011) suggests that with the growing sophistication in the application of models from organisational and social psychology within the field of HRM we should consider not just the presence of specific practices, but perceptions about the intentionality behind these practices. The same note of caution we suggest could be applied to the adoption of coaching within organisations. To what extent then is the intentionality around the adoption of coaching made transparent and open to discussion and debate?

Sensitivity to the Needs of Different Types of Employees

Our participants who were commissioners of coaching services pointed out how in an organisation that operates in different counties they need to be aware of the needs of individual who are from different cultures. Participant CP2 spoke of their organisation as being diverse as they operate across 22 different countries in the Asia Pacific region. He commented: 'We used to work together with different cultures. As executives, leaders from different cultures and ethnic group, we need to understand the work place and norm of each countries so as to work in a harmony manner' (CP2). This participant thus surfaces some important considerations about the knowledge base of those who both commission and deliver coaching services. Another of our participants (CP1) referred to offering chemistry session: 'With **external coaching partners**, we run a chemistry session to ensure that the coachee is comfortable with the coach to meet their coaching requirements' (CP1). Whilst this approach might seem a good practice, such practices could be fraught with tensions for individuals particularly for someone who has never worked with a coach before and thus may have a different understanding or indeed or expectation from the coaching relationship and process. This is an issue that we return to in the narrative accounts from coachees in the next section.

Having set out some of the factors that inform how those who commission coaching services define and approach coaching within their organisations, we move on now to set out and discuss how consumers of coaching (i.e., coaches) choose to be coached and what helped and hindered their learning from engaging in a coaching relationship.

Narratives of Being Coached

Rationale for Choosing to be Coached

When our participants were asked about the reason why they had chosen to be coached we identified some similar explanations:

> I feel like there are a lot of things that's inside my mind that it would be great to **have someone to help me think** about and process them.

Sometimes I feel like I am not **completely self-aware** so it is nice to have someone to point out things that I couldn't see or missed out.

(C1)

I felt that I needed a discussion partner—and there was no one that I could talk to at work. It is normal to talk about challenges in the business with your peers/colleagues, but it is not normal to talk about what are often very private/personal challenges.

(C3)

I frequently have a need to help me clarify my thinking. My own thinking can be convoluted and chaotic, even emotional. I find that a **coach can help me unpack issues**, think more effectively and **notice things that are obvious but not noticed by me**. I therefore engage in coaching quite frequently with small number of trusted coaches that I work with professionally.

(C2)

In the first two accounts it is clear that coachee participants find conversations with coaches helpful in terms of helping them unpack and clarify their thinking around particular issues. Whereas the female participants (C1 and C3) appear to work with a single coach, the male participant (C2) refers to working with a number of 'trusted coaches.' The different experiences of coaching in these examples challenges out own assumptions about the coaching dyad. Thus far we have been conceptualising coaching as a one-on-one dyadic activity and the assumption that an individual will work with one coach at a time. However participant C3's coaching experience introduces the possibility that individuals might want to work with multiple coaches at the same time.

Two of our participants refer to a further benefit of coaching being that of helping them become more self- aware. There is a link here then with the work of Luft and Ingham (1955)—Johari Window—or concept of the 'coach as the third eye.' The following quote is from an interview, conducted by one of the authors, with an Olympic sailing coach (Whatmore 1996). 'the coach is able to see what you cannot see—it's the only way to go forward. One's potential is limited if no coach.' Of course we recognise that a sailing coach operates in a context where s/he is in a better position to observe a sailor's actual performance, either personally, or through utilising different technologies. Coaches in other contexts may not have these same opportunities for actual observation of their coachee's performance/behaviour, thus would need to apply different questioning techniques to encourage coachees to be reflexive when recounting their thinking/behaviours from a specific encounter/experience. The idea of being observed in action by a coach over time is one, as far as we can ascertain, that is not mentioned in the coaching literature as part of a coaches' method. If the process of coaching is to remain private between the coach and the coachee; how can a coach, apart from the accounts provided by their clients, understand if the coachee is adopting the ideas that surface within their discussions?

Clearly our participants value the support of their coaches to help them develop their self-awareness. The sense of not feeling completely self-aware surfaces a question for us as to what other support mechanisms might be available to these individuals in their respective organisations to help with developing self-awareness. With the growing use of 360° feedback mechanisms and personal development and/or leadership development programmes within organisations, especially in the West, we are left with a question as to what coaches do differently to help their coaches develop greater self-awareness.

Assumptions About the Value of Coaching

Some of our participants were able to clearly articulate their expectations of what to expect from engaging in coaching.

> My assumption of the value of coaching is that coach helps the coachee to find his/her own insights. The assumption is still the same.
> (C1)

> I assume that a coach will listen and reflect back what they see, hear and don't see and hear. I expect that a coach will not get involved in my issue or be tempted to provide personal views and opinions. I expect the coach to be as neutral and accepting of my situation and of me as a person as is humanly possible. The more I am involved in coaching, the more picky I become regarding good coaching manners. I have become intolerant of coaches who are tempted to tell, or get involved in my issues or feel the need to advise.
> (C2)

The concept of coaching manners is a theme that we had not encountered before. One interpretation of this phenomenon is that participants are not expecting the coach to offer direct advice, thus those that do are perceived as demonstrating poor coaching manners. What we could be observing here is a contrast between expectations of mentoring and coaching, given the reference to the ambassadorial nature of mentoring discussed earlier in this chapter. Yet what neither participant elaborates on is whether their expectation of the coaching relationship was something that was discussed during the contracting stage of the relationship; clear contracting is something that is defined in the comparison of coaching competencies in Chapter 4.

However another of our participants had very different assumptions about what to expect from a coaching relationship. It appears that s/he was expecting something more directive:

> I (wrongly) expected the coach to map out a development plan in the same way that a teacher may do. In time I realised that coaching was about encouraging self-reflection—helping me to step back and look at my specific challenges from a different angle.
>
> (C3)

Again, we are left with a question regarding the way that coaching is positioned in organisations and how the contracting process works, that led to the comment, 'I (wrongly) expected the coach to map out a development plan.' Perhaps this coachees' experience is a reflection of how organisations perceive coaching, particularly when they are new to coaching as a developmental process and/or where they have very clear performance outcomes. In either scenario, the performance expectations associated with coaching may be a source of tension for individuals.

Coaching Conversations: What Worked and What Worked Least Well

There were some very emotive words and phrases used by participants in terms of what worked and what did not work form their experience of being coached.

> What works for me include having someone to tell me what I'm missing or not seeing clearly, having someone to help me process things, asking me questions that I have never thought of previously. One of the most important things is to help me think creatively, as I'm not a very creative person. Empathy is also important—although I don't consider that as the primary objective of a coaching session.
>
> (C2)

This same participant was very clear about what didn't work for her in coaching conversations: 'Interrogations don't work for me.' In this very crisp response, what might this participant be leaving unsaid? If in an actual coaching conversation, might the individual elaborate more on a particular critical incident that the coachee perceived as an interrogation? To what extent might a coach be attuned to what is missing in this crisp type of crisp response? How then might a coachee differentiate between good coaching questions aimed at gaining further insights/perspectives and those that might be construed by the coachee as interrogation.

The participant C2 appeared very clear about what a helpful coaching approach meant to her: 'Non-judgemental listening. Challenging my thoughts, beliefs and assumptions. Being accepted and not feeling judged. Effective reflection of my words and positions. Being made aware of my thoughts, assumptions and beliefs.'

Another participant (C1) was equally clear about what she perceived as a non-helpful coaching approach:

> Telling me what to do. Not listening. Making assumptions. Being part of a coach's games—trying to drop bombs, provoke, challenge— in non constructive ways or in ways that show off their ability to provoke instead of their ability to listen. Similarly, making invalid assumptions and then following those instead of helping me follow my interest or need.
>
> (C1)

In some cases, asking what appears to the coachee as asking very simple questions can help individuals engage in self-reflection which then leads to identification of future action plans:

> My coach asked very simple questions that I would never have otherwise taken the time to consider. In answering such questions, it quickly opens up branches of thought and identifies areas that I need to focus on. For example, in the very first session [coach] asked me what the main differences were between my new role and my previous role. This question helped me to articulate what I needed to focus on during the forming stage of my new role.
>
> (C2)

These accounts surface a question for us regarding the underpinning model/philosophy of coaching that underpin coachees' expectation? For example, is there an expectation of coaching as a social process? (Shoukry and Cox 2018). If so, how do coaches articulate their philosophy of coaching? Cushion and Partington (2016) suggest that many coaches are unable to articulate their personal philosophy of caching.

What is the coachee's understanding of the concept of empathy here and how might this differ to that of the coach? Perhaps we could draw on Bachkirova's (2016) work where she discusses the notion of the 'self of the coach' and how this affects the coaching relationship.

We received some very emotive responses in response to our question 'What worked less well for you in your coaching conversation?' Whilst the use of the word 'interrogations' is particularly emotive, the participant does not elaborate on what they understand by the concept of 'interrogation'. To what extent might the understanding of the notion of interrogation be aligned to the coachee's understanding and experience of authoritarianism, given her cultural background? How would a coach know how their coachee perceives/construes the concept of interrogation?

(see Heron's categories of intervention). Another consideration is where is the perceived boundary between the concept of interrogation and use of different questioning techniques aimed at helping coachees' to develop their self-awareness and reflexivity? The use of 'Powerful Questions' is one of the core competencies in ICF's (2018) core coaching competencies framework. Other Coaching Associations also include questioning techniques in their competency frameworks, e.g., 'Asks questions to challenge client's assumptions and elicit new insights' (Association of Coaching) (see Table 4.1 in Chapter 4).

Coaches Understanding of the Cultural Context—From the Coachees' Perspective

Our coaches narratives indicate that they assume coaches will be sensitive to cultural differences:

> I have had several coaches and all of them understand my cultural context enough to coach me.
>
> (C1)

> I never felt that coaches did not understand my cultural issues. I often, however, felt that they failed to put themselves in my shoes as a person. That they look at me from their perspective and would like to coach me from their truth. That's worse than a lack of cultural awareness.
>
> (C2)

As we discussed earlier in this chapter an understanding of the way that different cultures expect men and women to behave and the expectations around male/female roles in society is also something that needs to be considered too.

Perceived Constraints to Applying Learning From Coaching Conversations

In the accounts that follow participants refer to internal factors affecting their ability to apply the learning from coaching. For one participant this is about self-doubt: 'Probably my own self-doubts' (C1).

As the participant does not elaborate here on what she means, we are left wondering if this is something that was explored within the coaching dialogue, but the participant did not want and/or feel able to elaborate on when participating in our research. If this thought (about self-doubt) was not something that was explored in the coaching dialogue, is this perhaps a reflection of the cultural context within which coaching conversations occurred?

In contrast, another coachee participant referred to the need to feel personally ready to embrace change.

> Change readiness. I have found that I make changes when I'm ready—and this often takes time. I need to process things and coaching help to promote the readiness. However, no amount of coaching could force me to become ready. So, my learning depends on the time I take to accept understand myself and the courage to make the changes required to move on. Sometimes it is **insight, not courage** that is required. A specific insight that would make me "click" and then the changes would be easy.
>
> (C2)

Another participant referred to the need to be in the right frame of mind for coaching sessions, in order to get the most out of these session.

> The nature of coaching is that it is about reflection. So, if you are not **personally in the right mind-set for a session you will not get the most out of it.** There were certainly a couple of sessions that I entered unprepared and distracted by the day's events. These sessions were not the best in terms of productivity and outcomes.
>
> (C3)

This raises a question as to how coaches can help their coaches get into the 'right mind-set.' What different techniques can be applied?

Whilst individuals refer to individual factors affecting their ability to learn from and change as a result of participating in coaching, this raises a question as to how coaches (who have been commissioned by the organisation) manage the differing assumptions and expectations from these different stakeholders, particularly where coaching is assumed to bring about enhanced performance (Whitmore 2017). Managing Progress & Accountability is included in the list of competencies expected by some Coaching Associations (see Chapter 4). Yet, how do coaches' maintain their authenticity as a coach (i.e., remain true to one's own coaching philosophy and values) but at the same time manage their contractual obligations to the organisation that is paying for coaching services?

Summary and Conclusion

Commissioners of coaching refer to performance enhancing expectations from coaching, such as transitioning into more senior roles, enhance ability for strategic thinking, and help accelerate the pace of change and ensure acceptance of accountability for change. Coachees on the other hand refer to the rationale and value of coaching as helping them better understand themselves through the use of insightful feedback and to help them resolve issues in a more creative way. However coaches did not refer to needing/wanting to achieve specific performance goals/measures. This is perhaps surprising given that one of the commissioners of coaching referred to the use of the GROW model (Whitmore 2017), which is performance focused. Commissioners of coaching do clearly refer more to the performance enhancement expectations. Yet as one of our participants commented the benefits of leaders engaging in coaching can bring wider benefits that are potentially difficult to quantify:

> Through my experience I have come to value self-reflection. I now actively encourage self-reflection amongst my team. As [coach] told me, you cannot be creative without taking a time-out to think without distraction. I have also come to really value coaching. I now want to develop my own skills in the area so that I can coach my team and organisation better.
>
> (C3)

Commissioners of coaching also referred to the need to be mindful of the cost of coaching—'it all depends on the need of the hour and cost budgets' (CP1). As we saw in Chapter 4, there is a difference in the rates that different external coaches charge. Within the Asia Pacific region, coaches charge between $150 and $750; the rate changed varies depending on the seniority of the coachee (www.apacoaches.com); the rate charged is higher when working with Executives than other categories of workers. The responses from participants who commission coaching indicates that this is something they need to be mindful of, hence the reference to considering deploying different technologies to make coaching more accessible and cost effective; this includes piloting the use of Artificial Intelligence technologies. This is a development in the field of coaching that we discuss in more depth in Chapter 8.

References

APAC. (2016). *4th Asia Coaching Benchmark*. www.apacoaches.org/resources/country-regional-coaching-survey/ (accessed 25 March 2019).

Bachkirova, T. (2016). The self of the coach: Conceptualization, issues and opportunities for practitioner development. *Consulting Psychology Journal: Practice and Research*, 68(2), 143–156.

Carayol, R. (2017). *Spike: What Are You Good at?* London: LID Publishing Ltd.

Cushion, C. and Partington, M. (2016). A critical analysis of the conceptualisation of 'coaching philosophy'. *Sport, Education and Society*, 21(6), 851–867.

Guest, D.E. (2011). Human resource management and performance: Still searching for some answers. *Human Resource Management Journal*, 21(1), 3–13.

Hofstede, G.H. and Hofstede, G.J. (2005). *Culture and Organizations: Software of the Mind*. New York: McGraw Hill.

ICF. (2018). *ICF Core Competencies*. www.icf.com (accessed 25 March 2019).

Luft, J. and Ingham, H. (1955). The Johari window, a graphic model of interpersonal awareness. In *Proceedings of the Western Training Laboratory in Group Development*. Los Angeles, CA: UCLA.

Perlmutter, H.V. (1996). The tortuous evolution of the multinational corporation. *Columbia Journal of World Business*, 4(1), 9–18.

Shoukry, H. and Cox, E. (2018). Coaching as a social process. *Management Learning*, 49(4), 413–428.

Whatmore, J. (1996). *Managing Creative Groups: What Makes People Good at It*. Horsham: Roffey Park Management Institute.

Whitmore, J. (2017). *Coaching for Performance*. London: Nicholas Brealey Publishing.

7   Tensions Experienced by Coaches as They Develop and Practice Their Craft

Introduction

Our aim in this chapter is to draw together some of the tensions and challenges that coaches operating in different contexts face as they develop and practice their craft. The themes set out in this chapter are drawn from two main sources. First, conversations and papers presented during the Coaching and Mentoring stream at recent Universities Forum for Human Resource development (UFHRD) annual conferences. Some of the delegates at UFHRD conferences are engaged in delivering coaching programmes within a university environment, and are also practicing coaches. Second, additional analysis of the interview data gathered from coaches practicing in Hong Kong and Singapore as a way of comparing and contrasting experiences in these different contexts. Whilst we have alluded to a number of tensions and challenges in previous chapters, we feel that drawing these together will help provide more of a focus on how coaches develop their craft and the developmental processes that support this. We conclude this chapter with some reflective questions for individual coaches to consider when developing their practice.

Identity in Flux

A recurring theme from our informal conversations and more formal interviews with coaches relates the nature and status of coaching as perceived by themselves and clients. Whether coaching is, or en route to becoming a profession with its own distinctive identity, is a theme that has been debated in the existing literature as discussed in Chapter 4. Yet whether coaching can be considered a profession is not necessarily a concern for all practitioners. One of our participants from the Asia-Pacific region commented:

> The growth of the profession was of little consequence . . . generic coachers are becoming a "dime a dozen". The future of coaching rests in specialisation, the development of niches and the development

of specific knowledge bases that interested business leaders and are backed up with suitable deep experience.

Another participant, again from the Asia-Pacific region, noted, 'I view coaching as a skill set.' As we discussed in Chapter 5, the reference to skill set here seems to position coaching as an additional set of skills that might be seen as an enhancement of existing capabilities.

Many individuals entering the field of coaching join from aligned professions (e.g., Human Resource Development, Counselling) and/or transition from other careers (Yates et al. 2017), thus they potentially have relevant knowledge and or skills that can be transferred to their coaching practice. However given the diverse career backgrounds that coaches can come from, some authors suggest that coaches could be considered a liminal profession—betwixt and between (Saunders et al. 2018). The concept of liminality is drawn from what social anthropologists refer to as rites of passage, involving an individual moving from one identity state to another (Beech 2011). Liminality is a concept that has been adopted to make sense of a number of career transitions, particularly with the growing interest in boundaryless careers and other forms of boundary crossing that can have implications for an individual's identity (Daskalaki 2012). Indeed as we discovered in our own previous research that explored how those new to coaching describe themselves to others, supports this sense of liminality to some extent (Evans and Lines 2014).

The concept of identity is complex, fluid and dynamic; a social construction that is relational, informed, shaped, and expressed as a dialectic between self and significant others (Alvesson 2010; Beech 2011; Ibarra 1999; Parker, Hall and Kram 2008). Whilst individuals hold various identities (personal, social, professional), professional identity occupies an important role. Changing work environments, structures, and routines can result in an individual's identity becoming detached from the organisation (Weick 1996) and fragile (Alvesson 2010).

Professional identity in particular is integral to what the person strives for, is committed to, and values, his/her profession. Identity has been described as an opportunity of the self to 'become what it truly is' (Grey 1994: 482). Yet this process does not happen in isolation; social relations (i.e., the relational approach) play a significant role in helping shape our identities. The relational approach concept is rooted in the belief that by 'forming mutual and meaningful connections with others, individuals gain a greater sense of energy, purpose, and ultimately self-understanding (Walsh, Bartunek & Lacey 1998, in Parker, Hall and Kram (2008: 489). Social relations in the workplace are perceived as fundamental to identity development since they enable career growth 'identity and competence are continuously reshaped and affirmed through interactions with others' Parker, Hall and Kram (2008: 489).

Given the centrality of professional identity to professionals, they are more likely to be affected by structural changes, e.g., institutional or managerial practices, professional standards, or measures of accountability affecting performance that threatens their identity (Clarke, Knights and Jarvis 2012). Where this arises individuals engage in the notion of identity work (Alvesson 2010; Beech 2011; McInnes and Corlett 2012), defined as a processual approach involving the active construction of a self-identity that is 'constituted, negotiated and reproduced in various social settings' (Sveningsson and Larsson 2006: 207). Although it is argued that identity work does form part of individuals' day-to-day routine, particularly amongst professionals, it is more likely to be triggered by specific events 'where individuals experience a rupture in our sense of self, or at least a minimal amount of self-doubt' (Alvesson and Willmott 2002: 626).

A paper by Moore and Koning (2016), based on a narrative and autoethnographic account of sense making of participants on a university coaching programme and the relationship with identity work, highlights three intersecting aspects that influences the identity work performed by novice coaches. Their paper starts of by referring to the notion of 'dynamic complexity' of coaching consisting of three intersecting aspects. First, the complex personal and biographical reasons for joining a coaching programme. Second, how these personal conditions affect the learning context. Third, tension of trying to establish a professional identity in an emerging coaching industry, expressed as 'Trying to determine what it means to be/become a practitioner in an emerging industry (coaching) or reconciling conflicting identities as, for example, student, existing professional and aspiring coach, are examples of such tensions that require heightened professional identity work' (Moore and Koning 2016: 31). They draw on the work of Holt and Cornelissen (2013) who suggest that 'current sensemaking theories in organisation and management fail to consider the everydayness of certain situations in which "our usual frames no longer pertain" and the importance of "mood" and "openness" to the unknown in terms of restoring balance' (Moore and Koning 2016: 3).

Indeed, for those aspiring to work in occupations such as coaching, awareness to the ambiguity of 'life projects [being] inherently open, without specific direction or even form' (Holt and Cornelissen 2013: 3) is part and parcel of the job. (Moore and Koning 2016: 32). Drawing on the work Colville et al. 2012), Moore and Koning (2016), further suggest that the sensemaking of coaches-to-be has additional challenges as 'they find that their past can no longer serve as a reliable guide to what is going on.' The adult learning literature supports the notion that learning itself is instigated by conditions of dynamic complexity. For example, Mezirow (2000) refers to the concept of a 'disorienting dilemma,' and Jarvis (2009: 22) argues that 'disjuncture (the gap between biography and my current experience) . . . precedes all human learning.'

Ibarra and Obodaru (2016: 61) suggest that one way to measure, or get a sense of liminal experiences in careers, is to pose/gather responses to the question—'When meeting someone for the first time, I am at a loss to define myself.' 'There is no clear category to describe what I do.' or 'I feel like I am in limbo.' or 'When it comes to defining my identity, I often feel caught in between two stools'—such statements may have more resonance with individuals depending on the timing (temporal, or processual phases (Beech 2011: 287) of when such questions are asked and/or where coaching fits as part of an individual's overall identity and/or the level of investment made in becoming a coach.

But what if we conceptualised coaching not as a liminal profession per se but as a role/skill set that individuals choose (or perform) alongside other roles (manager, HRD professional, counsellor, educator), can we still classify coaching as a liminal profession? A study into the experiences of individuals training to become paratroopers (Thornborrow and Brown 2009, in Beech 2011: 288) only identified as being a paratrooper after a particular 'battle experience'—so a seminal moment where individuals felt able to say to self 'yes I feel worthy to say now, that I'm a paratrooper.' Something else for us to follow up is to what extent does the concept of 'liminality' and 'liminal career' makes sense for coaches (or others in career transition) in non-Western contexts? Question to whether liminality a perpetual state for coaches—given that coaching is a marginal/precious profession? Also consider tension of coaches may be working with people who are in a liminal space as they transition from phase to phase in career or life terms. How might coaches, then, who are mainly objective and goal driven, handle the confusion and chaos of the liminal space?.

Meeting Clients' Expectations: Coaching vs Mentoring

Several of our coach participants working in the Asia Pacific region referred to having to manage a mis-match in the expectations of coachees, as not all were clear around the differences between coaching and mentoring. Some coaches, as discussed in Chapter 5, were expecting mentoring. This feeling was summarised by one coach as: 'Generally speaking I feel that mentoring and coaching get confused in Hong Kong and there are times that a [client] is really looking for a mentor to share and advise on "how to do it" with them.'

This sense of mis-match of expectations surfaced in some of the narrative accounts in Chapter 6, both from those who commission coaching in organisations and coachees. One participant (a commissioner of coaching) commented:

> We have nurtured the coaching culture at our workplace. Mentoring program has been implementing for 3 to 4 years. The purpose of this

program is a more experienced employee to have a thorough knowledge of the company, a mentor will sometimes need to teach, to motivate and to offer feedback to help mentee to reach their goals such as career growth, interpersonal skills. . . . We assigned old employees as an ambassador to help new employees feel comfortable to ask questions about the company procedures and culture.

One of our coach participants commented:

I (wrongly) expected the coach to map out a development plan in the same way that a teacher may do. In time I realised that coaching was about encouraging self-reflection—helping me to step back and look at my specific challenges from a different angle.

It is the latter part of this comment that seems to resonate with the assumptions about the purpose of coaching amongst coaches. One coach referred to the notion of walking alongside their coachees, another spoke of coaching being about facilitating insights, learning, and results, and another as caching being facilitative rather than directive. The language expressed by these coaches implies a more balanced developmental relationship rather than the assumed power (or status) differences associated with mentoring.

As we speculated in Chapter 5, the mis-match in the assumptions and expectations with regard to coaching processes and outcomes could be a reflection of the educational culture of Hong Kong, where teachers are seen as experts in their subjects; thus coaching could be associated with the idea of being a 'teacher' amongst coachees. However, organisational context alongside cultural influences could equally explain different expectations. Several of our coaches worked in MNCs where coaching had been introduced as part of a larger leadership development process, that was being rolled out across business units in different country contexts. Here then what we may be seeing is insufficient attention being given to preparing the ground for caching as part of a wider development programme or organisational transformational change programme.

Finally, coach experience is also a consideration here, as one of our coaches commented:

I feel that when I started out as a coach I wanted to help others to solve their issues. I now realise that this puts me above the client and that it is not about saving them, or about me at all, but rather about letting them self-discover their unique purpose and unlimited potential, I am just there to help facilitate that process.

Using Assessments Tools in Coaching Practice: Choices and Dilemmas

Many coaches use psychometric tools in their practice. However deciding what, how many and at what point to use such tools can be source of tension for coaches in some contexts. Research conducted by Herd, Gettman and Stevens (2018) amongst faculty members delivering coaching on an Executive MBA at the University of Louisville surfaced a number of questions with regard to the use of tests in their coaching practice:

1. How many tools to use and what type of tools to use? Herd, Gettman and Stevens (2018) categorised the tools used in her practice tools that sign (where the coach draws inferences from the results from instruments used) and those (where the instrument provides evidence into actual behaviours).
2. Where in the timeline of the coaching relationship should specific tools be used?
3. To what extent is the relationship between assessments used in coaching and stages of adult learning? Are some coaches more aware of this than others?
4. To what extend might the use of assessments be construed as a form of interference?
5. To what extent is the use of tools a safety net for coaches, so a way of structuring coaching sessions—rather than working with what the client brings to each session to work on.
6. Might the use of psychometrics be construed as a form of control, thus changing the power dynamic—the coach perceived as the expert, rather than as someone facilitating new insights from coachees?
7. Might the use of tools lead to 'categorization of the coachee,' thus limiting any scope for exploring growth?
8. Where tools are used in the coaching process, is there a potential issue relating to the giving and receiving of feedback following the use of such tools, including the relationship (and relevance) with coachee's goals?

In a meta-analysis (comprising of a sample of 17 out of 54 studies that met the author's inclusion criteria) of the learning and performance outcomes of workplace coaching, Jones, Woods and Guillaume (2016) identified the benefits of using multi-source feedback tools in the coaching process was one that appeared to have smaller positive effects of the coaching outcomes. They concluded that 'practitioners and organizations should consider carefully the use of multi-source feedback,' as this appears to have smaller positive effects of coaching' (Jones, Woods and Guillaume 2016: 35). One plausible explanation for this finding, proposed by these authors, is that feedback (especially negative feedback) offered during a coaching session may divert the coachee's attention, so that they become more pre-occupied with the content of the feedback rather than focusing on other aspects of the coaching process. Another plausible explanation Jones, Woods and Guillaume (2016: 33) suggest relates to the choice of the instrument and what it is measuring: 'many multi-source feedback instruments often focus on leadership behaviour, which may be rather distal from the development objectives of the coachee'.

The research by Herd, Gettman and Stevens (2018) also identified that the recipients of the coaching provided on the MBA programme was not always positively received by participants. Whilst offering coaching was perceived by the university as a value—adding benefit to the MBA participants, not all participants shared this view; some didn't seem to want or value the coaching offered. This experience could be because where experiential work (such as coaching) is blended with academic work participants can become confused about the expectations of them. In addition they may find it difficult to switch into different learning modes. For example, switching between participating in an academic lecture, where they may have been in a more passive mode of learning, to participating in a coaching session where they are expected to take more control and be interactive and participative.

However, another factor to consider here is the importance of creating the right environmental conditions for fruitful coaching conversations to take place. This is something that was referred to in Chapter 5. The following comment by one of our coach participants draws attention to the multiple factors that need to be considered:

> Mine and the [clients] preparation for the session, our physical and mental condition on that day, and language capabilities, in the case of remote coaching, the quality of the internet or telephone connection. The environment, (quiet space, office environment, coffee shop . . .) and thus the presence or absence of distractions, my ability to be truly in the moment.

Another potential tension where coaching is offered as part of wider Executive development programme, such as an MBA, relates to how competition and market forces influences the content of University programmes. To compete in the global marketplace for education, Universities may feel under pressure to provide value-adding learning opportunities for students, even if these are not expected/valued by the students on such programmes (Parker, Hall and Kram 2008). Coaching delivered on Executive development programmes could be perceived as being extra-curricular by participants, thus optional, even when business schools position coaching an integral aspect of the programme. As Herd, Gettman and Stevens (2018) identified in their research coaches can struggle with the possibility of gathering more formal feedback of the coaching element of the MBA programme. However, the sense was that this approach that did not sit comfortably with all coaches, given that coaching is a very personalised service. Yet, as we discuss in the next section, feedback is a key mechanism for helping answer the question—as a coach, how do I know how well I am doing?

How As a Coach Do I Know How I Am Doing?

Our conversations with coaches working in different cultural and organisational contexts surfaced the different stakeholders who can provide feedback on the efficacy of the coaching provided and whether this is meeting expectations. These different stakeholders include: the commissioners of coaching, line managers, coaches, and of course the coach him/herself. As we saw in Chapter 5, some coaches commented on how their humanistic philosophy and approach to coaching created potential tensions with more immediate performance expectations by the organisation. So one coach commented 'providing them [the client] with that "much needed" space for [the] personal attention that supports them in their learning and development as both a professional and a private citizen,' whilst as another coach commentated 'at the same time, keeping the [clients] and eventually their organisation's desired outcomes in mind.' In both these accounts coaches appeared to listen and respond to the client's personal and professional agenda; the organisation's expectations may seemed to take secondary consideration.

Coaches referred to engaging in in the practice of self-reflection as one way of getting feedback to help answer the question 'How am I doing?', This was expressed by one coach as:

> Whether the outcome of the coaching session is "good" or "bad", I usually set some time aside to reflect or analyse what it was specifically that led to the outcome. Then I do my best to do more of what's working and eliminate or at least reduce what's not working.

Developing the skill and practice of using feedback from self and others to reflect critically on one's own professional practice is considered a key aspect of adult learning (Ciporen 2015; Cushion 2018; Iszatt-White, Kempster and Carroll 2017) and thus a key aspect of continuing professional development (CPD) in all professions, including coaching (de Haan 2007; Maltbia, Marsick and Ghosh 2014). Reflective learning is considered as an intentional process that enables deep learning, 'where social context and experiences are acknowledged, in which clients are active individuals, wholly present, engaging with others, and open to challenge, and the outcome involves transformation as well as improvement both for individuals and their organization' (Brockbank and McGill

2006: 27). As (Schőn 1983) argues, reflection on and in practice ought, over time, to become rooted in the cognitive unconscious-competent of professionals.

As discussed in Chapter 4, there is an expectation that all professionals engage in continuous CPD to build and enhance their practice. Yet the expectation that coaches will engage in reflective practice is not something that is referred to explicitly in ICFs Coach Competency Framework. Griffiths and Campbell (2008: 8) point out: 'Thus, the ICF competencies, by focusing on coach competency, fail to articulate reflection as an essential coaching process.' A similar omission can be identified in a synthesis of executive and organisational coaching competencies by Maltbia, Marsick and Ghosh (2014). The three categories that Maltbia, Marsick and Ghosh (2014) summarise in their paper ('Co-creating the relationship; Productive dialogue skill and Helping others succeed') appear to be focused more on developing effective caching relationships and outcomes for clients rather than developing oneself as a coach.

Whilst training to become a coach, we assume that feedback from trainers, peers, and self-reflection can be combined to assess and evaluate one's own performance (Egan 1988: 342). We might assume that reflective practice is something that is developed/assessed in the curriculum of coaching programmes? Only ten of the 29 formal coaching programmes delivered by UK universities refer to the development of reflective practice explicitly as part of the programme. However, as (Drake 2011: 148) points out,

> coaches need to regularly engage in reflective practice to become more aware of and pay attention to their own patterns, preferences and biases in coaching (vertical development) and in deliberate practice to increase their ability to adapt their approaches and increase their accountability.

We are thus left with the questions—where, when and how is the concept and skill of reflexivity learnt and developed amongst coaching professionals? How do they utilise feedback to enhance their practice?

Yates et al. (2017) suggest that there is a general lack of reflexivity amongst practicing coaches within the career profession. Drawing on the work of Patton and McMahon (2006), Yates et al. (2017: 90) point to the importance of coaching professionals understanding 'their own career influences so they are best placed to help their clients, although they do not elaborate on why this is important.' Cox, Bachkirova and Clutterbuck (2014) argue that that there is limited evidence on if, or how reflexivity, is embedded in coaches' daily practice, despite coaching being positioned as a 'reflective, dialogic practice.' They suggest that individual coaches are perhaps more likely to engage in reflexive practice to help mediate their own identity work.

Based on a review of the core competencies expected by three of coaching associations (ICF, EMCC, WABC), Maltbia, Marsick and Ghosh (2014: 174) point out how none of these appear to make any reference to the 'theories or related research, science, or other forms of evidence supporting these approaches in publically available documentation.' Yet drawing on different theories and concepts is one way of facilitating our own sense-making, or as Drake (2011: 141) points argues helps develop Mastery: 'a deepening, reflexive relationship with knowledge and evidence as they inform and are applied in one's practice.' However, the literature that coaches could potentially draw on in their practice is spread across a diverse range of journals, for example psychology, social sciences, education, leadership development and organisational development. Access to these journals is often dependent on the following factors: membership of a university library; membership in professional associations; subscription to specific journal often restricted via a subscription or 'Pay Wall'; all of these require sufficient financial resources to gain access.

Once initial coach training is complete and coaches are practicing in the field the opportunities for feedback (informal and formal), which could trigger reflections that result in transformative learning, are likely to differ depending on the context that coaches work in. Yet, as discussed in Chapter 4, coaches operate in different contexts, e.g., as internal coaches, as external coach providers to organisations, as well as possibly providing one-to-one coaching to individual clients. The feedback received from the commissioners and consumers of coaching might differ. Indeed the feedback may necessarily be consistent given the different expectations of these different stakeholders. In addition some of the feedback that a coach receives might be vicarious. In other words gained from conversations with others about a coachee's performance rather than from actual observations of behaviour in practice; in which case behaviours could be interpreted without the relevant contextualisation.

A study by Robson (2018) surfaced specific tensions with regard to feedback amongst internal coaches, i.e., individuals who volunteer to provide coaching to others within their organisation on top of their formal day job. This is an alternative coaching scenario to manager as coach, which has become popular within many organisations in recent years (Anderson 2013; Grant 2017). Whilst individual coaches reported that they gained personally from performing in a coaching role, they expressed a sense of feeling invisible and less valued as external coaches. Yet the notion of value we suggest could be influenced by how coaches and coaches perceive the coaching relationship. If coaching, like mentoring, is positioned as form of social exchange where 'individuals aim to maximise benefits and minimise costs' (Holtbrügge and Ambrosius 2015: 280), then for internal coaches at least, one might expect some form of organisational asymmetry (mutual gains) within this dyadic relationship (i.e., coach and coachee as with mentor and mentee). Based on research that investigated the effects of mentoring of employees of U.S. subsidiaries on expatriate assignments in the parent company in Germany, Holtbrügge and Ambrosius (2015) suggest that internal mentors benefit in several ways: enhanced reputation; moments of creative impulses; increased personal satisfaction; acquisition of new skills; plus greater appreciation of different work styles and approaches. Arguably internal coaches, like internal mentors, could derive similar benefits from performing their role. Yet contextual factors, as Holtbrügge and Ambrosius's (2015) research highlights, may influence the actual benefits. The nationality of the mentor-mentee dyads is one potential influencing factor. It their case study organisation mentors were always identified from the home country (i.e., the country that the expatriates were born and lived) rather than from within the host (i.e., the international parent) country. However, the rationale for this approach was not made clear in their research (might we speculate that this possible further evidence to support the notion of U.S. hegemony?).

The research by Robson (2018) surfaced additional questions for those entering the field of coaching to consider. First, where does coaching sit as part of an individual's self-identity and overall career schema when coaching is performed as additional to their formal role? To what extent does performing the role of internal coach support (or reinforce, or prop up) individuals' sense of subjective career success? (Briscoe and Hall 2006; Hall 1996, 2004). Whilst the distinction between objective (external—external markers, such as positions, roles) and subjective (internal—meanings people ascribe to their career) dimensions of career is not new (Hughes 1937, in Ibarra and Obodaru 2016), Ibarra and Obodaru (2016: 60) suggest that as 'external career has changed beyond recognition,' due to the changing nature of organisations and employment more broadly, this has generated more interest in the dynamics of the internal career. This observation would seem consistent with the growing interest, particularly amongst the academic community, with the notion of job crafting, i.e., the self-initiated changes that individuals make to the task, or relational, boundaries of their work in order to derive a more positive sense of meaning at work (Wrzesniewski and Dutton 2001). If performing the role of internal coach is thus consistent with an individual's subjective career and reinforces an individual's self-identity in a positive way, might this then spill over into other dimensions of an individual's work/life? If so in what way(s)? Second, do individuals at different levels in an organisation ascribe a different value to coaching depending on who is delivering the coaching? For example, might Executives value an external coach more so than a coach (however senior) who is internal to the organisation? External coaches, we suggest, could be more influenced by objective career success measures, e.g., fees, status, repeat business—to build a viable and sustainable coaching business as discussed in Chapter 3.

Coaches, as discussed earlier, often enter the field of coaching from diverse professional backgrounds and having completed very diverse coaching qualifications. These range from a short one-week introduction to coaching to an intensive one, or two-year Master's level programme delivered by universities. Thus the extent to which developing the theoretical knowledge and skills associated with deep reflection is something we suggest thus varies depending on the nature of the programme and the philosophical standpoint of those designing and delivering these diverse coaching programme.

Those coaching practitioners who see coaching as a profession, or en route to becoming a profession, advocate for the use of supervision to enhance their practice as with other reference professions (e.g., psychology, psychotherapy, and sports coaching). From their research into global coach supervision, Turner and Passmore (2018: 138) reinforce the need for qualified coaches to engage in reflection, pointing out that coach supervision 'can provide a place for supporting good decision-making, alongside other forms of reflective practice.' In addition they argue that coach supervision is particularly helpful for enabling coaches to reflect on ethical dilemmas and thus develop their ethical decision-making. Yet supervision isn't something that is explicitly mentioned in ICF's competency framework (see Chapter 4, Table 4.1), although evaluation of results (referred to gathering information on the effectiveness of own practice and contributes to a culture of evaluation of outcomes) is listed as one of the core competencies. Other Coaching Associations (e.g., Association of Coaching and World Association of Business Coaching), however, do refer explicitly to supervision in their competency frameworks.

As discussed in Chapter 5, whilst the importance of supervision in coaching is gaining ground (Clutterbuck, Whitaker and Lucas 2016; Turner and Passmore 2018), coach supervision is an emerging phenomenon that does not yet appear to be widespread in Asia. Some of our coach participants did comment on the support they gain from working with a supervisor. This included having someone with whom they can discuss difficult cases and also encouraging self-questioning such as 'I wonder what my supervisor would say [here]?' as a way of reflecting-in-practice.

Two observations come to mind here for us. First, particular tensions and difficulties with the practice of coaching in societies where power is invested in a formal hierarchy; something that may create additional tensions for internal coaches where there is pressure to break the rules of confidentiality. Second, difficulties in gaining access to high quality supervisors in an (entrepreneurial) profession that is still evolving in different countries, combined with the costs associated with accessing and integrating supervision into one's coaching business.

How Do I Know What Evidence to Draw On to Evaluate My Practice?

As the interest (and the business of coaching) has continued to grow, so too has the number of articles, books, and conference papers that address different dimensions of coaching in different contexts. In part, this increase in publications could be attributed to the renewed interest in evidence-based approaches to management more generally since the 1990s (Barends and Rousseau 2018; Briner, Denyer and Rousseau 2009). Briner, Denyer and Rousseau (2009) define evidence-based management as:

> 'making decisions through the conscientious, explicit, and judicious use of four sources of information: practitioner expertise and judgment, evidence from the local context, a critical evaluation of the best available research evidence, and the perspectives of those people who might be affected by the decision.
>
> (Briner, Denyer and Rousseau 2009: 19)

In his analysis of the shifting focus of the different generations of coaching over a 35 year period, Grant (2017: 38) argues that the current generation (which he defines as the third generation) is 'increasingly evidence-based and typically draws on peer-reviewed coaching research, including that from specialist university centres,' which he then lists several in the UK, Australia, and the U.S. based. Grant (2017) also argues that 'Organizations have increasingly recognised that workplace coaching methodologies can do more than mere "performance enhancement" . . . coaching is now seen as a vital tool in the organisational change process' (Grant 2017: 43).

In Table 7.1, we set out some of the characteristics associated with an evidence-based approach, as defined by (Briner, Denyer and Rousseau 2009: 21), with our own commentary as to how these characteristics might apply to an evidence-based coaching practice.

The participants in our own research certainly referred to drawing on their own 'expertise and judgements' when trying to make sense of the decision-making processes during and after coaching dialogues. The terms 'gut feelings,' 'intuitions,' and 'imagination' were referred to in the narrative accounts of coaches set out in Chapter 5. One coach participant elaborated further commenting that on one of the bigger challenges is that of 'being able to properly distinguish material arising from the client, from projections and countertransference reactions in ourselves.' This particular participant would appear to be referring implicitly to theoretical knowledge about transference and projection in dyadic relationships, and possibly research evidence too, to help focus and make

Table 7.1 Comparing Evidence-Based Management With Evidence-Based Coaching

Evidence-based management (Briner, Denyer and Rousseau 2009: 21)	Evidence-based approach to coaching (Authors' commentary)
Something managers and practitioners do	When coaching senior managers caches may rely on others (HRD professionals) to tease out and promote the benefits of coaching so that coaching programmes deliver the expected organisational benefits. However, as Cox, Bachkirova and Clutterbuck (2014: 140) point out 'the eclectic use of theory creates uncertainty and an unnecessary mystique, leading sometimes to the denigration of coaching as atheoretical . . . This in turn leads to difficulty in judging the value of coaching for HR.' A further consideration here is the relationship between theory and practice and the extent that coaches feel comfortable engaging with theory, or indeed persevering with the eclectic amount of theory that can potentially be drawn in coaching. Does this depend on how the theory is used in a given context? Other professions, e.g., nursing could equally be classified as an eclectic profession, yet links are made between the theories it draws on and the activities it encourages in practice. Is there as Bachkirova and Borrington (2019) suggest, the need for coaches to work with the overarching theory of philosophical pragmatism? Might line managers performing the role of coach, feel more comfortable working with a combination of more formulaic models and their own experience, rather than drawing on different theoretical perspectives to help make sense of a particular coaching situation?
Something practitioners already do to some extent	This we speculate depends upon a number of factors: a) Type of coaching practice and whether coaching is a significant part of an individuals' business b) Level of qualification and familiarity/ease of access to different types of evidence, including underpinning theories. As Akkermans and Kubasch (2017: 597) point out 'the field of coaching in general is still there is a lack of theoretical development.' By this they mean a stronger theoretical basis for developing an understanding of why specific coaching interventions are effective.

(Continued)

Table 7.1 (Continued)

Evidence-based management (Briner, Denyer and Rousseau 2009: 21)	Evidence-based approach to coaching (Authors' commentary)
	c) Networks and Associations that coaches have access to. This will potentially differ depending on where geographically coaches are based. In theory in the networked society with more information available online, this should not present a problem. But information sources are censured in some countries, thus access could be problematic.
A family of related approaches to decision making— 'making it [practice] more explicit, mindful, critical, and systematic'	Yet as Cox, Bachkirova and Clutterbuck (2014) point out that many of the current coaching approaches have been drawn from other subject disciplines e.g., adult learning theories and therapeutic approaches.
About using a wide range of different kinds of research evidence depending on the problem	This can be limited though by the rigour and transparency in the way that coaching studies have been conducted: 'We acknowledged earlier that our selection of practice moderators was somewhat governed by those factors that were described and operationalized in the studies we examined. This observation speaks to a broader limitation of many studies of coaching effectiveness, namely a lack of detail in the descriptions of coaching interventions employed. Failing to completely describe coaching techniques and approaches employed in empirical studies prevents later classification in meta-analyses such as ours. We therefore encourage greater thoroughness on the part of researchers in this area to specify precisely the nature and format of coaching employed in empirical studies' (Jones, Woods and Guillaume 2016: 33). This point is echoed by Akkermans and Kubasch (2017) who call for greater detail in relation to the methods and processes adopted in the research, so others can make informed decisions with respect to the research findings and conclusions.
A means of getting existing management research out to practitioners	Differing classifications of coaching research and publications. For example more practitioner focused journals, e.g., International Journal of Coaching in Organisations, where the editorial board is largely made up of coaching practitioners.

Evidence-based management (Briner, Denyer and Rousseau 2009: 21)	Evidence-based approach to coaching (Authors' commentary)
	Publications aligned to a specific Coaching Association, e.g., Coaching: An International Journal of Theory, Research and Practice—available as a member benefit of the Association of Coaching.
	Publications written by academics delivering and /or researching coaching programmes and published in peer review journals that fall into the ABS journal rankings, e.g., *Journal of Occupational and Organizational Psychology, Management Learning, Human Relations.*
	However, as many of these journals are subscription based, this can limit access depending on whether practitioners have access to these journals, either through affiliation with a university, or a professional institution that provides access to peer reviewed articles and databases such as EBSCO, as part of the membership package.
About questioning ideas such as 'best practice'	Has coaching sufficiently matured enough to get beyond a pre-occupation with 'best practice?'; best-practice has been a feature of HRD for some time, despite calls to adopt more context specific HRM/HRD practices.
	Sonesh et al. (2015) point out that peer-reviewed empirical work on coaching is scarce, despite the growing popularity of coaching in business. They cite the work of Dagley (2006) and Grant (2013), who argue that 'a significant proportion [of coaching research] remains uncontrolled, anecdotal and lacking theoretical foundation' (Sonesh et al. 2015: 74); by implication then perpetuating the notion of 'best practice'?.

sense of particular outcomes of coaching conversations. Another coach participant commented:

> Without question the most valuable development tool in my own approach has been reflections on how the material I work on with my clients might relate to my own experience and difficulties. Accessing that has often required supervision . . . with other experienced coaches, to widen my own perspective on the situation, the client and my own agency in the case.

However, when we asked our coach participants in the Asia Pacific region specific questions about the research evidence they draw on in their practice and whether this reflected specific challenges in the Asia Pacific region, we identified some mixed responses. One participant commented: 'Not easy. I do not think of any means to research for coaching practice. May be Corporate Board . . . but frankly, I have not thought of it [research] to enhance my coaching practice.' Another referred to research published by Coaching Associations: 'ICF publish research on coaching which is easily accessible. That said I don't use it so much. . . . I tend to rely on coaching tools and techniques I learn through CPD rather than research'. Another participant was more positive: 'Relatively easy through my membership of [particular coaching institute] and alumni status with [Business Schools] and through paid subscriptions to organisations like SAGE Publications, Elsevier etc.' However, this same participant commented that the research available to him was 'skewed towards a client base in multinational organisations. Where I to try to develop a practice focused on more local organisations I am not sure the research support would be as good.' This latter comment resonates with the point made by Kim and McLean (2015), who argue that there is often a lack of transparency of contextual and methodological information provided in HRD research more broadly, for comparisons and conclusions to be drawn and thus perceived as a useful source of evidence. Finally, the cost of accessing high quality peer-reviewed journals by coaching practitioners is potentially a restricting factor for individuals when developing a coaching practice. This is an observation that we discuss further in Chapter 9.

Chapter Summary

In this chapter we have drawn together some of the tensions and challenges that coaches operating in different contexts face as they develop and practice their craft. These include: issues relating to identity; meeting the expectations of different clients; choices over if, when, and where to use assessment tools (e.g., psychometrics) in a coaching practice; gathering and using feedback to get a sense of 'How well am I doing?'; and, finally, tensions with what evidence to draw on to help with decision-making in coaching. As with other chapters we have drawn on insights gained from the field as a start point, then analysed further with reference to other published work.

Based on the previous discussion, we offer the following reflective questions for coaches:

- Where does coaching fit as part of your self-identity and overall career schema?
- Who might support you with the identity-work that others argue is an inevitable aspect of being part of an emerging profession?

- How might you build an understanding of what evidence-based coaching is and why it matters?
- How will you set about gaining access to evidence-based coaching research? How will you learn to assess the quality of this research?
- How will you ensure that you gain access to good quality supervision to help you makes sense of the different coaching situations and decisions that you are encountering, using this as another way of reflecting critically on your practice?

References

Akkermans, J. and Kubasch, S. (2017). #Trending topics in careers: A review and future research agenda. *Career Development International*, 22(6), 586–627.

Alvesson, M. (2010). Self-doubters, strugglers, storytellers, surfers and others: Images of self-identities in organization studies. *Human Relations*, 63(2), 193–217.

Alvesson, M. and Willmott, H. (2002). Identity regulation as organizational control: Producing the appropriate individual. *Journal of Management Studies*, 39(5), 619–644.

Anderson, V. (2013). A trojan horse? The implications of managerial coaching for leadership theory. *Human Resource Development International*, 16(3), 251–266.

Bachkirova, T. and Borrington, S. (2019). Old wine in new bottles: Exploring pragmatism as a philosophical framework for the discipline of coaching. *Academy of Management Learning and Education*, 18(3), 337–360.

Barends, E. and Rousseau, D.M. (2018). *Evidence Based Management: How to Use Evidence to Make Better Organizational Decisions*. London: Kogan Page.

Beech, N. (2011). Liminality and the practices of identity reconstruction. *Human Relations*, 64(2), 285–302.

Briner, R., Denyer, D. and Rousseau, D. (2009). Concept clean up time? *Academy of Management Perspectives*, 23(4), 19–32.

Briscoe, J.P. and Hall, D.T. (2006). The interplay of boundaryless and protean careers: Combination and implications. *Journal of Vocational Behavior*, 69(1), 4–18.

Brockbank, A. and McGill, I. (2006). *Facilitating Reflective Learning Through Mentoring & Coaching*. London: Kogan Page.

Ciporen, R. (2015). The emerging field of executive and organizational coaching: An overview. *New Directions for Adult and Continuing Education*, 148, 5–15, Winter.

Clarke, C., Knights, D. and Jarvis, C. (2012). A labour of love? Academics in business schools. *Scandinavian Journal of Management*, 28(1), 5–15.

Clutterbuck, D., Whitaker, C. and Lucas, C. (2016). *Coaching Supervision: A Practical Guide for Supervisors*. Oxon: Routledge.

Colville, I.D., Brown, A.D. and Pye, A.J. (2012). Simplexity: Sensemaking, organizing and storytelling for our time. *Human Relations*, 65(5), 5–15.

Cox, E., Bachkirova, T. and Clutterbuck, D. (2014). Theoretical traditions and coaching: Mapping the territory. *Advances in Developing Human Resources*, 16(2), 139–160.

Cushion, C.J. (2018). Reflection and reflective practice discourses in coaching: A critical analysis. *Sport, Education and Society*, 23(1), 82–94.

Dagley, G. (2006). Human resources professionals' perception of executive coaching: Efficacy, benefits and return on investment. *International Coaching Psychology Review*, 1(2), 34–44.

Daskalaki, M. (2012). Personal narratives and cosmopolitan identities. An autobiographical approach. *Journal of Management Inquiry*, 21(4), 430–441.

De Haan, E. (2007). Becoming simultaneously thicker and thinner skinned. *Personnel Review*, 37(5), 526–542.

Drake, A.B. (2011). What do coaches need to know? Using the mastery window to assess and develop expertise. *Coaching: An International Journal of Theory, Research and Practice*, 4(2), 138–155.

Egan, G. (1988). *The Skilled Helper: A Problem-Management Approach to Helping*. Pacific Grove: Brookes, Cole Publishing Company.

Evans, C. and Lines, D. (2014). Which hat do I say I'm wearing? Identity work of independent coaching practitioners. *European Journal of Training and Development*, 38(8), 764–779.

Grant, A.M. (2013). The efficacy of coaching. In, Passmore, J., Peterson, D. and Freire, T. (Eds.), *Handbook of the Psychology of Coaching and Mentoring* (pp. 15–39). West Sussex: Wiley-Blackwell.

Grant, A.M. (2017). The third 'generation' of workplace coaching: Creating a culture of quality conversations. *Coaching: An International Journal of Theory, Research & Practice*, 10(1), 37–53.

Grey, C. (1994). Career as a project of self and labour process discipline. *Sociology*, 28(2), 479–497.

Griffiths, K.E. and Campbell, M.A. (2008). Regulating the regulators: Paving the way for international, evidence-based coaching standards. *International Journal of Evidence Based Coaching and Mentoring*, 6(1), 19–31.

Hall, D.T. (1996). Protean careers of the 21st century. *Academy of Management Perspectives*, 10(4), 8–16.

Hall, D.T. (2004). The protean career: A quarter-century journey. *Journal of Vocational Behavior*, 65(1), 1–13.

Herd, A., Gettman, H. and Stevens, C. (2018). *Coaches' and Clients' Perspectives on Using Various Assessment Tools in Executive Coaching: Toward a Data-Driven Conceptual Decision Framework*. UFHRD Annual Conference. Northumbria University, Newcastle, 6–8 June.

Holt, R. and Cornelissen, J. (2013). Sensemaking revisited. *Management Learning*. Epub ahead of print 22 May. DOI: 10.1177/1350507613486422

Holtbrügge, D. and Ambrosius, J. (2015). Mentoring, skill development and career success of foreign expatriates. *Human Resource Development International*, 18(3), 278–294.

Hughes, E.C. (1937). Institutional office and the person. *American Journal of Sociology*, 43(3), 414–413.

Ibarra, H. (1999). Provisional selves: Experimenting with image and identity in professional adaptation. *Administrative Science Quarterly*, 44, 764–791.

Ibarra, H. and Obodaru, O. (2016). Betwixt and between identities: Liminal experience in contemporary careers. *Research in Organizational Behaviour*, 36, 47–64.

Iszatt-White, M., Kempster, S. and Carroll, B. (2017). An educator's perspective on reflexive pedagogy: Identity undoing and issues of power. *Management Learning*, 48(5), 582–596.

Jarvis, B. (2009). Learning to be a person in society. In, Illeris, K. (Ed.) *Contemporary Theories of Learning*. Abingdon: Routledge.

Jones, R., Woods, S. and Guillaume, Y. (2016). The effectiveness of coaching: A meta-analysis of learning and performance outcomes from coaching. *Journal of Occupational and Organizational Psychology*, 89(2), 249–277.

Kim, J. and McLean, G.N. (2015). An integrative framework for global leadership competency: Levels and dimensions. *Human Resource Development International*, 18(3), 235–258.

Maltbia, T.E., Marsick, V.J. and Ghosh, R. (2014). Executive and organizational coaching: A review of insights drawn from literature to inform HRD practice. *Advances in Developing Human Resources*, 16(2), 161–183.

McInnes, P. and Corlett, S. (2012). Conversational identity work in everyday interaction. *Scandinavian Journal of Management*, 28(1), 27–38.

Mezirow, J. (2000). Learning to think like a scholar. In, Meziro, J. (Ed.) *Learning as Transformation: Critical Perspectives on a Theory in Progress*. San Francisco: Jossey-Bass.

Moore, L. and Koning, J. (2016). Intersubjective identity work and sensemaking of adult learners on a postgraduate coaching course: Finding the balance in a world of dynamic complexity. *Management Learning*, 47(1), 28–44.

Parker, P., Hall, D.T. and Kram, K.E. (2008). Peer coaching: A relational process for accelerating career learning. *Academy of Management Learning & Education*, 487–503.

Patton, W. and McMahon, M. (2006). The systems theory framework of career development and counseling: Connecting theory and practice. *International Journal for the Advancement of Counselling*, 28(2), 153–166.

Robson, M. (2018). *Preliminary Findings of an Exploration of the Experience of Being an Internal Coach*. UFHRD Annual Conference. Northumbria University, Newcastle, 6–8 June.

Saunders, M., Gray, D., Nyfoudi, M. and Curnow, B. (2018). *Professional Identity, Commitment and Self-Esteem in Emerging Professions: A Necessary Condition Analysis of Coaching Practitioners*. UFHRD Annual Conference. Northumbria University, Newcastle, 6–8 June.

Schön, D. (1983). *The Reflective Practitioner: How Professionals Think in Action*. New York: Harper & Collins.

Sonesh, S.C., Coultas, C.W., Lacerenza, C.N., Marlow, S.L., Benishek, L.E. and Salas, E. (2015). The power of coaching: A meta-analytic investigation. *Coaching: An International Journal of Theory, Research & Practice*, 8(2), 73–95.

Sveningsson, S. and Larsson, M. (2006). Fantasies of leadership: Identity work. *Leadership*, 2(2), 203–224.

Thornborrow, T. and Brown, A. (2009). Being regimented: Aspiration, discipline and identity work in the British Parachute Regiment. *Organization Studies*, 30(4), 355–376.

Turner, E. and Passmore, J. (2018). A global perspective of coaching supervisors' practice in coach ethical decision-making. *International Journal of Evidence Based Coaching and Mentoring*, 16(1), 126–142.

Walsh, K., Bartunek, J.M. and Lacey, C.A. (1998). A relational approach to empowerment. In, Cooper, C.L. and Rousseau, D.M. (Eds.). *Trends in Organizational Behaviour* (Vol. 5: 103–126). Chichester: Wiley.

Weick, K. (1996). Enactment and boundaryless careers: Organizing as we work. In, Arthur, M. and Rousseau, D.M. (Eds.) *The Boundaryless Career: A New Employment Principle for a New Organizational Era*. New York: Oxford University Press, pp. 40–57.

Wrzesniewski, A. and Dutton, J. (2001). Crafting a job: Revisioning employees as active crafters of their work. *Academy of Management Review*, 26, 179–201.

Yates, J., Oginni, T., Olway, H. and Petzold, T. (2017). Career conversations in coaching: The contribution that career theory can make to coaching practice. *Coaching: An International Journal of Theory, Research and Practice*, 10(1), 82–93.

Part 3

Contemporary Debates and Dilemmas

Coaching as a Business vs Coaching as a Respected Profession

8 AI and Automation
New Challenges for the Business of Coaching?

Introduction

Our aim in this chapter is to extend current debates on a specific aspect of the changing wider eco-system that coaches operate within. Since starting the process of writing this book we have become more aware of the growing interest and debates around the adoption of AI and Automation technologies, particularly within HRM/HRD and other coaching reference professions (Bachkirova and Borrington 2019). In this chapter we draw out and discuss some of the tensions associated with the adoption of AI and Automation technologies more generally, before focusing on potential tensions for coaching.

The specific questions that this chapter aims to address are:

- What impact are new technologies such as Artificial Intelligence (AI) having on the work that coaches do? Should these new technologies be perceived as an opportunity or threat for coaching? With the rise in the concept of the 'internet of things' (Marr 2018; Nord 2019), how might this help, or hinder, the development of coaches business and/or identity?
- To what extent might coaching remain a viable and sustainable occupation/profession as we see more developments in the field of AI and Automation?
- With changing organisational needs might coaching become yet another example of the precarious work and worker phenomenon? If this is the case, how might this affect coaches' professional identity?

Emergence of the 4th Industrial Revolution and the Rise of AI and Automation

The digital age, generally referred to as the 4th Industrial Revolution, appears as with other industrial revolutions to be a key resource that is both disrupting, as well as enabling, the transformation of industries and individual organisations (CIPD 2019a; HM Government 2017; Seldon and Abidoye 2018; PWC 2018; WEF 2016). It is argued that the 4th Industrial Revolution is different to previous technological revolutions in that we are experiencing 'exponential changes to the way we live, work and relate to one another due to the adoption of cyber-physical systems, the Internet of Things and Internet of Systems' (Marr 2018, in CIPD (2019a: 3). Yet, as the World Economic Forum (2016: 4) point out 'In this new world, analog incumbents—large, successful companies that predate the digital revolution—can feel like they are being ' "hunted" from all sides, with hundreds of startups attacking traditional markets.'

Yet even in the mid-1980s, Porter and Millar (1985: 152) cautioned that 'technological transformation is expanding the limits of what companies can do faster than managers can explore opportunities.' The information revolution as Porter and Millar (1985) refer to it affects competition in three ways: it changes industry structure, enables competitive advantage, and leads to new businesses, often grown from within an existing company. However, one of the case examples in Porter and Millar's (1985: 152) paper, where General Electric was able to store and access the 'accumulated experience and (often intuitive) knowledge of its appliance service engineers to provide customer support' might now be classed as old technology (expert systems). In contrast, IBM's Watson Assistant technology is a more recent example of how a technology company (that started building mainframes in the 1950s) is developing new AI technologies (www.ibm.com).

It is perhaps inevitable then given the competitive nature of global business that organisations will seek to adopt new digital technologies (including AI and Automation technologies) where it is believed these will enhance productivity/performance and thus ultimately reduce business costs. In the field of HR for example, a profession that perhaps ought to be more proactively engaging with AI, Hogg (2019: 47) suggests that 'AI, like analytics before it, has huge potential. The main advantage is increased productivity—repetitive tasks are completed by the technology in a faster and more accurate manner, giving HR professionals more time to work on human-centric tasks.'

However as Frey and Osbourne (2017) point out whereas historically computerised technological developments have been confined to the automation of routine rule-based tasks, current technological advancements that enable the manipulation of big data through computer algorithms that are expert at pattern recognition are already being used in business environments that involve non-routine cognitive tasks. This change is thus generating increasing demand for existing roles (e.g., computer scientists), as well as generating the need for new roles, such as Humanisers, individuals who use their knowledge of linguistics to help develop more authentic Chatbots, as well as cognitive engineers who can 'build and implement new cognitive functionalities, including: business processes, episodic memories, knowledge ontologies &

automation components' (Kerr and Moloney 2018: 22). The technologies deployed in the 4th Industrial revolution would thus appear to be creating new opportunities: 'while it is evident that computers are entering the domains of science and engineering, our predictions implicitly suggest strong complementarities between computers and labour in creative science and engineering occupations' (Frey and Osbourne 2017: 268).

Despite research into AI dating back to the mid-1950s (Cantu-Ortiz 2014), one of the difficulties with the concept of AI is the lack of definitional clarity, thus ambiguity, around what AI is and AI is not. For instance to what extent is AI different to the concept of expert-systems that have been utilised in some professions such as Auditing for around 20 years as a means to imitate the judgments of experts (Omoteso 2012). In his research Omoteso (2012: 841) draws on a definition of expert systems produced by the British Computer Society:

> An expert system is regarded as the embodiment within a computer of a knowledge-based component, from an expert skill, in such a form that the system can offer intelligent advice or take intelligent decision about a processing function. A desirable additional characteristic, which many would consider fundamental, is the capability of the system, on demand, to justify its own line of reasoning in a manner directly intelligible to the enquirer.

Expert systems, then, are based on explicit knowledge, extracted from human experts who are able to articulate particular types of knowledge in a way that can be programmed into rule-based logic, as opposed to generating algorithmic solutions. They are thus appropriate tools for initial diagnostics, which may then lead to signposting to more expert sources of help. One example here is the NHS Direct online platform [https://digital.nhs.uk/services/nhs-111-online] that users can access to get an initial diagnosis of a presenting medical condition, before contacting a GP or visiting a hospital. Users are asked a series of questions about their symptoms, followed by a series of questions about their general health (so questions can be multi-layered). Based on the information provided the system will present a suggested next steps, which could either be sign-posting the user to sources of further help and/or trigger a phone call from a health professional.

Organisations thus deploy Expert Systems to enable them to reach a larger customer/user base, where they are better able to control the quality of information provided. Thus if the question asked by the customer is not in the pre-programmed script, the customer/user will be directed to someone more knowledgeable. Here then we move into the terrain of tacit knowledge, as opposed to explicit knowledge which can be more easily coded.

Systems based on AI, then, are thought to be more advanced than Expert Systems in so much as they have some form of in-built intelligence, a similar capability to that of humans, together with the ability to learn:

> Technologies with the ability to perform tasks that would otherwise require human intelligence, such as visual perception, speech recognition and language translation . . . Machine learning: a type of AI that allows computers to learn rapidly from large datasets without being explicitly programmed.
>
> (HM Government 2017: 36)

> AI is at least as effective already as humans at some tasks which require the application of intelligence.
>
> (Seldon and Abidoye 2018: 106)

> AI is an intelligent agent (i.e., device) that distinguishes between different environments and can take a course of actions to increase the success of achieving predetermined objectives.
>
> (Oana, Cosmin and Valentin 2017, in van Esch, Stewart Black and Ferolie 2019: 215)

> Software/equipment that uses AI i.e., able to learn from data reasoning, or self-correction.
>
> (CIPD 2019a: 36)

> But the nature of AI—which the Oxford English Dictionary defines as "the capacity of a computer to perform operations analogous to learning and decision-making in humans"—means the algorithms can not only make reliable analyses and predict outcomes, but they also learn from these predictions over time. So in some areas at least, they can improve on what humans do.
>
> (Simms 2019: 17).

In reviewing the previous definitions of AI, it appears that a key distinction between AI and Automation and Expert Systems, and an indication of why there is a growing interest in these technologies, is a) AI's ability to manipulate vast amounts of data (typically referred to as Big Data) made possible by the concept of 'the internet of things' (Dellott, Mason and Wallace-Stephens 2019; Marr 2019a; Nord 2019; Seldon 2018) and b) the concept of machine learning, in particular the notion of 'deep learning' (Davis 2019; Faust et al. 2018; Jackson 2019).

One of the advantages of machines is that they have the capacity to retain vast amounts of explicit knowledge. Thus why machine learning (ML) is a key assumption underpinning the adoption of AI and

Automation. But how do machines learn? In essence, they learn through the use of algorithms that seek out and analyse patterns in vast amounts of data (enabled through the internet of things) that then informs decision-making of some form (Harrison, Nichol and Gold 2019). Having processed all available data in response to a given task, the machine will present the 'closet match' (result) to the user. But it is the user then who has to interpret and decide whether the data provided by the AI system is useful data. Depending on the level of sophistication of the AI system they use may be able to provide feedback to the system. AI systems, through the process of 'reinforcement learning' (a concept applied to human and biological systems), learns how to respond better to user needs in the future (Jackson 2019). The next time then that a similar search/question is made by a user the machine (as the intelligent agent) has more data and connections between data to draw on; hence the concept of machine learning.

Based on a review of 53 academic papers on deep learning drawn from the field of medicine, Faust et al. (2018: 2) suggest that one of the limitations of expert systems is that they 'don't reflect the concept of suspicion and common sense'; characteristics typically associated with humans and one that many readers would associate with the notion of tacit knowledge. However Faust et al. (2018) suggest machines can learn to develop a form of tacit knowledge through learning (or mimicking) examples, which is enabled though several hidden layers within the Artificial Neural Network structure, which is designed to model the functionality of the biological brain. Faust et al. (2018: 7) concluded that even though the concept of deep learning as applied to the field of medicine is still in its infancy, it has 'the capability of faster and more reliable diagnoses in physiological signals.'

The concept of deep learning as applied to the field of AI is different in some respects to the concept of deep learning as understood and applied in the field of education. Drawing on the work of Bransford, Brown and Cocking (2000), Kolb and Kolb (2005: 208) point out how

> effective learning requires not only factual knowledge, but the organization of these facts and ideas in a conceptual framework and the ability to retrieve knowledge for application and transfer to different contexts . . . such deep learning is facilitated by deliberate, recursive practice on areas that are related to the learner's goals.

This observation by Kolb and Kolb (2005), reinforces the point about the notion of intentionality, or motivation, in relation to learning, a key facet of learning amongst humans (Bandura 1971). Encouraging and practising deep reflection Kolb and Kolb (2005) suggest is a key process in supporting deep learning. With machine learning, perhaps what we need to question is the intentionality of those developing the algorithms that facilitate machine learning and the uses that such learning is applied to.

Marr (2019a) points out that although AI technologies have been around for over 50 years, it is only now that technology firms have developed the technological capabilities to gather, store, and manipulate large amounts of data given the concept of the 'internet of things' that new applications are emerging. Yet one of the potential unintended consequences of the 'internet of things' is that individuals can become overwhelmed by the 'tsunami of data from the web,' which can result in cognitive overload (CIPD 2019c).

A further sceptical view of AI's current capabilities is suggested by Dave Coplin of the Envisioners:

> AI in its current state at least is neither artificial, nor intelligent. It is just automation—the equivalent of the Spinning Jenny 250 years ago.
> (CIPD 2019b: 16)

A similar cautionary message about the current capabilities of AI appears in a paper by Omoteso (2012), which is based on a review of existing research into the adoption of AI by the audit profession over the past 20 years. Omoteso (2012) suggests that whilst AI (which takes the form of a combination of expert systems and neural networks) is adopted to facilitate judgements made by auditors, it is not meant to replace these. Omoteso (2012: 8491) concludes 'artificial intelligence tools adopted by auditors are considered as mere "agents" being hired for the accomplishment of a particular task. The onus is on the auditor to ensure the relevance, reliability and effectiveness of such tools for his/her purpose.'

Based on a systematic review of academic publications submitted to International AI conferences, Cantu-Ortiz (2014) identified the top four areas of research interest are: data mining, machine learning, neural networks and robotics. These collective AI technologies, according to Cantu-Ortiz (2014: 784) are 'silently permeating and enabling all of the technological advances in computing, telecommunications, automotive engineering, aerospace, biotechnology, medicine, logistics, military activities and other important industrial sectors of world economies.'

The Impact Technologies Such as Artificial Intelligence (AI) are Having on the Work of Professionals

Although in the past the adoption of new technologies (such as automation in the manufacturing industry) has presented more of a threat to low-skilled, or semi-skilled workers, some writers predict that the current wave of technological developments i.e., Artificial Intelligence (AI), could potentially present a threat to some categories of skilled workers (CIPD 2019a; Frey and Osbourne 2017; Omoteso 2012; Wakefield 2015).

Based on a combination of a meta-analysis of existing literature that has researched the historical impact of technological change on occupations and analysis of current O*NET data Frey and Osbourne (2017) have categorised specific occupations as low, medium and high risk of computerisation over the next couple of decades. Their research indicates that occupations that involve assisting and caring for others, use of persuasion, negotiation, social perceptiveness and originality are classified as low probability of computerisation. Specific occupations that utilise these attributes listed in Frey and Osbourne's (2017: 269) research include: occupational therapists, psychologists (all); clinical, counselling and school psychologists; human resources managers; training and development managers; educational, guidance, school, and vocational counsellors and career/technical education teachers.

Other researchers (see Osbourne) suggest that the extent to which AI and Automation will replace jobs depends on a number of factors, such as government regulation and the cost of developing AI technologies. Osborne has identified three bottlenecks that he suggests affect where jobs are likely to be susceptible to AI and Automation: the level of originality required in a job role; the social intelligence needed to carry out a role, e.g., negotiation, persuasion; and the ability for autonomous perception, i.e., ability to see things in a given context. Given these bottlenecks, Hogg's (2019: 48), view that 'Whilst baristas and digital transformation leaders need not worry—their jobs aren't going to be taken over by robotic employees any time soon' may be a comfort to these categories of employees. Yet the situation would appear more precarious for other categories of workers, where firms would appear to be investing heavily in AI and robotics. In China, news reports suggest that there is growing investment in AI and robotics: 'Since September last year, a total of 505 factories across Dongguan have invested 4.2bn yuan (£430m) in robots, aiming to replace more than 30,000 workers, according to the Dongguan Economy and Information Technology Bureau' (Wakefield 2015).

Cooke (2019) echoes this investment in new technologies, including AI, particularly in countries like China. Speaking at the 2019 Universities for Human Resource Development (UFHRD) annual conference, Cooke (2019) referred to the investment by Bosch group in developing the concept of a 'smart city' developing in Taijin in China. The 'smart city' concept is one that has been introduced in other countries, such as Singapore. What this appears to mean is having more integrated mobility, energy, buildings, security, and e-governance systems that are underpinned by the concept of bid data and the Internet of Things. But as Cooke (2019) argued, digitally enabled innovation needs to be implemented in a socially responsible way, given the potential negative implications for employees and citizens. Being part of a society where individuals are subject to constant monitoring and surveillance, enabled through various AI and automation technologies, is likely to have negative effects on individuals' mental health. Cooke (2019) posed the question 'How should we (re)conceptualise HRD in the digital context economy?' given that increasingly nations are not in sole control of technological developments. However, Cooke (2019) did not elaborate on how she thought HRD might/should be re-conceptualised. Others suggests that there is a role for HRD professionals to help ensure that individuals come to understand the critical role of learning where societies and organisations are undergoing radical change, including helping employees develop the new skills needed to thrive in the digital economy. Whilst Cooke (2019) does not refer specifically to the role of coaches (who might be considered part of the HRD community), we suggest that there is a role for them in helping individuals makes sense of the changing eco-system that they are part of and how this might affect their identity.

Carlsson (2018) points out that the digitisation age creates particular tensions for managers, since not all have the knowledge of the key concepts, or the cognitive abilities, to work out how to make use of the complex analytics that digitisation enables. One option to enhance the skill set of managers, according to Carlsson (2018), is to utilise 'digital coaching'. Digital coaches are

> software constructs (artefacts) that we can (i) design and work out jointly with the coming users in co-creative processes; (ii) the artefacts can be validated and verified for design and construct errors, the usability of the artefacts can be tested, and (iii) the functionality of the services can be worked out in the context and with the users for which they were designed.
>
> (Carlsson 2018: 15)

Digital coaching thus acts as bridging tool: 'analytics representation of explicit knowledge built from data and information collected from [a particular process] and the fuzzy ontology representation from partly explicit, linguistic knowledge and partly tacit knowledge collected through work with experienced engineers' (Carlsson 2018: 12). In essence, then, the Digital Coach provides a means to transfer tacit knowledge (from a more experienced knowledgeable skilled worker) to explicit knowledge (which can be understood by a novice/less experienced worker). Arguably this seems more like mentoring than coaching, given that the focus for the Digital Coach would seem to be more knowledge transfer as opposed to utilising conversational methods (i.e., Dialogue Systems) aimed at helping individuals resolve issues, dilemmas and problems for themselves.

Coaching however does not appear in Frey and Osbourne's (2017) analysis of occupations predicted to be affected by AI and Automation technologies. As coaching is a new and emerging occupation, it does not currently exist as a discrete occupational category in the U.S. Standard Occupational Classification (SOC) System (www.bls.gov/soc/2018/

major_groups.htm.) Moreover, coaching conducted in the world of business, as opposed to the world of sport, only appeared in the 2010 UK Standard Occupational Classification (SOC) (www.ons.gov/uk).

This may account for why coaching does not yet have much coverage in the numerous survey research/consultancy reports that refer to occupations/professions at risk from AI and Automation. However given that the work of aligned professions such as Human Resource Management and Development and Industrial-Organisational and Clinical and Counselling Psychologists are changing to some degree through the adoption of new technologies which fall under the broad definition of AI, then coaching is likely to be affected at some future point in time (Carter 2018; CIPD 2019a; Stone et al. 2015). As the cost of AI and Automation technologies fall, and consumers start to feel more comfortable with using these technologies, then demand is likely to increase. Based on the adoption of AI in organisational recruitment, some authors suggest that a combination of the novelty aspect and ease of use of systems that are AI and Automation enabled are key factors in the adoption and acceptance of these technologies (van Esch, Stewart Black and Ferolie 2019; Niehues and Boak 2019).

A growing number of reports suggest that the application of AI is both transforming and in some instances displacing the work which historically would have been carried out by skilled professionals. Table 8.1 sets out some examples of this.

Despite the examples of the application of AI set out in Table 8.1, there is a lack of consensus around both the extent and speed at which AI is replacing existing jobs. Agrawal, Gans, and Goldfarb (2017), for example, point out that

> the current generation of machine learning systems is particularly suited for augmenting or automating tasks that involve at least some prediction aspect. . . . These cover a wide range of tasks, occupations and industries, from driving a car (predicting the correct direction to turn the steering wheel) and diagnosing a disease (predicting its cause) to recommending a product (predicting what the customer will like).
>
> (see Brynjolfsson, Rock and Syverson 2017: 20)

Recent survey research by the CIPD (2019a), completed in partnership with PA Consulting, also suggests that AI is augmenting work rather than replacing it at the current point in time. The CIPD (2019a) research focuses on AI and Automation, rather than just AI. Collectively, AI and Automation consists of strong AI (i.e., system that can mimic human brain activity), weak AI (i.e., discrete smaller tasks that perform specific cognitive tasks that would otherwise be performed by humans, such as probabilistic reasoning), robotics (that can perform to a higher degree

Table 8.1 Examples of Where AI is Transforming the Work of Professionals

Professional field	Application	Source
Medicine, Health and Wellbeing	Application of Virtual Reality technology to aid diagnosis and/ or help with training of new professionals: 'Visualising what is happening in someone's body . . . on the one hand you get a more detailed picture of what has happened to a patient and the other thing is you can display to an untrained person what is happening to their [patients] body to a greater degree, far more simply, using 360 degree or 4D technology, and change behaviours or reduce training time.'	BCS (2018: 63)
	Using Virtual Reality technology to help individuals overcome phobias, such as fear of heights: 'There are very few conditions VR can't help . . . because in the end every mental health is about dealing with a problem in the real world, and VR can produce that troubling situation for you. It gives you a chance to coach people in the way of responding.'	The Guardian Weekend (2018: 25)
	Growing use of E-coaching applications to help people develop a healthier lifestyle e.g., exercise, sleep, nutrition: 'Emerging technology enables us to implement personalized, cooperative, and empathetic mobile agents (not only artificial social agents but also nonsocial agents) that provide a basis for integrating coaching principles in smartphones.'	Beun et al. (2017)
	Introduction of humanoid units on wheels to support the work of careers in residential homes for people with dementia and schools that support young people with autism. 'The robot (humanoid) works in residential homes— typically playing vintage videos to stimulate the memories of residents with early onset dementia'	People Management (2018: 44)

Professional field	Application	Source
HRM: Recruitment and selection	AI-driven games based assessment applied in graduate level recruitment in major Multinational companies.	CIPD (2019b)
	Robots that are programmed to conduct non-biased job interviews.	Savage (2019)
	Use of HireVue technology at Vodafone to help reduce the bias in their automated recruitment process. This technology would appear to combine AI and big data techniques that analyses 'visual and verbal cues, and compares with word choice, facial movements. Body language and tone to help employers find the very best candidate.'	Kerr and Moloney (2018: 11); HireVue (2018)
	Adoption of Second Life Virtual Environment to replace traditional job fairs.	Stone et al. (2015: 218)
Career transition and outplacement	Lee Hecht Harrison Penna, a global career and transition company, use a number of AI enabled technologies to deliver career support to individuals experiencing some form of transition in the workplace. The organisation clearly differentiates the services offered to Executives and those services that are mediated through AI technologies 'giving us new and enhanced ways to assist employees at all levels find better jobs, faster, while supporting our clients with real-time data and insights on the progress of their impacted employees.' The benefits of using AI enabled tools in the service offering is that clients can have access to career support tools and advice 24/7.	www.lhh.com/ lhhpenna/en/ our-services/ career-transition- and- outplacement/ our-technology
Coaching	Coaching Apps and Chatbots: 'Coaching is a very personal process. How could a computer do it? . . . Coaching is about questions. AI can be handed prompts to start a conversation and then tailor its follow-up accordingly . . . But who would open up to AI? . . . Research actually suggests that because we don't feel "judged" or	People Management (2017: 26)

(Continued)

Table 8.1 (Continued)

Professional field	Application	Source
	intimidated by the digital coach's presence, we're more likely to be candid and open.'	
	'This year's winner of the AXA Health Tech & You Awards in the Mental Health in Workplace Challenge is Emoquo, a confidential coaching app that has aggregated advice from trained coaches and therapists to guide individuals through workplace stresses and anxieties'	The Guardian Weekend (2018: 55)
	Characterscope. A digital coaching tool (APP) that can augment other learning and development interventions for leaders.	https:// characterscope. com/for-coaches/
	AI virtual reality coaching tools, such as 'Instant Coach' developed at Arizona State University. The Instant Coach is based on a similar concept to flight simulation technologies. Using this AI enabled tool enables an individual to practice specific behaviours that would enhance their overall performance.	https:// trainingindustry. com/magazine/ may-jun-2018/ artificially- intelligent- coaching-has- arrived/

of accuracy and performance to humans), and automated systems (that involve a combination of robotics and rule-based automated processing systems). To support the argument that AI is augmenting work, not replacing it, the CIPD (2019a) research cites a case example from Atkins engineering who are using AI and Automation to enhance the process for diagnosing defaults in the extensive pipe networks that they install and manage. The use of AI technologies in the context supports skilled engineers in providing a more efficient and effective service to users of the network.

Whilst the CIPD (2019a) research concludes that AI and Automation is currently a long way from replacing the tacit knowledge (i.e., the contextualised and situated knowledge) that professionals in many fields can apply in their day-to-day work, others are more optimistic. Brynjolfsson, Rock and Syverson (2017) point out AI and other machine—language learning methods now incorporate aspects of perception and cognition that are fundamental in many tasks/activities carried out by humans.

In the world of medicine there would appear to be great optimism around the benefits that the use of AI and associated technologies can bring in order to alleviate some of the resourcing pressures associated with diagnosing particular types of patient illnesses, e.g., those at risk of heart failure. This optimism is such that the UK Government has pledged investment in the development of artificial intelligence technologies within the NHS: 'AI could be used to identify those most at-risk of life-threatening diseases, as well as upskilling the NHS workforce so they can use the new technologies' (Davis 2019; Faust et al. 2018; National Health Executive 2019). The attraction of AI would appear to be around its ability for 'deep learning' (Faust et al. 2018). But what is not fully explained, or indeed critically debated, in the growing number of news items and reports on AI is how deep learning in AI works and why it is perceived that AI is better at deep learning than humans.

Within the field of HRD it would seem that given the prominence of the concept of the internet of things, HRD professionals are having to adjust and adapt to the way that employees are now able to acquire knowledge and learn. This of course is not a new phenomenon. The adoption of e-learning has been used within organisations and educational establishments since the 1990s. However the increasingly diverse way in which individuals can access learning resources appears to be making HRD/Learning and Development professionals reconsider what their offering is. Speaking at the CIPD 2019 Festival of Work (CIPD 2019c), the Learning Solutions Manager from TUI, discussed how their organisation is developing their learning and development delivery strategy and methods. As with other professions the need to adopt more agile ways of working and delivery is something that the HRD function recognises is necessary if they are to meet the needs of business leaders. The organisation is thus transitioning from a more rigid Learning Management System (LMS) approach to a more agile approach where leaders can acquire knowledge and learn in more agile ways mediated through a range of different technologies, e.g., learning content accessed through a mobile phone or other smart device, with content curated from sources such as YouTube, Webinars, Podcasts, and web enabled Chatbots. Some of this curated content has been developed through the use of an AI-enabled content creation tool, developed by Donald Clark, which uses voice and natural language in its interface: 'You can do the whole elearning experience just by speaking to it; all of the navigation—front, back, next; creates elearning in minutes' (Learning News 2018). Through adopting a curated learning methodology, which is more agile and responsive to learner needs, the learning and development team hope to ensure that the learning resources accessed are pulled form more credible sources.

Are Coaches at Threat From AI and Automation?

As with other professions, AI and Automation does appear to be encroaching into the eco-system that coaches operate within. So at a time when coaching is still seeking to establish its own identity as a profession is the rise of AI and Automation likely to affect its evolution, and if so in what way?

One way of answering this question is to consider current developments and debates around the effect that AI and Automation is having (or predicted to have) on aligned professions e.g., Human Resources, Human Resource Development, and Coaching Psychologists. As indicated in Table 8.1, technology is already influencing the work of HR professionals, particularly in the areas of Recruitment and Selection. The adoption of AI is positioned as a way of potentially eliminating biases in recruitment and selection (Savage 2019); robots, for example, can be programmed not to engage in pre-interview chit-chat and to pose all questions to applicants in an identical way, in the same tone, and typically, in the same order, thus providing a fairer and more objective interview (Savage 2019). However given that robots have to be pre-programmes by someone, then the issue of bias may occur at the programming stage given that there is a lack of diversity working in the IT sector (Guerrier et al. 2009; Lambrecht and Tucker 2016; Smith 2019). Smith (2019) argues that given that algorithms are designed to solve real—world issues through simplification, then it is imperative that the team designing news systems using AI and Automation are more diverse to help eliminate bias.

But is asking a question in an identical way more equitable when we live in a more diverse and multicultural society? Hall and Hall (1990) for example identified from their research that people from different cultures differ in the way they communicate with each other. So they differentiate between high context cultures (that use a more indirect form of expression and communication) and low context cultures (where information is clearly verbalised). In addition some individuals take language more literally as opposed to being comfortable and able to engage with a more ambiguous/metaphorical form of communication. Individuals with Autism is one example here. Equally individuals living temporarily in different culture may mis-interpret colloquialisms. I am mindful here of an International student who was initially confused by the term milkround (as applied to graduate recruitment). He referred to the milking shed in his assignment, when discussing employer sessions aimed at offering information about career opportunities after graduating.

In their evaluation of the strengths and limitations of the adoption of new and emerging technologies on HRM, Stone et al. (2015) acknowledge that whilst the adoption of automated technologies can increase the efficiency and lower the cost of specific HRM activities, e.g., recruitment, they caution against losing sight of the strategic goal of attracting and retaining a talented and diverse workforce: 'The danger is that the more HR becomes technology-focused, rather than employee-focused, the field of HR as a whole may be viewed as more of management "tool" and less as a strategic partner' (Stone et al. 2015: 227).

Another consideration, as Omoteso (2012) points out AI tools are 'agents' themselves: agents that need to be coached to present information in the way that the user requires in order to be most useful to the user. Research by Duan et al. (2012: 5539) into how 'intelligent software agents assist business executives to make effective decisions' identified that

> an agent should be able to adapt to changing situations and individual executive's information processing behaviour through learning and coaching . . . It is important for the system to learn within itself (learning) or through user feedback (coaching) . . . Most participants suggested that great efforts are needed in order to coach the agent and to enhance its learning capability.

However, it would seem that the model of coaching that is utilised in educating 'intelligent software agents' is different to the coaching models we referred to in Chapter 2. First, the coaching seems directive: 'The coaching attribute enables executives to train the system by giving explicit feedback in order to increase its robustness' (Duan et al. 2012: 5544). Second, the coaching mechanism appears more simplistic. This would seem intentional in order to avoid cognitive overload in the executive users. However, trustworthiness is something that would appear to be a common theme: 'The implication for agent system developers is that the simple, workable and trustworthy personalised software agents are what business executives want' (Duan et al. 2012: 5545).

However if we dig deeper into the current positive discourse associated with AI, a shadow side of AI emerges. As we have already pointed out in earlier chapters, there are both different genres and types of coaches. Whilst the work of Burnett (2017) suggest that the application of AI in coaching will lead to greater democratisation of coaching (i.e., bringing coaching to the masses), we suggest that this may widen the gap between the quality of coaching received by different coachees. Whilst providing a Coaching App (The Guardian Weekend 2018), or 'intelligent chat box mentors' (People Management 2018) may enable organisations to extend its coaching/mentoring support to more of its employees, there is a danger that more complex performance and personal issues go undetected.

Digitally Enabled Coaching Case: Pemberton Asset Management Group: Augmenting Face-to-face Coaching With AI Enabled Coaching

Pemberton Asset Management Group is an independent asset management firm that was established in 2013 to benefit from the changing European Financial markets. The firm has around 80 employees, including the Executive team, supporting clients in seven locations across Europe (www.pembertonam.com/).

As part of its commitment to developing its talent, Pemberton Asset Management has introduced digital enabled coaching as part of its overall development strategy. The Head of People and Performance, Paul Aldrich, explained how the overarching rationale for adopting a blended approach to coaching—digital enabled coaching supported with face-to-face coaching sessions—is one of cost effectiveness and accessibility. Whilst he can provide regular one-to-one coaching for the Executive team this approach is not as feasible for other staff in the firm. Augmenting the use of a digitally enabled coaching tool with other development tools and face-to-face coaching sessions is a way of helping develop greater self-ownership of personal and career development.

Pemberton Asset Management has been working with Character-Scope a technology company that provides 'a digital coaching platform that helps leaders and their teams perform at their best' (https://characterscope.com/). CharacterScope's approach to coaching is focused on developing personal strengths that underlie leadership capabilities. Their digital platform provides a structured process for helping individuals discover these strengths, through providing a number of diagnostic and peer feedback tools as well as curated learning content to help build and extend leadership self-insights and encourage continuous self-coaching. The content is structured through a series of 34 different 25-day development plans, guiding users through daily, bite-sized workouts to create new habits and capabilities. The firm has integrated the use of CharacterScope's digital coaching platform into a broader development offering and process. The process started with an all staff briefing on the benefits of continuous self and career development, which CharacterScope helped to facilitate. Staff were then offered the opportunity to complete various psychometric tests, such as the Watson-Glaser Cognitive Ability and Hogan Personality Inventory psychometrics. The use of these psychometrics, combined with 360° feedback enabled though Characterscope, help inform an individual's development plans.

The digital coaching platform, Aldrich explained, can be used in a similar way to how individuals might supplement specific sessions with a personal fitness trainer; using the digital platform between coaching session (online, or face-to-face) to help to monitor and set new goals. Aldrich explained that the overall coaching philosophy underpinning their development approach is strengths-based, something that is also core to the CharacterScope approach. Once the leaders in Pemberton Asset Management are familiar with the CharacterScope offering and have experienced it themselves, they can then draw on this knowledge in their day-to-day leadership and team-working.

Aldrich acknowledges that there is a difference in the quality and type of coaching that could be delivered through a digital coaching platform than that provided in face-to-face coaching sessions facilitated by an experienced coach. In a face-to-face coaching session the coach can go deeper into a specific situation/issue by using different questioning approaches to draw out the contextual factors affecting a specific situation/issue that the coachee wants to explore and work on, as well as drawing on a range of coaching models (e.g., CBT, Solutions Focused Coaching) as appropriate for a given coaching scenario. The assumption (or philosophy) behind this thinking is that the coach wants to support people find meaning and purpose and fulfil their potential. In face-to-face coaching sessions, then, the coach can move beyond the goal-orientated approach (widely promoted in some of the coaching literature) to focus more on the here and now issues. The skilled coach is thus better able to pick up on non-verbal as well as verbal cues, whereas coaching delivered through a digital platform may not be able to do this until the underlying technologies (AI) has developed the learning to pick up on these subtleties—and even then, its role is likely to remain as a support to and extension of the work of a coach.

In terms of monitoring the effectiveness of tools such as CharacterScope, Aldrich explained that this will happen though a number of mechanisms; for example, through the one-to-one coaching session that he offers staff personally, as well as through the firm's performance management process.

A further consideration for individual users of Coaching Apps is whether, and/or at what point, they identify a need for a different kind of support from a human coach. The challenges that individuals working in organisations that are experiencing digital transformation may encounter, suggest that the need for coaching may become even greater. This quotation from the WEF (2016) Digital Transformation Report, surfaces a number of tensions for organisations and individuals that suggests that there might be a greater need for experienced coaches during periods of organisational transformation:

> This report takes a look at how enterprises can attract, retain and develop the right talent. The report also highlights the imperative for organizations to embrace the cultural transformation and encourage millennials to join their workforce. Finally, it assesses how companies need to adapt to different ways of working, whether it's integrating robots or on-demand workers.
>
> (WEF 2016: 4)

It is the latter sentence in the previous comment that draws attention in particular to the challenges that organisations and individuals face from technological transformation. The integration of robots into existing work systems and routines, particularly where this displaces existing workers will inevitably create stress and marginalisation for some categories of workers. Equally being in an environment that utilises 'on-demand' workers, which includes outsourced and temporary project workers WEF (2016), again may lead to a segregated and marginalised workforce. The question arises though as to whether these categories of workers will benefit from the changes in technology that could enable the democratisation of coaching (Burnett and Malafronte 2017).

David Clutterbuck (2019a) suggests that the coaches most at risk of being displaced by AI and Automation are those that follow more simplistic/prescriptive coaching models such as the GROW model (Whitmore 2017). It is these types of model that could be replaced by simple rule based algorithmic technologies including Chatbots/CoachBots. An example here is the CoachBot developed by Saberr (www.saberr.com/coachbot). However, as Clutterbuck (2019b) suggests, there are potential synergies for coaches and AI. Referring to the information, knowledge, skills and wisdom deployed in coaching he suggests that AI can provide greater depth of information, but limited depth of knowledge (we assume he is referring to tacit knowledge here) and potentially higher levels of observation (enabled through other technologies and the internet of things) than coaches. However coaches are better able to draw interpretations from dialogue and observations given that they can apply wisdom (i.e., the ability to integrate knowledge and experience in the moment) to coaching scenarios, problems and narratives; something that is outside the scope of the current generation of AI technologies.

AI and Coaching: A Potential Scenario

I am an expert coach (however we define that). I have used a CoachBot to gather some initial diagnostics from a new client. I have a report in front of me. I start to make some assumptions about the individual's coaching needs based on the initial diagnostics. There is something in the initial diagnostic report that raises an alarm bell—not sure the information provided is revealing the full picture.

I have the first coaching session—the niggle I had about not having the full picture is still with me. So now I access my SupervisorBot—that can help me identify what models, theories and tools I could draw on to try and discover more about where the client is at currently (principle of start from where the client is at currently—what is their reality?).

Who provides (and who owns) the data gathered and utilised for these two systems CoachBot and SupervisorBot?

1.   Recording device, worn by the coach that records all coaching conversations—the data is then available for someone, or something, to analyse further. Ethical issue—confidential and sensitive information being captured/stored on a platform for which neither coach, or coachee, has access and control.

2. After the coaching session has ended the CoachBot then initiates a dialogue with the coach based on the captured data: What made you ask that question then? Or Why did you suggest that approach then? Here we are moving into the realm of tacit knowledge—making tacit knowledge more explicit. The responses from the coach are stored and added to a database that can then be accessed by other CoachBots. The AI then knows more (it is assumed to have learnt), thus able to offer a range of suggestions to support other 'novice coaches' in the future.

Whilst we acknowledge that this is a hypothetical scenario, it is conceivable that coaches who use more simplistic/prescriptive coaching models may find that they are in need of additional support to help develop the coaching relationship with clients, or where the presenting issue(s) requires drawing on more sophisticated coaching models. Where this is the case coaches have a choice. They could utilise a Supervisor Coach-Bot, or seek to engage with a more traditional Supervision arrangement. Equally there is potentially the opportunity to utilise AI technologies (CoachBot) in coach training/education to present coaching scenarios that novice coaches can reflect on, formulate their proposed coaching solution and possibly get feedback from a particular type of CoachBot.

Whilst we can see that CoachBots may be attractive to organisations (and individuals) enabling coaching to become more accessible to employees at different levels in the organisation, we suggest that executives will still expect a more (dyadic) coaching relationship. Potentially we could envisage a more differentiated service offering; more traditional dyadic coaching provided for senior leaders and wider access to caching to other categories of employees enabled through the use of CoachBots.

If the pace of technological change is increasing and thus radically changing the nature of businesses, nature of work and jobs and careers, arguably there could be a growing need for more coaching to help individuals make sense of and navigate a sustainable career, as well as help ensure that they look after their mental health (The Psychologist 2018). Thus there could be potential benefits if organisations were to provide employees with a Coaching type app, possibly combined with a wearable device that can monitor stress levels, which are connected. These combined technologies could thus capture 'live data' that could be used in future face-to-face coaching conversations. This may be more beneficial in helping individuals understand and plan behavioural change. This approach is similar to the observational filming (using GoPro technology) used by Sports Coaches to help monitor and provide feedback on athletes' performances.

In addition, given the shortage of mental health practitioners, there may be a role for coaches to work with individuals who are experiencing stress from the pace of change in organisations. This could be more ethically appropriate and sustainable to practising mindfulness alone using an app (The Guardian 2019).

As Burhouse et al. (2015) point out

> People with long-term mental health conditions are increasingly looking for alternatives to pharmacological management alone and seeking out psychological, emotional, spiritual and educational perspectives to better understand and manage their conditions. Specialist NHS adult mental health services are not currently designed or resourced for the volume of demand that is emerging in the area of self-management.

However, we offer a word of caution here: should coaches work with clients who have been diagnosed with mental health issues? Where do the boundaries of professional knowledge and responsibilities fall? The article by Pick (2018) raises questions around whether coach education fully prepares coaches to recognise mental health issues and/or the emotions that arise in coaching conversations. If this is the case then it is rather worrying to think that CoachBots could replace human coaches. Who will programme these technologies to recognise signs of mental health? Who will monitor the ethics of these new technological applications? Whilst new roles are emerging, such as AI Ethics Officers, which appear to be a combination of ethics and compliance, there is no legislation currently to ensure that organisations have someone appointed to this role. Within Europe, the European Commission's High-level Expert group on AI has started to draft some ethical guidelines for developing trustworthy AI systems (Fernando 2019). The guidelines are based on some fundamental principles: 'AI is human centric, ethical and developed for the common good' and given that AI is in its infancy the ethical frameworks 'offers this overtly values-based approach. It is hoped that this will allow innovation to be designed in an ethical way' (Fernando 2019: 27). Whilst we can see that these guidelines are likely to be welcomed by AI developers across Europe, this leaves us with a question as to who is driving similar initiatives in other countries. If the development of AI enabled coaching tools is the way forward, then arguably there is a need for Coaching Associations to engage with the process of establishing ethical guidelines for the development and application of such tools. Furthermore, in the future is there a role for coaches, especially those working with executives to help them reflect on the ethics (and unintended consequences) of the adoption of AI technologies on the wellbeing of their employees?

With AI Enabled Coaching Might Coaching Become Yet Another Example of the Precarious Work and Worker Phenomenon?

Despite the reach in terms of the applications that AI and Automation is being utilised in specific fields such as medicine, the adoption of AI in coaching would appear to still be at the early stages. A blog post on ICF's website by Barney (2018), an organisational psychologist who uses coaching in his practice, suggests that there is a role for technology-enabled coaching and face-to-face coaching to complement each other. In other words, technology can be utilised to help reinforce behavioural change in coachees. For coaches this means positioning AI tools as a useful extension of an already established developmental relationship with their coachees. The benefit to individuals (and thus by implication businesses) is that this will ensure better transfer of learning, compared with other more traditional training/development approaches. Barney (2018) suggests that AI enabled coaching is unlikely to affect the take up of coaching amongst Executives and other senior leaders, a point that we also suggest is likely to be the case as discussed earlier in this chapter. He also suggests that coaches could use AI tools in order to scale up their business. In other words, to offer coaching to a wider group of individuals who may not have the resources to pay for face-to-face coaching.

One of our participants suggested that the use of AI enabled coaching is perhaps a logical evolution of coaching services, not dissimilar to the way that the Outplacement and Executive Search industries have evolved over the past 20 years as more people have become familiar with what these services are designed to achieve and as the technologies to develop these services evolve. We suggest that as organisations (as the client) take a more cost-benefit approach to the adoption of these types of development services, irrespective of how much they see these as supporting business transformation, it is inevitable that providers of such services in a crowded marketplace will seek to identify more cost-effective solutions. The application of different technologies is seen as one way to achieve this.

Might Coaching Become a Liminal or Precarious Profession?

Previous work by the authors (Evans and Lines 2014) identified that it is hard for some to make a viable living out of coaching alone. Getting established in the field takes time, and not all individuals have the resources to invest in getting established. There are other tensions too, relating to professional identity. In a study of individuals transitioning into coaching, Gray, Saunders and Curnow (2017) refer to the notion of a liminal professional identity, i.e., betwixt and between identities, as they transition from one form of professional work into another. Whilst we accept that developing another dimension of one's professional identity creates tensions with regard to an individual's identity, given that identity is fluid and dynamic (Alvesson 2010; Alvesson and Willmott 2002), then any work transition will inevitably involve some form of identity work (Alvesson and Willmott 2002; McInnes and Corlett 2012). However, the extent to which those new to coaching might be considered to be experiencing a liminal professional identity may vary depending on where individuals perceive coaching as part of his/her overall professional identity. In other words, to what extent are they seeking to make coaching a dominant part of their professional identity or something to augment other professional roles/identities?

Establishing a viable coaching business as discussed in Chapter 3 is something that is influenced by a number of factors: economic, socio-political, regulatory, and, at the organisational level, having the right organisational environment and investment for coaching to become an accepted development approach. Arguably it is easier to introduce coaching in particular types of organisations where there is an established commitment to investing in learning and development. Yet as one of our participants pointed out there is arguably a limited platform (stage) for coaches who might be considered equivalent to 'celebrity chefs' and thus have achieved sufficient status to command the highest fees.

Building a viable coaching business that has one or more recognised influential founder member(s) in the coaching firm is arguably one way of legitimising the business offering. Yet to develop the wider global reach needed to become and remain competitive in the global coaching world, would appear to also need investing in some form of digital technologies too. One example of this is the online coaching company BetterUp, based in San Francisco. The organisation has a number of recognised thought leaders on their Board who provide the science behind the organisation's coaching offering (www.betterup.co/en-us/why-betterup/our-science/). One of the BetterUp Board members is Martin Seligman, who is acknowledged as the initial thought leader behind positive psychology. Another is Josh Bersin, founder of Bersin by Deloitte. In a news item, Bersin (2019) appears to be making a case for adopting coaching as a new way of developing leadership capabilities. Thus the tools BetterUp offer provide a means for individuals to self-assess their coaching needs, connect with and select the right coach for themselves, as well as engage with other customised/curated learning solutions and products. Bersin (2019) argues that the old way of developing leadership is broken. Instead, organisations need to adopt an approach to leadership development that acknowledges that 'Leadership is a craft . . . you learn by doing it, through coaching and apprenticeship, and by leaning and reflecting on your mistakes,' Digitally enabled coaching, according to Bersin (2019), is key to helping people develop their leadership and development needs.

However, as Paul Aldrich suggests (see Pemberton Asset Management case), the growing interest in applying occupational psychological tools and techniques in the workplace has created a platform that coaches can align themselves to, thus potentially differentiating their offering. However, there is a trade-off to be made here. Developing the necessary competencies and accreditations to use occupational psychological tools in their practice involves coaches making an additional financial investment in their own learning and development. Before making this type of invest-ment, coaches will need to research the market that they intend to prac-tice in. As one of our participants, who provides coaching in the Middle East, pointed out, the use of psychometric tools in coaching is not neces-sarily accepted in all cultures. In the Middle East, for example, the use of psychometric tools in coaching has become more acceptable as more sophisticated HRM approaches have evolved—for example, incorporat-ing more sophisticated recruitment and selection tools that involve the use of psychometric testing.

George (2013) offers an alternative perspective on building a viable coaching business. She suggests that a tight-loose dichotomy could be advantageous where coaches aim to differentiate themselves from related therapeutic occupations, or where coaches aim to expand their reach to areas of work that are not seen to be part of their scope, e.g., into areas of wellness and stress management. This suggestion resonates one we made earlier in this chapter about coaches, perhaps complementing the work of other aligned professions. Where this is feasible this might then affect the longer term occupational viability of coaching.

Summary and Conclusion

This chapter has explored how the emergence of new technologies such as AI and Automation are impacting on the work of the professions in general and more specifically the work of coaching professionals. Whether coaching can be considered a profession is still the subject of much debate, something that we have discussed in Chapter 4. However the work that coaches perform does not seem to be immune from devel-opments within the field of AI and Automation.

There are several aspects of these developing AI and Automation technologies that we suggest coaches need to consider. First, the issues that clients may bring to a coaching session as a result of the impact that the pace and reach of technological change is having on their current work performance, as well as concerns about the impact these tech-nologies may have on their future careers. Senior leaders and middle managers may feel particularly overwhelmed by technological change and potentially most at risk as organisations restructure to ensure they remain a viable entity. Second, coaches will need to think about the impact AI and Automation technologies could have on their own coach-ing business.

Some of the more positive accounts of the adoption of AI and Automa-tion suggest that organisations can benefit from seeking ways of ensur-ing AI and human intelligence work synergistically together. What some commentators refer to as finding the 'sweet spot' between AI and humans (Marr 2019b). Thus the term 'augment' is one that we should perhaps focus on rather than the more negative term 'displace.' Yet separating the hype of AI and Automation from the reality is problematic even for IT professionals (Fernando 2019). The AI industry is shrouded in mystique, and it is not helped by the impenetrable language used by those working in this field. In addition, the pace at which AI technologies are being adopted in different sectors and different countries could make developing a sustainable coaching business more difficult, particularly for coaches working with global clients and businesses. In Chapter 9, we discuss where awareness of technological developments and the impact (and benefits) this can bring on coaching as a business should fit within coach education and development.

References

Agrawal, A., Gans, J.S. and Goldfarb, A. (2017). *What to expect from Artificial Intelligence*. MIT Sloan Management Review. https://sloanreview.mit.edu/arti cle/what-to-expect-from-artificial-intelligence/ (accessed 26 February 2020).

Alvesson, M. (2010). Self-doubters, strugglers, storytellers, surfers and others: Images of self-identities in organization studies. *Human Relations*, 63(2), 193–217.

Alvesson, M. and Willmott, H. (2002). Identity regulation as organizational control: Producing the appropriate individual. *Journal of Management Studies*, 39(5), 619–644.

Bachkirova, T. and Borrington, S. (2019). Old wine in new bottles: Exploring pragmatism as a philosophical framework for the discipline of coaching. *Academy of Management Learning and Education*, 18(3), 337–360.

Bandura, A. (1971). *Social Learning Theory*. New York: General Learning Press. www.asecib.ase.ro/mps/Bandura_SocialLearningTheory.pdf (accessed 21 August 2019).

Barney, M. (2018). *Is Coaching Extinct?* Blog post. https://coachfederation.org/ blog/is-coaching-going-extinct (accessed 27 September 2019).

BCS. (2018). Inside the Bristol VR Lab. *IT Now, June 2018*. Swindon: BCS.

Bersin, J. (2019). *Why Leadership Development Feels Broken*. https://joshber sin.com/2019/07/why-leadership-development-feels-broken-and-how-were-fixing-it/ (accessed 20 September 2019).

Beun, R.J., Anderson, J., Ham, J., Klein, M., Roefs, A. and Westerink, J. (2017). Special issue on supporting a healthier lifestyle with e-coaching systems. *Personal and Ubiquitous Learning*, 21(4), 621–623. https://doi.org/10.1007/ s00779-017-1029-x.

Bosch. (2017). *A Smart City in China: Bosch to Make Tianjin Intelligent*. www. bosch-presse.de/pressportal/de/en/a-smart-city-in-china-bosch-to-make-tian jin-intelligent-111680.html (accessed 10 August 2019).

Bransford, J.D., Brown, A. L. and Cocking, R.R. (2000). *How People Learn: Brain, Mind Experience, and School*. Washington DC: National Academy Press.

Brynjolfsson, E., Rock, S. and Syverson, C. (2017). *Artificial Intelligence and the Modern Productivity Paradox: A Clash of Expectations and Statistics*. NBER Working Paper No. 24001. www.nber.org/chapters/c14007.pdf (accessed 1 September 2018).

Burhouse, A., et al. (2015). Coaching for recovery: A quality improvement project in mental health care. *BJM Quality Improvement Report*, 4(1). www.ncbi.nlm.nih.gov/pmc/articles/PMC4693036/ (accessed 26 June 2019).

Burnett, N. (2017). E-coaching: Theory and practice for a new online approach to coaching. *Coaching: An International Journal of Theory, Research and Practice*, 11(1), 91–93. www.tandfonline.com/doi/abs/10.1080/17521882.2017.1348372?journalCode=rcoa20. (accessed 10 August 2019).

Burnett, N. and Malafronte, O. (2017). The democratisation of coaching – Artificial Intelligence (AI) Coaching. *Australian Educational Leader*, 39(4), 44–46.

Cantu-Ortiz, F.J. (2014). Advancing artificial intelligence research and dissemination through conference series: Benchmark, scientific impact and the MICIA. *Expert Systems with Applications*, 41, 781–785.

Carlsson, C. (2018). Decision analytics mobilized with digital coaching. *Intelligent Systems in Accounting Finance & Management*, 25, 3–17.

Carter, D. (2018). How real is the impact of artificial intelligence? The business information survey 2018. *Business Information Review*, 1–17. http://journals.sagepub.com/doi/abs/10.1177/0266382118790150?journalCode=bira (accessed 21 August 2019).

CIPD. (2019a). *People and Machines: From Hype to Reality*. London: CIPD.

CIPD. (2019b). *HR Will Wreck AI: Work. Because Business Is About People*. London: CIPD. www.festivalofwork.com/prereading-day1/; www.festivalofwork.com/prereading-day2/.

CIPD. (2019c). *Artificial Intelligence in Learning—How AI Will Change Everything*. CIPD Festival of Work Conference, Olympia, London, 12–13 June.

Clark, D. (2018). *Artificial Intelligence in Learning*. https://learningnews.com/news/learning-news/2018/ai-in-learning-donald-clark-at-ltsf-2018 (accessed 13 June 2019).

Clutterbuck, D. (2019a). *The New AI Coach—Explore How AI Will Help Humans Deliver Better Coaching*. CIPD Festival of Work, Olympia, London, 12–13 June.

Clutterbuck, D. (2019b). *Coach Versus Bot: How Do They Compare?* www.davidclutterbuckpartnership.com/coach-versus-bot-how-do-they-compare/ (accessed 18 August 2019).

Cooke, F.L. (2019). *Digitally-Enabled Innovation in a Socially Responsible Way: The Role of the State and Firms as Key Institutional Actors for HDR*. UFHRD 2019 Annual Conference, Nottingham Business School, Nottingham Trent University, 24–26 June.

Davis, N. (2019). AI 'on a par with humans' in making medical diagnoses. *The Guardian*, 25 September.

Dellott, B., Mason, R. and Wallace-Stephens, F. (2019). *The Four Futures of Work: Coping with Uncertainty in an Age of Radical Technologies*. London: RSA. www.thersa.org/globalassets/pdfs/reports/rsa_four-futures-of-work.pdf (accessed 13 June 2019).

Duan, Y., Ong, V.K., Xu, M. and Mathews, B. (2012). Supporting decision making process with "ideal" software agents—What do business executives want? *Expert Systems with Applications*, 39, 5534–5547.

Evans, C. and Lines, D. (2014). Which hat do I say I'm wearing? Identity work of independent coaching practitioners. *European Journal of Training and Development*, 38(8), 764–779.

Faust, O., Hagiwara, Y., Hong, T.G., Lih, O.S. and Acharya, U.R. (2018). Deep learning for healthcare applications based on physiological signals: A review. *Computer Methods and Programmes in Biomedicine*, 161, 1–13.

Fernando, R. (2019). *Living with AI: A Personal Perspective*. IT NOW. Swindon: BCS, September.

Fister Gale, S. (2018). Artificial intelligence may power the next generation of mentors, but can technology really replace a human touch? *Chief learning Officer*, April 2018. https://www.chieflearningofficer.com/

Frey, C.B. and Osbourne, M.A. (2017). The future of employment: How susceptible are jobs to computerisation. *Technological Forecasting & Social Change*, 114(217), 254–280.

George, M. (2013). Seeking legitimacy: The professionalization of life coaching. *Sociological Inquiry*, 83(2), 179–208.

Gray, D.E., Saunders, M. and Curnow, B.J. (2017). *Professional Identity: Liminality, Fragmentation and the Trauma of Career Transition*. UFHRD Annual Conference, Lisbon Portugal, 7–8 June.

The Guardian. (2019). *The Mindfulness Conspiracy Capitalist*. www.theguardian.com/lifeandstyle/2019/jun/14/the-mindfulness-conspiracy-capitalist-spirituality (accessed 13 June 2019).

The Guardian Weekend. (2018). After, I feel ecstatic and emotional: Could virtual reality replace therapy? *The Guardian Weekend*, 17 October 2017. https://www.theguardian.com/technology/2017/oct/07/virtual-reality-acrophobia-paranoia-fear-of-flying-ptsd-depression-mental-health

Guerrier, Y., Glover, J., Evans, C. and Wilson, C. (2009). 'Technical, but not very . . .' Constructing gendered identities in IT-related employment. *Work, Employment and Society*, 23(3), 494–511.

Hall, E.T. and Hall, M.R. (1990). *Understanding Cultural Differences: Germans, French and Americans*. Yarmouth, ME: Intercultural Press.

Harrison, P., Nichol, L. and Gold, G. (2019). *The Impact of Machine Learning on Future HRD Practice and Research*. UFHRD 2019 Annual Conference. Nottingham Trent University, 24–26 June.

HireVue. (2018). *Hirevue Hiring Intelligence*. www.hirevue.com/blog/hirevue-hiring-intelligence (accessed 13 June 2019).

HM Government. (2017). *Industrial Strategy: Building a Britain Fit for the Future*. Policy Paper, November.

Hogg, P. (2019). Artificial intelligence: HR friend or foe? *Strategic HR Review*, 18(2), 47–51.

IBM. (2019). www.ibm.com/ibm/history/exhibits/mainframe/mainframe_FT2.html; https://developer.ibm.com/components/watson-assistant/) (accessed 8 August 2019).

Jackson, P.C. (2019). *Introduction to Artificial Intelligence* (Third Edition). New York: Dover Publications, Inc.

Kerr, W.R. and Moloney, E. (2018). *Vodafone: Managing Advanced Technologies and Artificial Intelligence*. Boston, MA: Harvard Business School Publishing.

Kolb, A.Y. and Kold, D.A. (2005). Learning styles and learning spaces: Enhancing learning in higher education. *Academy of Management*, 4(2), 193–212.

Lambrecht, A. and Tucker, C.E. (2016). *Algorithmic Bias? An Empirical Study into Apparent Gender-Based Discrimination in the Display of STEM Career Ads*. SSRN. https://papers.ssrn.com/sol3/papers.cfm?abstract_id=2852260 (accessed 10 June 2019).

Marr, B. (2019a). *AI and the Internet of Things in the Future Workplace— Exploring the Interconnected Benefits for Organisations.* CIPD Festival of Work, 12–13 June.

Marr, B. (2019b). *The Fascinating Ways PepsiCo Uses Artificial Intelligence and Machine Learning to Deliver Success.* www.forbes.com/sites/bernard-marr/2019/04/05/the-fascinating-ways-pepsico-uses-artificial-intelligence-and-machine-learning-to-deliver-success/#19dde4a7311e (accessed 26 July 2019).

Marr, B. (2018). The 4th Industrial Revolution is here – are you ready? Forbes. 13 August. Available at: www.forbes.com/sites/bernardmarr/2018/08/13/the-4th-industrialrevolution-is-here-are-you-ready/#5fd8f95d628b.

McInnes, P. and Corlett, S. (2012). Conversational identity work in everyday interaction. *Scandinavian Journal of Management*, 28, 27–38.

National Health Executive. (2019). *Government Pledges £250m for NHS National Artificial Intelligence Lab.* www.nationalhealthexecutive.com/News/government-pledges-250m-for-nhs-national-artificial-intelligence-lab) (accessed 26 September 2019).

Niehues, W. and Boak, G. (2019). *Artificial Intelligence: Attitudes Towards New Technology in a Human Resources Function: Implications for Training and Development.* Paper presented at UFHRD 2019 Annual Conference. Nottingham Trent University, 24–26 June.

Nord, J.H. (2019). The internet of things: Review and theoretical framework. *Expert Systems with Applications*, 1–45, May.

Oana, O., Cosmin, T. and Valentin, N.C. (2017). Artificial intelligence – a new field of computer science which any business should consider. *Ovidius University Annals, Economic Sciences Series*, 17(1), 356–360.

Omoteso, K. (2012). The application of artificial intelligence: Looking back to the future. *Expert Systems with Applications*, 38, 8490–8495.

ONS (2010). *Standard Occupational Classifications.* www.ons.gov.uk/methodology/classificationsandstandards/standardoccupationalclassificationsoc (accessed 26 July 2019).

People Management. (2017). These are the experts deciding the future of HR . . . shouldn't you know who they are? *People Management, August 2017.* London: Haymarket Media Group.

People Management. (2018). *Does AI Mean the End of HR?* www.peoplemanagement.co.uk (accessed 26 October 2019).

Pick. (2018). *Coaching in a Crisis: Part 1—Working with Mental Health Issues.* https://performanceandwellbeing.com/blog/2018/11/special-report-coaching-in-a-crisis-part-1-working-with-mental-health-issues/ (accessed 26 July 2019).

Porter, M.E. and Millar, V.E. (1985). How information gives you competitive advantage. *Harvard Business Review*, 149–160, July–August.

The Psychologist. (2018). *Coaching Has Great Potential in the World of Work.* https://thepsychologist.bps.org.uk/volume-31/may-2018/coaching-has-great-potential-world-mental-health (accessed 26 July 2019).

PWC. (2018). *Will Robots Really Steal Our Jobs? An International Analysis of the Potential Long Term Impact of Automation.* www.pwc.co.uk/economic-services/assets/international-impact-of-automation-feb-2018.pdf (accessed 21 October 2019).

Savage, M. (2019). *Would You Be Happy Being Interviewed by a Robot?* www.bbc.co.uk/news/business-47442953 (accessed 12 March 2019).

Seldon, A. and Abidoye, O. (2018). *The Fourth Education Revolution: How Artificial Intelligence Is Changing the Face of Technology.* Buckingham: The University of Buckingham Press.

Simms, J. (2019). AI will wreck HR: HR will wreck AI. In, *Work.* London: CIPD, Spring.

Smith, R.E. (2019). The dark heart of the algorithm. In, *Work.* London: CIPD, Summer.

Stone, D., Deadrick, D.L., Lukaszewski, K.M. and Johnson, R. (2015). The influence of technology on the future of human resource management. *Human Resource Management Review*, 25(2), 216–231.

van Esch, P., Stewart Black, J. and Ferolie, J. (2019). Marketing AI recruitment: The next phase in job applications and selection. *Computers in Human Behaviour*, 90, 215–222.

Wakefield, J. (2015). *Intelligent Machines: The Jobs Robots Will Steal First.* www.bbc.co.uk/news/technology-33327659 (accessed 8 August 2019).

WEF. (2016). *World Economic White Paper: Digital Transformation of Industries.* http://reports.weforum.org/digital-transformation/wp-content/blogs.dir/94/mp/files/pages/files/digital-enterprise-narrative-final-january-2016.pdf (accessed 1 September 2018).

Whitmore, J. (2017). *Coaching for Performance.* London: Nicholas Brealey Publishing.

9 Reflecting Back Looking Forward
Speculating on the Future of Coaching

Introduction

In this chapter we draw together the key themes with further reflections from our meta-analysis of coaching as a global phenomenon. Our aim in this chapter is to intentionally provoke further discussion and debate that will stimulate future research into the arena of coach education, practice, and governance that reflects the diversity of organisational and individual needs.

Despite the numerous reports that indicate that coaching has become a global business from our own analysis of these sources, together with interviews with coaching practitioners and commissioners of coaching, we have identified tensions with the phenomenon of coaching. Despite the positive discourse associated with coaching, i.e., the performance-enhancing benefits, as we discuss later in this chapter there is a shadow side to coaching which we suggest has not yet had sufficient critical debate either in the academic literature, or amongst the coaching practitioner community. We believe this critical debate is needed, given the way the various narrative accounts of the evolution of coaching have been positioned, combined with narrative accounts of the future trajectory of coaching as a field of practice that is at risk from AI and Automation.

We thus provide some further observations on what we see as the opportunities/threats for coaching in a world where everyone has the potential to be, or has been developed to coach themselves, and whether new and emerging technologies, e.g., AI and Automation, pose a threat to the personalised support that coaches have traditionally provided.

We conclude this chapter with some final reflections on the implications for coach education, coaching practice and future research on coaching.

Situating Coaching in a Wider Eco-system

Coaching as we have already seen in earlier chapters does not exist in a vacuum but has emerged and is situated with a wider socio-cultural and political system, which we refer to as the coaching eco-system. Each of the entities in the coaching eco-system (see Figure 9.1) is shaped by other factors (entities), but at the same time influences other entities. These entities are multi-layered: macro, meso, and micro, which we elaborate on later in this section. Whilst the observation that coaching is situated in wider socio-cultural system is not new, our intention here is to draw out different dimensions of the coaching eco-system that other authors have either not considered, or fully explored to-date.

The historical roots of coaching, as discussed in Chapter 2, have been presented in other work as emerging from a distinctive socio-political and educational context. Several authors (Brock 2008; Garvey 2011) assert that coaching has emerged from and is embedded within the Socratic tradition of teaching and learning, thus Socrates is considered one of the original coaches. By implication, coaching has emerged from an Athenian eco-system. However, as discussed in Chapter 2, one of the main elements of the Socratic story that we believe has been left out is the unfortunate consequences of Socrates' life and career as an educator of young Athenian talent. Fry (2018: 404), for example, suggests that Socrates was accused of offending the 'gods' of Athens, which was his major offense.

However as we pointed out in Chapter 2, the 'gods' of Athens were figments of the Greeks' imagination. They were part of a mythology that the Athenians held onto when they found their power base was under threat. We included this aspect of the story of Socrates, as we feel it draws attention to the risks for coaches of coaching senior leaders and major influential organisations. Here then we are alluding to the metaphorical 'gods' that exist in organisations that are often revered and unchallenged; a shadow side then of the eco-system that coaching and coaches are a part of.

Whilst we are unable to accurately re-present what happened to the process we, and others, call coaching in between Athenian Greece and the present day, we have argued that the models and processes adopted by contemporary coaches operating in the work of business have been influenced by the work of Gallwey (1986) and Whitmore (2017) who brought coaching from the world of sport into the world of business. We feel this is an important point given that as Rogers (cited in the foreword to Wildflower 2013) suggests: 'Coaches need to know where our ideas come from. When we are furnished with such knowledge we are in a much better position to understand where and when to call on one technique rather than another.' Here then we need to recognise and distinguish between different types of knowledge: explicit and tacit knowledge. Explicit knowledge, as we discuss later, is associated with formal learning, whereas tacit knowledge evolving from experience. Part of the tacit knowledge that coaches need to develop, we suggest, is knowing when to question universalist assumptions about coaching, the processes

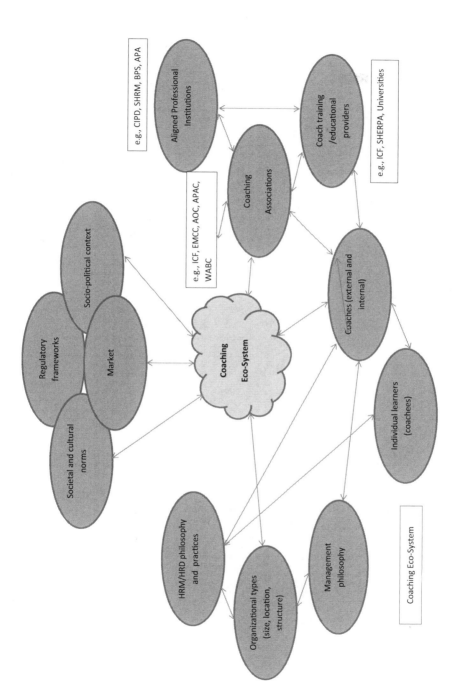

e.g., CIPD, SHRM, BPS, APA

Aligned Professional Institutions

Coach training /educational providers

Coaching Associations

e.g., ICF, SHERPA, Universities

e.g., ICF, EMCC, AOC, APAC, WABC

Socio-political context

Regulatory frameworks

Market

Societal and cultural norms

Coaching Eco-System

Coaches (external and internal)

Individual learners (coachees)

HRM/HRD philosophy and practices

Organizational types (size, location, structure)

Management philosophy

Coaching Eco-System

Figure 9.1 Coaching Eco-System

involved, and the efficacy. For example, the widely held assumption that coaching is performance-enhancing: 'It seems that the main drivers of coaching activities are performance-related rather than being used to address "softer" issues like improving work-life balance, or increasing motivation' (CIPD 2008: 9).

The assumption that coaching is performance enhancing is one that, as already discussed, has been transferred from the world of sport. Yet the eco-system within which the performance of athletes and other sports are assessed, nurtured and developed to ensure they deliver the expected performance is different to the eco-system within which employees are assessed on their performance. An example here to illustrate this point is the recent news story about the marathon runner, Eliud Kipchoge, who completed a marathon in under two hours; a world first (Murray 2019). Yet if we analyse this story more deeply we see the amount of planning and support that went into making this performance possible. Murray (2019: 3) reports that Kipchoge's marathon performance was special 'but was highly manufactured. He was running on a carefully selected flat course with long straights. He was also accompanied by a rotating seven—man team of elite pacesetters, all running in a V formation to cut wind resistance.' Whilst this might seem an outlier example, comparing the performance of a high-performing athlete with the performance of individuals who have been through a coaching programme in organisations, there are a number of key points we wish to draw attention to. First, the coaching eco-system to produce a world-class athlete has to work in synergy (macro, meso, and micro layers). Second, high performers need support from others around them, including team members, who may not necessarily be receiving the same level of investment in their development in order to perform consistently at a particular level. Third, the use of the term 'pacesetters' also attunes us to the need that performance needs to be paced; something that organisations arguably may not necessarily have the option to do, given the much quoted VUCA world (CIPD 2015) that businesses now operate in. Fourth, although not referred to explicitly in the story about Kipchoge's success, the psychological and mental health needs of high performers is something that any coaching eco-system needs to take into account.

Another news story about a high performance sports individual, this time a gymnast (Williams 2019), refers to the technologies that judges have access to help those competing at the highest level in sport:

> Her every movement, and those of her 546 rivals, was being captured by three-dimensional laser sensors hidden inside boxes placed around the floor of the Stuttgart arena. Developed by Fujitsu, the system is based on AI technology. Body measurements are taken from the competitors—in the case of the few who declined in Stuttgart, a standard template was used—and their movements are then tracked

for position, angle and speed, instantly processed and fed to the competition judges in graphic form as a clear real-time analysis of every performance.

Williams (2019) goes on to point out that access to this technology will also help caches to fine tune the performance of their coachees. Of course we realise that we are a long way from similar technologies being used in caching, or are we? As we saw in Chapter 8, other professionals, in aligned fields such as health and wellbeing, are encouraging the use of wearable devices that are able to capture different types of user data (e.g., heart rate, pulse rate) that could act as an early warning system by users and health professionals to more serious health issues/needs. What might happen, then, if coaches started to encourage the use of similar types of wearable devices that are cable of capturing real-time data about their coachee's performance in different contexts? There are a number of issues that need to be considered: ethical considerations, including issues of confidentiality, data security and privacy, the possibility that the use of such technologies may change the dynamics of the relationship between the coachee and others within the organisation, and potential mis-use of power if senior leaders in an organisation ask to have access to this type of data.

The reference to coaching not addressing 'soft' issues in organisations (CIPD 2005) is another assumption that needs further scrutiny, given that coaching is adopted in many organisations to develop the organisation's future leadership pipeline (Gray, de Haan and Bonneywell 2019; O'Neil, Hopkins and Bilimoria 2015). Yet if work-life-balance tensions are not brought into coaching conversations, aimed at enhancing performance and/or developing future leaders, this could marginalise those (particularly women) where work-life-balance tensions are known to act as a barrier to women's career fulfilment and development (Gray, de Haan and Bonneywell 2019; O'Neil, Hopkins and Bilimoria 2015). Coaches, then, we suggest, need to take into account the wider eco-system that coaching is being delivered and in particular to tease out those meso-level entities (e.g., management philosophy and HR policies and practices) that lack congruence with the espoused aims and outcomes of a coaching programme.

A further consideration here with regard to the eco-system within which coaching is situated that we want to draw attention to is how the story of coaching has been told largely through a Western lens (the hegemony of the West). McLean (2017), as pointed out in Chapter 2, argues that the dominance of the English language in international high-quality journals inhibits the publication of articles by authors where English is not their first, or even second, language. Our participants, many of whom have been socialised in the Asia-Pacific region (e.g., Hong Kong and Singapore), or in the Middle East (e.g., Saudi Arabia, Dubai), have provided us with a different perspective on the coaching eco-system which they are part of. First, language is a distinctive aspect of individuals' understanding. As discussed in Chapter 5, in the Chinese language there is no literal translation of the word *coach*. Coaches and coachees have had to embrace a concept that emerged in the West and adapt to their own cultural context. When commissioners of coaching and coachees in Singapore and Hong Kong spoke of their experience of coaching, they used language which we might typically associate with mentoring. For example we noticed participants positioned the mentor as someone who is: seen as the 'expert,' and thus there is an explicit recognition of his/her expertise, or someone who is generally a more experienced person who shares their successes and failures with a less experienced person, so they can learn from those experiences, or from a trusted friend and advisor. Based on our understanding of the cultural influences in Asia, we suggest that mentoring might be considered more acceptable and perhaps a better with the societal and organisational structures as well as the educational philosophy that system that traditionally has not encouraged independent thought or, the questioning of espoused wisdom of elders.

Language we suggest influences how concepts and ideas are socially constructed. Familial situation, educational experience, as well as political systems all influence (and shape) our understanding of particular concepts and phenomena. Even where concepts have been translated into different languages, the subtleties and nuances associated with different concepts invariably do not translate well. One of our participants, an academic working in the Middle East, spoke of some of the difficulties that she and her peers had experienced when trying to translate concepts that originated from other languages/cultures. It is these hidden stories, or voices, that we feel have been missing from the coaching literature to date.

Figure 9.1 represents our view of the coaching eco-system. Whilst we recognise that no model can fully capture the complexities of a particular eco-system, our aim is to highlight the different factors that have and continue to influence how coaching is perceived and positioned as something that is beneficial to businesses, society, and individuals.

Within the coaching eco-system that we have mapped out in Figure 9.1, we can draw out three distinctive layers: macro, meso, and micro; each of these interact with each other to create a fluid and dynamic system within which coaching is practiced and received.

At the macro level, regulatory frameworks set the context for how organisational entities are established and governed, including legislation aimed at protecting the rights and need of employees. In addition, regulatory frameworks influence the governance of professions more broadly, and the professional conduct of individuals within particular professions. However with coaching, as we have already discussed in Chapter 4, there is no single governance structure. What we have instead is a number of

Coaching Associations that have (or aspire to) a global reach, for example ICF (U.S), EMCC (Europe), AOC (UK), WABC (Canada), Asia Pacific Association—APAC (Singapore), Coaching Psychology Forum (UK), and Australian Institute of Coaching (Melbourne). Each of these associations have defined their own codes of conduct that coaches are expected to follow. However these codes of conduct are not subject to scrutiny by any higher institutional authority. Furthermore, Maltbia, Marsick and Ghosh (2014) question whether there is a conflict of interest when the professional associations that 'accredit' providers also certify individual members. In addition each of these associations have contributed in different ways to the positive coaching narrative that organisations have bought into, even though, as we have seen in Chapter 3, the actual benefits can be difficult to quantify.

At the meso layer organisational structure, culture, HRM philosophy and practices each have an influencing effect on when and how coaching is adopted and practised. Several authors (Eastman 2019; Gray, de Haan and Bonneywell 2019) draw attention to the relationship between organisational culture and coaching effectiveness. One aspect that we discuss in more detail later in this chapter is the assumed gender neutral nature of organisational practices. An example to illustrate this point relates to organisational talent management approaches which are invariably presented as meritocratic, despite research evidence that indicates that women's career aspirations, experiences and trajectories differ to those of men (Harris and Foster 2010; O'Neil, Hopkins and Bilimoria 2015). Coaching then may be offered as a way to help women 'fit in' (or survive) in cultures where masculinity is valued, rather than as a means to surface, question and change the underlying structures and discourse that reproduce gender inequalities in organisations (Lewis et al. 2017).

We are aware of course that HRM philosophy and practice are influenced by broader external forces, such as government policies and legislation that affects the employee relations landscape, as well as the influences from particular HRM professional institutions. As discussed in Chapters 5 and 6, a particular tension here is the hegemony of Western HRM/HRD practices that are presumed to work and bring benefits to organisation and individuals despite cultural differences. The behaviour of MNC's is a contributing factor here where standardisation perpetuates the practice of knowledge flowing in a unidirectional manner (from the MNCs HQ out to subsidiaries), as opposed to encouraging bidirectional knowledge flows.

Revisiting the 'Coaching as a Business' Success Narrative

Karakusevic (2017), who is from an organisation that develops coaches, operating in the UK and in Singapore, cites the work of Hillman (1993), which questions the benefits of psychotherapy (as an individualised therapy) without taking into account the wider system (social, economic, and political) that individuals who undergo therapy live in. Karakusevic (2017) suggests that the same criticism can be applied to Executive Coaching. As discussed in Chapter 3, coaching is reported in numerous survey reports as a growing global business. Boersma (2016) for example cites ICF figures that indicate that coaching is a $2 billion global business. Yet the 2016 ICF Global Coaching Study, based on research conducted in partnership with PWC, indicates that coaching revenues vary across world regions considerably. The Oceania region is quoted in the ICF (2016) survey as having the largest revenue stream ($73,100), whereas Eastern Europe has the lowest ($18,400). However, separating out the revenue gained from coaching, as distinct from other forms of personal development, is problematic, given the difficulties in drawing boundaries around different personal development interventions. Actual coaching revenue data (or predications) aside, difficulties remain with evaluating the benefits, or return on investment (ROI) of coaching (Grant 2012; Whitmore 2017). Grant (2012: 75) questions whether ROI is a meaningful measure: 'What is in debate is the notion that financial ROI can provide a fundamental or meaningful benchmark of coaching success.' What he is questioning here is the issue of making causal links between coaching interventions and financial return. This is an issue that has been levied at other HRM/HRD interventions (see Guest 2011 for a more in-depth critique).

Another factor to consider here, we suggest, is where organisations are not specific (or transparent) about what they want to get out of coaching. The CIPD's (2008) survey research, for example, lists several broad outcomes from coaching: deliver tangible benefits to organisations and individuals, promote learning in organisations, and help with the transfer of learning from training/development back in the workplace. Another outcome quoted in this report was 'When coaching is managed effectively it can have a positive effect on an organisation's bottom line' CIPD's (2008: 8). However, the report does not elaborate on what is meant by being 'managed effectively' or, indeed, who in the organisation should be accountable for this. As we discussed previously, coaching is not always aimed at developing 'soft skills,' or perhaps focused enough on individual outcomes. Yet as Grant (2012) argues, organisations could consider more 'humanistic measures' when evaluating coaching outcomes, which he defines as enhanced employee wellbeing and employee engagement; constructs which he argues already have pre-existing validated measures that can be incorporated into an evaluation framework.

But as Karakusevic (2017) points out, other factors may account for why Executive Coaching does not always deliver the expected outcomes: insufficient emphasis given to the contracting phase, where all relevant stakeholders are involved to ensure that the expectations of all parties are fully explored; or, coaching session take place without any meaningful baseline data about the coaches, gathered through, for example, 'meaningful 360° feedback' and coaches not having the opportunity to observe the actual behaviour of coaches in their 'natural habitat.' Each of these points relate to the meso layer of the coaching eco-system, where coaching needs to be aligned with other HRM/HRD processes and practices.

A further consideration here is acknowledging that the providers of coaching services have their own performance targets. In a competitive marketplace this could result in the service provide proposing a coaching service that does fully address the complexities of the coaching eco-system that coaching will be delivered, or proposes a differentiated service for different categories of workers. As in other industries, providers of coaching services are likely to seek out technological solutions to ensure that the coaching services they provide are cost effective and sustainable. As we discussed in Chapter 8, AI and Automation technologies are now being adopted in many business sectors/professions, including similar professions to coaching, such as those working in mental health services. Whilst we are perhaps a long way from seeing the adoption of robotics in coaching, other AI technologies that are reportedly based on 'super intelligence' (Fernando 2019: 33) are transforming business processes. Fernando (2019: 32–33) cautions that in the future IT professionals need to 'sprinkle a bit of deep learning and some neural networks to make their CVs glow,' and experienced IT professionals 'need to spend time learning AI. We should be able to identify the hype from reality and be responsible for communicating to the general public and our governments what is and isn't possible with AI.' Coaches, as with other HRD professionals, will also need to invest in keeping up-to-date with developments that involve disruptive AI and Automation technologies.

A recent PWC (2018) report that provides an international analysis of jobs at risk of automaton indicates that jobs in the Financial Services sector have already been affected by the first wave of AI and Automation (referred to as the algorithmic phase). This is where simple computational tasks, or rule-based tasks, are reportedly being replaced by AI and Automation of some form, e.g., scripted apps, or Chatbots. But what about coaches? What might AI and Automation mean for them in the future? Coaches who use simple coaching models that draw on a more formulaic set of questions, combined with simple goalsetting, that arguably fit with the algorithmic wave of AI, are those considered most risk of being displaced by coaching apps and Chatbots (Clutterbuck 2019; Whitehouse 2019).

A paper by David, Clutterbuck and Megginson (2014) based on research amongst 194 coaches from the U.S. and Europe into the influences and extent to which they use goal-setting techniques in their practice, identified some interesting findings. First, coaches in the U.S. were more likely to draw on goal-setting techniques on their practice compared to coaches based in Europe. Second, as coaches gained more experience they were less likely to use goal-setting techniques in their coaching practice. Based on their findings, David, Clutterbuck and Megginson (2014: 141) speculated that

> It is equally possible that these data represent the opposite: a signalled increase in goal orientation in Europe over time. Perhaps coaches who have been newly trained or introduced to the field are more goal-focused than their predecessors, representing a new wave of coaching professionals who will gradually raise the level of goal orientation in the European field.

We find this finding interesting for two reasons. First, it draws attention to what is taught on coach training/education programmes and the dangers of over-promoting particular models of coaching. We suggest that is another example of the hegemony of the U.S. influence on coach training/education influence, particularly given the dominance of ICF, as discussed in Chapter 4. Second, if, as discussed previously, CoachBots are capable of delivering simplified formulaic coaching, then are coach training providers being disingenuous if they continue to promote coach training that is arguably formulaic?

Accessibility and timeliness of coaching interventions are some of the key benefits being promoted from the use of coaching mediated through technology. However a more worrying application of AI and Automation technologies is where these are being deployed in the development of digital coaches. Call centres have long been criticised for their use of surveillance techniques and technologies (Sinha and Gabriel 2013), that enable supervisors to listen to live calls between call centre advisors and customers. An extension of this approach would now appear to the adoption of AI technologies to replace human coaches (supervisors) with a digital coach that tracks language and voice tone and energy. Where call centre employees do not meet the expected performance standard a digital coach pops up to encourage employees 'to display more empathy, increase their vocal energy, speak more slowly or respond more quickly' (Field 2019).

Coach Education and Development: Future Considerations

In Chapter 4 we discussed some of the tensions and challenges associated with coach training, education and continuing development. In particular the tensions of evaluating the equivalence of the diversity of training/educational programmes and qualifications that coaches might pursue to present themselves as credible coaches. The proliferation of online coaching programmes, open to a global audience, has compounded the issue of assessing equivalency of programmes and qualifications. Other tensions include difficulties in identifying affiliations with a particular Coaching Association and potential governance issues where Coaching Associations accredit coach training/education programmes, as well as certifying individual coaches, where there is no clear independent audit or regulatory frameworks that coach training/education providers are held accountable to.

An initial unsystematic review of the literature using the keyword 'coach education' in Google Scholar identified a rather limited set of academic papers on the theme of coach education. Most papers were focused on the education of sports coaches. However, from this search we identified a couple of papers that we found particularly helpful in developing our thinking about coach education more generally, particularly relating to the underpinning theories and models that coach development programmes draw on. Behavioural change is assumed to be an outcome generally associated with coach development programmes (Allan et al. 2018). Yet a systematic literature review conducted by Allan et al. (2018) of coach development programmes aimed at sports coaches, identified that only six of the 29 programmes reviewed referred explicitly to behaviour change theory as one of the underpinning theories on the development programme.

Intrigued by this finding by Allan et al. (2018), we widened our search terms to include 'coach development' and 'development of executive coaches,' a distinction between coach education and coach development in relation to coaching in the world of business, as distinct from coaching in the world of sport, began to emerge. Based on research into critical incidents in specific scenarios that experienced executive coaches were engaged in, de Haan (2007) makes two observations which perhaps explains the lack of literature on coach education outside the world of sport coaching. His first point relates to the roots of coaching: 'While personal development through coaching may have grown out of remedial action, management education and sports coaching, it actually has more in common with the field of psychotherapy' (de Haan 2007: 527). However de Haan (2007) goes on to point out how, despite some common ground with the field of psychotherapy, the educational backgrounds and competencies of coaches and therapists are different. Whilst he doesn't elaborate on the different educational backgrounds of therapists and coaches, de Haan (2007) does emphasise the importance of Continuing Professional Development (CPD) for experienced coaches; this includes engaging in coach supervision, coaching practice, and structured reflection, as a way of addressing existential and instrumental doubts about their practice. Whilst we recognise the importance of these additional CPD activities for developing a sustainable coaching practice, the focus and content of the dialogues that take place in CPD might not develop a coach's knowledge base, or question their understanding of key concepts that underpin their coaching practice.

Writing in the *International Review of Sports and Exercise Psychology*, Allan et al. (2018) suggest that coach development programmes can be categorised into one of three types: formal (aligned to specific certifications, that require ability to demonstrate specific competencies), non-formal (the development of specific coach behaviours in specific domains, which are often aligned to specific research programmes), and professional and intra-personal (developing skill of self-reflection and practising mindfulness). De Haan's (2007) research would seem to align with Allan et al.'s (2018) category of Professional and intra-personal development.

From our own review of the design and learning content covered on Master's level coaching qualifications in UK universities (see Chapter 4, Table 4.2), we can see some parallels with Allan et al.'s (2018) categorisation of coach development programmes, particularly the category of professional and intra-professional development. Yet only eight of the 29 programmes listed in Table 4.2, refer to these programmes developing specific competencies aligned to certifications, as defined by different by Coaching Associations. In several cases, the participants of these educational programmes were expected to engage in other personal development work in to order to produce a portfolio of evidence that demonstrates the competencies required by specific Coaching Associations.

The ability to critically reflect is considered a key skill and practice that coaches need to demonstrate (Cushion 2018; Drake 2011). Drake (2011: 141) argues that this is key to coach Mastery, the path by which coaches grow 'in technical/professional proficiency and personal and relational maturity . . . essential to handle the increasing complexity in which they [coaches] and clients work.' Drake (2011: 142) draws on the work of Dirkx and Mezirow (2006) to emphasise how reflection and reflexivity enables coaches to progress from 'knowing what works, to how it works, to why it works, to when it works.'

Cushion (2018) points out that reflective practice is now central to coach development programmes. Whilst this may be the case in coach development programmes aimed at sports coaches, our analysis of Masters level coaching programmes set out in Chapter 4 — Table 4.2, shows that only ten of the 29 programmes listed explicitly refer to the development of reflective practice. On some programmes the knowledge and skills associated with reflective practice is not something that appears to be addressed unless participants complete the full Master's programme. Based on auto ethnographic account of transitioning to become a coach, Moore and Koning (2016) refer to their assumptions about coaching courses providing 'resources to help manage the issue of intransigence.' These take the form of what we describe as *sense-enabling* devices, such as theoretical literature, assignments, and coaching supervision, as well as coaching as a 'reflective, dialogic practice.' They suggest that these processes are fundamental in enabling the identity work required to move towards an aspirational identity. We suggest that the understanding of the theory of identity work and the practices to build an aspirational identity is not something that we would observe being covered in the plethora of short coaching courses.

Cushion (2018) argues that coach educators (and coach practitioners) should adopt a more critical perspective on reflection and reflective practice, arguing that: 'Most sociological approaches show coaching as an institution that has a dynamic, complex and diffused network of power relations . . . where coaches are "empowered" or made "autonomous"' (Cushion 2018: 83). He also draws attention to the importance of considering the wider eco-system within which coaching philosophy and practice, and knowledge more generally, is situated. Without this consideration, Cushion (2018) suggests there could be a denial of differences affecting the coaching relationship, as a result limited enquiry (critical reflection) into the assumptions, or theoretical bases, underpinning the work of coaches.

An example to illustrate Cushion's (2018) point about the institutionalised nature of coaching, limiting critical enquiry relates to the often unchallenged assumption about coaching as 'gender neutral' (Gray, de Haan and Bonneywell 2019; O'Neil, Hopkins and Bilimoria 2015; Swan 2017). Swan (2017) argues that the performativity of coaching, given the emphasis on facilitative and non-directive language, reflects Lewis's (2014) notion of 'relational entrepreneurial femininity.' Here, then, Swan (2017) is drawing attention to how feminine ways of behaving when coaching, for example demonstrating empathy, listening and empowerment, have become valorised amongst coaches in business. Paradoxically, these same behaviours when performed by female leaders as part of their day-to-day leadership often have negatives connotations as they are not perceived as congruent with the notion of the 'ideal worker', characterised as 'a rational, strong leader, committed to work and unencumbered by family or other responsibilities' (Gray, de Haan and Bonneywell 2019: 663). The gendered nature of organisations is something that those who coach female Executives Leaders need to become more attuned to (Gray, de Haan and Bonneywell 2019; O'Neil, Hopkins and Bilimoria 2015). As O'Neil, Hopkins and Bilimoria (2015) point out, those who coach female Executives also need to recognise the organisational and societal structures that make performing their leadership role more challenging for women. This observation resonates with the tension that Hearn et al. (2016) highlight about the gendered experiences of women professionals in masculinised professions (which they suggest includes professional managers) where women experience tensions in creating 'coherent narratives of their lives and work in masculinist working environments.'

Where assumptions associated with concepts such as the 'ideal worker' are left unchallenged in organisations, and we suggest in society more generally, this is likely to limit the career progression of female workers, regardless of how much coaching they receive. Managing the tension

258   *Contemporary Debates and Dilemmas*

between work and life, with or without the support of a coach, can result in women opting out of organisations that privilege masculinity over femininity (Hearn et al. 2016)—hence the notion of the 'ideal worker.' However, the notion of the 'ideal worker' is not necessarily a straight forward or binary concept. Implicit within the label 'ideal worker' are assumptions about masculinity and femininity; concepts that are culturally and historically dependent and thus 'are forms of subjectiv-ities (orientations in thinking, feeling and valu-ing) that recognise that 'men as well as women are capable of acting in what may be labelled masculine and feminine ways' (Mavin 2008: 76). Whilst women who perform masculinity can be perceived by co-workers as 'Queen Bees' (Mavin 2008), men in what might be considered feminised professions, such as nursing and teaching, use their masculine characteristics to ' " add value" to caring skills, rendering them superior to those of their female counterparts' (Simpson 2009: 44). Simpson's (2009) research into the lived experiences of men working in four occupational groups (librarianship, primary school teaching, cabin crew, and nursing), occupations typically considered feminised occupations/professions, identified that whilst the care performed by women in these occupations was undervalued, given the 'essentialized notions of femininity,' the work performed by men was 'rendered visible and celebrated as an asset. . . . The special status arose because of claimed differences form women (more rational, more detached), as well as claimed differences from privilege over other (traditionally masculine)' (Simpson 2009: 45).

From our own conversations and interviews with coaches and coachees in the Asia Pacific region, the issue of gendered organisations was not something that they specifically spoke of. In response to our question about whether as a coach they adapt their coaching style when working with female coaches, one participant pointed out 'adapting coaching styles based on gender is subtle' (Chapter 5, p6). However, we did identify distinct categories of responses to this particular question; coaches who did not consciously take gender into account the those who on reflection expressed that they did subconsciously. As one coach elaborated 'not consciously. But this question has made me think that perhaps I could subconsciously be more "supportive" to female clients to encourage them to take on leadership roles' (Chapter 5, P7). Yet we are aware that in the Asia Pacific region the action of 'encouraging female clients to take on leadership roles' can create tensions for the individual where the cultural expectations of women mean that leadership roles are not part of the cultural norm. As discussed in Chapters 5 and 6, what we also identified is the notion of internal coaches playing the role of Ambassadors (in Honk Kong and Singapore) and family members acting as mentors—opening doors for their protégés (Middle East); implicit within these terms is a power dynamic that reinforces the position and status of men and women in particular cultural contexts. Whilst we recognise that exploring the notion of gendered organisations and the 'ideal worker' could be problematic areas for coaches to bring into coaching conversations, if not raised this could perpetuate the situation of certain (i.e., female) voices remaining invisible. O'Neil, Hopkins and Bilimoria (2015) provide some helpful questions that could be incorporated in coaching conversations with female leaders: 'Why do you feel as though you always need to be "tough and decisive?"' and 'Are there leaders in your organization (both men and women) who balance being "tough and decisive" with being "caring and competent?"' However, we would argue that these would be helpful questions to surface in coaching conversations with all leaders, not just female leaders.

Paradoxically the entrepreneurial professional route that women who opt out of organisational structures often take is coaching (see Gray, de Haan and Bonneywell 2019). What we want to draw attention to here is the importance of organisational culture, or industry culture (Eastman 2019), the meso layer in the coaching eco-system in Figure 9.1, and how this influences the experiences and efficacy of coaching in organisations. Drawing on the observations of Shoukry and Cox (2018), Eastman (2019) suggests that coaches may feel pressured into adopting a coaching approach that encourages organisational and societal conformity rather than focusing on and encouraging personal growth. She elaborates this point by suggesting the focus in industry on 'coaching in a training setting, rather than in a more appropriate educational context' (Eastman 2019: 224) is a factor that contributes to this narrow view of coaching. However it is not clear whether the reference to 'industry' in Eastman's (2019) work is the growing coaching industry, which promotes itself as a service provider that enhances organisational performance.

A final reflection here on why coach education, aimed at coaches operating outside the world of sport, as distinct from coach development is not something that appears to have been discussed as a potential issue in other work is perhaps a reflection of the diversity of routes by which individuals become coaches. From our review of the target audience for formal coaching programmes, we can see that a number of Higher Education institutions aim for as wide an audience as possible. Some examples to illustrate this, extracted from Chapter 4—Table 4.2, include:

> The programme aims to equip coaches, consultants and HR professionals to work with groups and individuals at relational depth in organisations in the role of career coach, coach or consultant.
>
> (Birkbeck, University of London)

> You might already be a practising business coach seeking to enhance your coaching methodology and skills, an executive who wants to add coaching to your consultancy portfolio, or a human resources director.
>
> (Leeds Beckett University)

This course is aimed at internal or external coaches, consultants, mentor co-ordinators, coaching psychologists, counsellors, managers, human resources development or leadership professionals from the voluntary, public and private sectors.

(Oxford Brookes University)

This programme is aimed at leaders, managers and training professionals who want to develop their skills, knowledge and understanding in this rapidly developing field.

(University of Portsmouth)

Where a programme is aimed at a diverse group of professionals, the existing knowledge that individuals from these different professions can draw on will inevitably vary. Whilst some may have a greater awareness and understanding of relevant theories drawn on in coaching (e.g., learning, including learning styles, humanistic and positive psychology, behavioural change), given their prior education, professional qualifications and experience, others may not have this same depth of knowledge. Without ongoing supervision, within the context in which coaching is subsequently practiced, coaches and coachees could find themselves in a vulnerable and precarious situation. By this we mean that, depending upon whether coaching is seen as a skill set rather than a profession with a unique knowledge base, this skill set could be replaced through wider adoption of self-help coaching tools delivered through AI and Automation technologies, a trend which appears to be meeting employers (and employees) need for learning systems that 'provide performance support at the point of need' as opposed to 'learning [something] just in case' (CIPD 2015: 39).

So how might coach education need to change in the future to reflect the evolving eco-system that coaching will be delivered in? First, we believe it should cover the history, philosophy, and the socio-political roots of coaching. The history of how a profession has come into being and thus what makes it distinctive is an integral part of the educational curriculum of other professions. Second, introduce novice coaches to a wider repertoire of coaching model and theories and how these contribute to a more holistic view of coaching. Whilst we realise that coach education programmes will invariably draw on concepts and theories drawn from 'reference disciplines' such as psychology, psychotherapy, and sociology (Bachkirova and Borrington 2019: 338), we suggest that coaches need to be encouraged to reflect critically on the limitations of the concepts and knowledge gained from such reference disciplines for their situated caching practice within organisations. Aligned with this is developing a coaching curriculum that teaches coaches how to make sense of the different types of research evidence that has informed and is informing coaching practice. Third, help coaches develop strategies for delivering a coaching practice that is sustainable. This many mean that coach educators may need to partner with other professionals from a different part of the coaching eco-system, e.g., technology developers and ecologists.

Chapter Summary and Suggestions for Future Research on Coaching

In this chapter we have drawn together the key themes explored throughout our book. In writing this concluding chapter, we have been become more attuned ourselves to the dynamism of the coaching eco-system. Our approach to developing the ideas presented in this book, i.e., gaining insights for the field of coaching in different geographical contexts, has heightened our own awareness of the different narratives (positive and negative) associated with coaching.

Coaching, as we have discussed in Chapter 4, is an example of what Dent et al. (2016: 1) refer to as the new wave of 'entrepreneurial professions' who have 'no mandatory [professional] membership of or official credentials.' Whether coaching will eventually achieve its own independent status as a profession is still uncertain. We have highlighted factions within the coaching practitioner community itself, even amongst those who have sought coach accreditation by one of the largest Coaching Associations and tensions too between coaches and other reference disciplines who have achieved recognition of their professional status, e.g., coaching psychologists.

In the future, could coaching follow a similar trajectory as the HRM/HRD profession, where changing organisational expectations has given rise to different roles (not intentionally meant as hierarchical), which has resulted in identity struggles for some HRM professionals, for example those working in the HR Shared Service Centres (see Pritchard and Symon 2011). Thus are we likely to see a similar stratification emerging within coaching, possibly aligned around a specialist/generalist divide? As the coaching market matures (so moves out of the Gold Rush phase as discussed in Chapter 3), combined with the growing acceptance of AI and Automation tools, could less experienced coaches find themselves in the lowest strata, or possibly displaced by technology as others suggest? At the middle strata, might we see opportunities for coaches who draw on particular specialist areas of expertise, e.g., health and wellbeing, career growth and transitions, or possibly evolve into hybrid-professionals (Glover 2013; Kirkpatrick 2016)? As managers are now expected to integrate coaching into their existing managerial role, might this potentially displace the need for generalist coaches in the future? Or might their role evolve into something that we might recognise as a form of supervision?

As Kirkpatrick (2016) points out, there has been a rise in the number of hybrid professionals given the growing emphasis on professional-managers.

These hybrid roles are defined as a 'recombination of existing elements, often in tension' rather than a completely new role (Kirkpatrick 2016: 175). Using an example from the health sector, for example where clinicians also take on the role of Clinical Director, Kirkpatrick (2016) suggests that in those in hybrid roles 'form part of a wider control strategy, a means of subtly encouraging professionals to internalise financial disciplines . . . and organisational priorities' (180). The research conducted by Glover (2013) amongst hybrid knowledge workers working in the UK IT sector identified other tensions. Hybrid professionals in this context were considered by organisations as 'ideal workers, since they were able to combine 'technical expertise with prosocial behaviours, popularly known as "soft skills"' (Glover 2013: 105). However, the hybrid nature of their roles meant that these professionals had to become self-provisioning in order to keep their technical knowledge up-to-date to maintain their 'ideal worker' status. One participant in Glover's (2013: 111) research noted, 'I actually schedule time in my weekly schedule, to do technical development stuff . . . I am really lucky that I'm able to do this.' The reference to self-provisioning we suggest applies equally to those who run their own independent coaching business, where resources for continuing professional development need to be self-funded and self-managed.

Finally, will the top strata become (or as some may argue remain) the exclusive domain of the 'celebrity' or 'A status' coaches referred to in Chapter 8? Might coaches with a deeper understanding of business become more highly sought after by the most senior Executives? Or as de Haan and Kasozi (2014) suggest, with the increasing pressure for Executives to be held to account for their 'derailing behaviours,' might we observe a new wave of Executive Coaches emerging? Those with the confidence and reputation to challenge and confront the shadow side of leadership, or possibly help Executives to understand that traditional warrior, or heroic forms of leadership are counter-productive in the world of work? If this were the case, how might female coaches differentiate themselves in the market? Would their essentialist pro-social behaviours become valuable, or as in other occupations, as discussed previously, remain undervalued?

Another area of future research we suggest that is much needed is monitoring the extent to which the feminisation of coaching could perpetuate the occupational segregation that can be observed in other professions. If female coaches, given their current or previous organisational roles, have not had the opportunity to develop the deep understanding of business that we are led to believe that Executives want, does that mean that they will remain invisible when organisations choose coaches? Or might female coaches be perceived as the 'ideal coaches' to help soften executive behaviours? Either way, research into how sustainable the careers of male and female coaches are would be valuable.

References

Allan, V., Vierimaa, M., Gainforth, H.L. and Côté, J. (2018). The use of behavioural change theories and techniques in research-informed coach development programmes: A systematic review. *International Review of Sport and Exercise Psychology*, 11(1), 47–69.

Bachkirova, T. and Borrington, S. (2019). Old wine in new bottles: Exploring pragmatism as a philosophical framework for the discipline of coaching. *Academy of Management Learning and Education*, 18(3), 337–360.

Boersma, M. (2016). *Coaching No Longer the Preserve of Executives*. www.ft.com/content/60d6ae0a-d0b2-11e5-92a1-c5e23ef99c77 (accessed 10 October 2019).

Brock, V. (2008). *Grounded Theory of the Roots and Emergence of Coaching*. A Dissertation Submitted in Partial Fulfilment of the Requirements for the Degree Doctor of Philosophy in Coaching and Human Development, International University of Professional Studies, Maui.

CIPD. (2005). *Coaching and Buying Coaching Services: A Guide*. London: CIPD.

CIPD. (2008). *Coaching and Buying Coaching Services*: Guide, Second Edition. London: CIPD. Survey coaching.

CIPD. (2015). *L&D Evolving Roles, Enhancing Skills*. Research report. London: CIPD.

Clutterbuck, D. (2019). *Coach Versus Bot: How Do They Compare?* www.davidclutterbuckpartnership.com/coach-versus-bot-how-do-they-compare/ (accessed 18 August 2019).

Cushion, C.J. (2018). Reflection and reflective practice discourses in coaching: A critical analysis. *Sport, Education and Society*, 23(1), 82–94.

David, S., Clutterbuck, D. and Megginson, D. (2014). Goal orientation in coaching differs according to region, experience and education. *International Journal of Evidence Based Coaching and Mentoring*, 12(2), 134–145.

De Haan, E. (2007). Becoming simultaneously thicker and thinner skinned. *Personnel Review*, 37(5), 526–542.

De Haan, E. and Kasozi, A. (2014). *The Leadership Shadow*. London: Kogan Page.

Dent, M., Bourgeault, I.L., Denis, J-L. and Kuhlmann, E. (2016). General introduction: The changing world of professions and professionalism. In, *The Routledge Companion to the Professions and Professionalism*. Oxon: Routledge.

Dirkx, J.M. and Mezirow, J. (2006). Musings and reflections on the meaning, context, and process of transformative learning. *Journal of Transformative Education*, 4(2), 123–139.

Drake, A.B. (2011). What do coaches need to know? Using the mastery window to assess and develop expertise. *Coaching: An International Journal of Theory, Research and Practice*, 4(2), 138–155.

Eastman, C.A. (2019). The development needs of coaches and coachees. *International Journal of Mentoring and Coaching*, 8(3), 217–227.

Fernando, R. (2019). *Living with AI: A Personal Perspective*. IT NOW. Swindon: BCS, September.

Field, H. (2019). When being empathic is your full-time job, burning out is only human. *Entrepreneur Europe*. www.entrepreneur.com/article/340207 (accessed 15 October 2019).

Fry, S. (2018). *Mythos—The Greek Gods Retold*. London: Penguin Random House.

Gallwey, T.G. (1986). *The Inner Game of Golf*. Basingstoke: Pan Books Ltd.

Garvey, B. (2011). *A Very Short, Fairly Interesting and Reasonably Cheap Book About Coaching and Mentoring*. London: Sage Publications.

Glover, J. (2013). Digital Taylorism: Hybrid knowledge professionals in the UK ICT sector. In, Evans, C. and Holmes, L. (Eds.) *Re-Tayloring Management: Scientific Management a Century On*. Farnham: Gower Publishing Limited.

Grant, A.M. (2012). ROI is a poor measure of coaching success: Towards a more holistic approach using a well-being and engagement framework. *Coaching: An International Journal of Theory, Research and Practice*, 5(2), 74–85.

Gray, D., de Haan, E. and Bonneywell, S. (2019). Coaching the 'ideal worker': Female leaders and the gendered self in organizations. *European Journal of Training and Development*, 43(7–8), 661–668.

Guest, D.E. (2011). Human resource management and performance: Still searching for some answers. *Human Resource Management Journal*, 21(1), 3–13.

Harris, L. and Foster, C. (2010). Aligning talent management with approaches to equality and diversity. *Equality, Diversity and Inclusion: An International Journal*, 29(5), 422–435.

Hearn, J., Biese, I., Choroszewicz, M. and Husu, L. (2016). Gender, diversity and intersectionality in professions and potential professions. In, Dent, M., Bourgeault, I.L., Denis, J-L. and Kuhlmann, E. (Eds.) *The Routledge Companion to the Professions and Professionalism*. Oxon: Routledge.

Hillman, J. (1993). *We've Had a Hundred Years of Psychotherapy and the World's Getting Worse*. New York: HarperCollins.

ICF. (2016). *2016 ICF Global Coaching Study*. https://coachfederation.org/app/uploads/2017/12/2016ICFGlobalCoachingStudy_ExecutiveSummary-2.pdf (accessed 10 October 2019).

Karakusevic, A. (2017). *Advanced Coaching Skills Part 3: Paying Attention to the Wider System*. www.roffeypark.com/coaching/advanced-coaching-skills-part-three-paying-attention-to-the-wider-system/ (accessed 10 October 2019).

Kirkpatrick, I. (2016). Hybrid managers and professional leadership. In, Dent, M., Bourgeault, I.L., Denis, J-L. and Kuhlmann, E. (2016). General introduction: The changing world of professions and professionalism. *The Routledge Companion to the Professions and Professionalism*. Oxon: Routledge.

Lewis, P. (2014). Postfeminism, femininities and organization studies: Exploring a new agenda. *Organization Studies*, 35(12), 1845–66.

Lewis, P., Benschop, Y. and Simpson, R. (2017). Postfeminism, Gender and Organization. *Gender, Work and Organization*, 24(3), 213–225.

Maltbia, T.E., Marsick, V.J. and Ghosh, R. (2014). Executive and organizational coaching: A review of insights drawn from literature to inform HRD practice. *Advances in Developing Human Resources*, 16(2), 161–183.

Mavin, S. (2008). Queen bees, wannabees and afraid to bees: No more 'best enemies' for women in management? *British Journal of Management*, 19(1), 75–85.

McLean, G.N. (2017). *The Case of the Misguided Researcher: A Fairy Tale of Ethnocentricity (Evil Witch) Versus Indigenization (Good Witch)*. Presentation at the 18th International Conference on HRD Research and Practice across Europe (UFHRD/AHRD) Lisbon, Portugal, 8 June.

Moore, L. and Koning, J. (2016). Intersubjective identity work and sensemaking of adult learners on a postgraduate coaching course: Finding the balance in a world of dynamic complexity. *Management Learning*, 47(1), 28–44.

Murray, E. (2019). Kipchoge gallops to athletic immortality in Vienna sprint. *The Observer, Sport*, 13 October.

O'Neil, D.A., Hopkins, M.M. and Bilimoria, D. (2015). A framework for developing women leaders: Applications to executive coaching. *The Journal of Applied Behavioural Science*, 51(2), 253–276.

Pritchard, K. and Symon, G. (2011). Identity on the line: Constructing professional identity in a HR call centre. *Work, Employment and Society*, 25(3), 434–450.

PWC. (2018). *Will Robots Really Steal Our Jobs?* www.pwc.co.uk/economic-services/assets/international-impact-of-automation-feb-2018.pdf (accessed 10 October 2019).

Shoukry, H. and Cox, E. (2018). Coaching as a social process. *Management Learning*, 49(4), 413–428.

Simpson, R. (2009). *Men in Caring Occupations: Doing Gender Differently*. Basingstoke: Palgrave Macmillan.

Sinha, S. and Gabriel, Y. (2013). Call centre work: Taylorism with a facelift. In, Evans, C. and Holmes, L. (Eds.) *Re-Tayloring Management: Scientific Management a Century on*. Farnham: Gower Publishing Limited.

Swan, E. (2017). Postfeminist stylistics, work femininities and coaching: A multimodal study of a website. *Gender, Work and Organizations*, 24(3), 274–296.

Whitehouse, E. (2019). Would you let a chatbot coach you? *People Management*, 11 July. www.peoplemanagement.co.uk/long-reads/articles/would-let-chatbot-coach-you (accessed 15 October 2019).

Whitmore, J. (2017). *Coaching for Performance* (Fifth Edition). London: Nicholas Brealey Publishing.

Wildflower, L. (2013). *The Hidden History of Coaching*. Maidenhead: McGraw-Hill Education, Open University Press.

Williams, R. (2019). *Armchair Viewers Get a Glimpse of the Future and It Looks to Be Laser Guided*. www.theguardian.com/sport/blog/2019/oct/14/armchair-viewers-laser-guided-rugby-union-kipchoge (accessed 15 October 2019).

Index

Page numbers in *italics* and **bold** indicate Figures and Tables, respectively.

274   *Index*